# The Profit *MAGIC* of Stock Transaction Timing

## J. M. HURST

**Traders Press, Inc.®**
**PO Box 6206**
**Greenville, SC 29606**

*Serving Traders since 1975*

**Reprinted February 2000 by Traders Press, Inc.®**
**Special arrangement with Prentice Hall, Inc.**



**ISBN: 0-934380-62-7**



*Cover Design by: Teresa Darty Alligood*
*Editor & Graphic Designer*
*Traders Press, Inc.®*

**Traders Press, Inc.®**
**PO Box 6206**
**Greenville, SC 29606**

*Serving Traders since 1975*

# *Biography*

James M. Hurst was educated at Kansas State, Brown, and Washington Universities, majoring in physics and mathematics. World War II and the advent of radar stimulated interest and training in electronics and the theory of communications.

Following the war, Mr. Hurst specialized for 25 years in electronics systems design for aerospace applications. An interesting project related to antisubmarine warfare provided experience with and appreciation of the power of large digital computers as applied to the problem of extracting information from time-series data.

Numerical analysis methods were first applied by Mr. Hurst to negotiable equity data in the search for a solution to the classical cost-effectiveness problem. This effort led to the discovery of the spectral signature phenomenon in price data (cyclicality), and to a *Theory of Irrational Decision Processes*. *The Wave Theory of Price Action* described in this paper is the first practical application of *The Decision Theory* to be developed.

In 1969, Mr. Hurst founded **Decision Models, Inc.** for the purpose of further developing decision theory and wave concepts as applied to the equity markets. The **CycliTec** aids to cyclic analysis of equities resulted and were initially published in 1971.

Mr. Hurst has authored several treatises on the Wave Theory of Price Action. The first was the book *The Profit Magic of Stock Transaction Timing,* published by **Prentice-Hall** in 1970. The paper *Cycles for Profits in Stocks and Commodities* was presented to the Society for the Investigation of Recurring Events on 15 June 1971. The paper *Predictive Implications of Periodicity in Stock and Commodity Prices* followed (presented to the Technical Security Analysts of San Francisco, 18 October 1972). The last, and by far most extensive treatment is in the form of the *CycliTec Services Training Course*, initially published in 1973 by **CycliTec Services,** San Francisco. This course has been reproduced and preserved by Traders Press, Inc., Greenville, SC and has been renamed the *J. M. Hurst Cycles Trading and Training Course*. It is available exclusively through Traders Press.

**TRADERS PRESS, INC.®**
**PO BOX 6206**
**GREENVILLE, SC 29606**

*7 Secrets Every Commodity Trader Needs to Know* (Mound)
*A Complete Guide to Trading Profits* (Paris)
*A Professional Look at S&P Day Trading* (Trivette)
*A Treasury of Wall Street Wisdom* (Editors: Schultz & Coslow)
*Ask Mr. EasyLanguage* (Tennis)
*Beginner's Guide to Computer Assisted Trading* (Alexander)
*Channels and Cycles: A Tribute to J.M. Hurst* (Millard)
*Chart Reading for Professional Traders* (Jenkins)
*Commodity Spreads: Analysis, Selection and Trading Techniques* (Smith)
*Comparison of Twelve Technical Trading Systems* (Lukac, Brorsen, & Irwin)
*Complete Stock Market Trading and Forecasting Course* (Jenkins)
*Cyclic Analysis* (J.M. Hurst)
*Dynamic Trading* (Miner)
*Exceptional Trading: The Mind Game* (Roosevelt)
*Fibonacci Ratios with Pattern Recognition* (Pesavento)
*Futures Spread Trading: The Complete Guide* (Smith)
*Geometry of Markets* (Gilmore)
*Geometry of Stock Market Profits* (Jenkins)
*Harmonic Vibrations* (Pesavento)
*How to Trade in Stocks* (Livermore & Smitten)
*Hurst Cycles Course* (J.M. Hurst)
*Investing by the Stars* (Weingarten)
*It's Your Option* (Zelkin)
*Magic of Moving Averages* (Lowry)
*Market Rap: The Odyssey of a Still-Struggling Commodity Trader* (Collins)
*Pit Trading: Do You Have the Right Stuff?* (Hoffman)
*Planetary Harmonics of Speculative Markets* (Pesavento)
*Point & Figure Charting* (Aby)
*Point & Figure Charting: Commodity and Stock Trading Techniques* (Zieg)
*Private Thoughts From a Trader's Diary* (Pesavento & MacKay)
*Profitable Grain Trading* (Ainsworth)
*Profitable Patterns for Stock Trading* (Pesavento)
*RoadMap to the Markets* (Busby)
*Short-Term Trading with Price Patterns* (Harris)
*Single Stock Futures: The Complete Guide* (Greenberg)
*Stock Patterns for Day Trading (2 volumes)* (Rudd)
*Stock Trading Based on Price Patterns* (Harris)
*Study Helps in Point & Figure Techniques* (Wheelan)
*Technically Speaking* (Wilkinson)
*Technical Trading Systems for Commodities and Stocks* (Patel)
*The Amazing Life of Jesse Livermore: World's Greatest Stock Trader* (Smitten)
*The Handbook of: Global Securities Operations* (O'Connell & Steiniger)
*The Opening Price Principle: The Best Kept Secret on Wall Street* (Pesavento & MacKay)
*The Professional Commodity Trader* (Kroll)
*The Taylor Trading Technique* (Taylor)
*The Trading Rule That Can Make You Rich** (Dobson)
*Top Traders Under Fire* (Collins)
*Trading Secrets of the Inner Circle* (Goodwin)
*Trading S&P Futures and Options* (Lloyd)
*Twelve Habitudes of Highly Successful Traders* (Roosevelt)
*Understanding Bollinger Bands* (Dobson)
*Understanding Fibonacci Numbers* (Dobson)
*Viewpoints of a Commodity Trader* (Longstreet)
*Wall Street Ventures & Adventures Through Forty Years* (Wyckoff)
*Winning Edge 4* (Toghraie)
*Winning Market Systems* (Appel)

# *Publisher's Foreword*

The work of J.M. Hurst has become legendary among serious technical analysts. The material in this book presents the results of his extensive and painstaking research into the cyclical nature of price movements in the stock market and the principles he proposed with respect to these movements and how they might be used to predict future price movements. This book has become a classic. Many customers of ***Traders Press*** have told me, over the years, that this has been one of the most valuable books (if not THE most valuable) they have ever acquired to give them insight into the market and how to predict its movements.

Unfortunately, the previous publisher of this book has allowed it to go out of print and it was no longer available to the investing public. I felt that it would be a worthwhile project and undertaking to bring this book back into print, making it available once again to investors. One of the main goals of ***Traders Press*** is to preserve quality research and literature for the investing public, especially if these works have become unavailable through any other source, and this book certainly fits into this mold.

Hurst produced two other works of major importance for those interested in the cyclical nature of price movements: a 1974 work entitled ***Cyclic Analysis: A Dynamic Approach to Technical Analysis***, and an extensive training course designed to teach the student precisely how to use his principles espoused in this book. Those interested in the cyclical approach will find these additional materials valuable. Those who are intimidated by the intense math in this book will be comforted to know that Hurst's other works are not as rigorous in the theoretical approach, and are more concerned with the practical application of the principles explained herein. Both of these other works are available through ***Traders Press.***

Another relevant publication of ***Traders Press*** is ***Channels and Cycles: A Tribute to J. M. Hurst***, authored by Brian Millard, a British technician who found Hurst's work to be an enormous inspiration. In his book he interprets and summarizes the principles which Hurst set forth in ***The Profit Magic of Stock Transaction Timing*** and gives updated chart examples.

We at ***Traders Press*** are proud to be associated with research and literature of the high caliber of that produced by J. M. Hurst, one of the true pioneers in technical analysis whose work is held in exceptionally high esteem by serious technicians and students of the market.

***Traders Press*** produces an extensive catalog which describes hundreds of books, courses, and other educational materials of interest to traders and investors in stocks, options, and futures. Readers who wish to obtain a copy are encouraged to contact the publisher of this book.

Edward Dobson

Edward D. Dobson, President
Traders Press, Inc.®
Greenville, SC

February 3, 2000

*To Pat*

# How This Book Can Boost Your Profit Performance

Can a $10,000 investment yield $1,000,000 in a year? In five years? If so, what is the risk involved?

These are the kinds of questions to which this work is addressed. Such fantastic results are possible in the stock market. Individual issues fluctuate widely enough and often enough to permit this and more. Techniques are presented here that put an average yield on invested capital of 10% per month well within the realm of possibility. Compounding profits at this rate, such a yield can return $1,000,000 on a $10,000 investment within 50 months!

An actual trading experiment will be described using these principles which produced an 8.9% yield per transaction—every 9.7 days. Such a yield, if continued, compounds $10,000 to $1,000,000 in 15 months. If such results can be attained in the market – *why isn't everyone doing it*?

The answer is complex, but the elements are simple: *effort, knowledge,* and *psychological barriers.* Any goal this worthwhile requires time and effort. Most investors, amateur and professional, do not have the kind of analytical background needed to shear through rumor, opinion, and adage to get at the basis of why stock prices change. And finally, even with knowledge in hand, many investors lack training in the emotion-logic balance required for success.

Nevertheless, *all of these obstacles can be overcome*. It is the purpose of this book to provide you with the essentials. The results are yours if you care to apply yourself with sufficient intensity. Investment operations will be presented here in a deliberately unorthodox manner. We will turn our backs firmly on all cliches, adages, and market lore that will not withstand critical scrutiny. Where necessary, we will not hesitate to form new ones that *do* fit the facts.

The results discussed were derived using the most modern available methods of computerized data analysis and were researched for nine years before making their debut here. However, the presentation is directed to all kinds of investors. The techniques involved are simple, are not overly time-consuming, and do not presuppose extensive academic background. The work involved on your part is concerned with the need to grasp and integrate an understanding of why stock prices change with the mechanical transaction-timing techniques described.

You will find here that the big money in investing stems from the principle of "profit compounding"—of short-term trades. It is further shown that this potential cannot be exploited in an optimum manner without a *large* improvement in transaction-timing capability, that cannot be achieved using traditional investment methods.

You will be guided through a plausible introduction to the basic tenets of price change, an understanding of which is essential to the success of your operations in the market. You will find that one particular element of the price change concept is ideally suited to the improvement of transaction timing.

You will see demonstrated dramatic new transaction methods which can result in startling potential. These are simple to apply and can be handled by anyone who will take the time to learn what they are and why they work.

You will be exposed to:

- A concept of profit maximization.
- A model of stock price motion with prediction implications.
- An explanation of why chart patterns form—and how to use this knowledge to your profit.
- Step-by-step methods for using the price-motion model to generate definitive "wait," "buy," "hold," "sell," "sell short," "cover short," and "protect profit" signals.
- An explanation of why moving averages work and how to design your own for use in transaction timing.
- A complete trading method: how to select issues, how to analyze them for action signals, and how to improve your chances of turning and keeping a profit.
- The extent to which you should be concerned by chance factors; whether or not you should sell in case of war or financial crisis.
- The reasons why psychological considerations can affect your profits and what you can do about it.
- An introduction to numerical analysis and spectral analysis, upon which the results in the book are based.

The problems of trading techniques and methods are dealt with directly. As a side benefit (and confined chiefly to the Appendix), enough in the way of methods, results, and references is included to permit those so inclined to repeat and carry forward the research on which the book is based.

*Good luck, and large and consistent profits!*

*J. M. Hurst*

## Acknowledgments

This book is a strange entity—almost an afterthought. For the real effort involved was not in the writing, but in the years of experience and research that went before. As a result of those years, the book almost wrote itself. It is only natural, therefore, that the author's obligations stem mostly from "before"—and are literally beyond fulfilling. From the host of those that shaped background, firmed ideas, and lent moral support, a few can be singled out, however.

What value an understanding wife? How can thanks be expressed to mine for the patience and fortitude required through endless evenings and weekends when I was not there to share life, but was lost in intricate manipulations of numbers, ideas, and other intangibles of seemingly dubious work-a-day value? To Pat also go thanks for the midnight typing sessions which ultimately resulted in not only a finished manuscript but also in my graduation from the "single finger" to the "two finger" stage of expertise.

Along the way there were also several who contributed hard-wrested time from family affairs, laboriously collecting data to be later digested by computer, or slaving under a drafting light with slide-rule in hand. Dutch Fink and Wally Dunn will recognize the characterization.

Stan Levine read and constructively criticized the manuscript in its most embryonic form—and still had words of encouragement to offer.

Bart, Eric, Gordon, John, and Juanita all shared the excitement, labor, and tension of the "trading experiment"—while Fred Kayne and Tim Buginas never faltered in their moral (and other) support. When photo work was required, it was Doug and Sheri Edwards who came to the rescue.

It was Gian Rende who endured the stress and strain of the final critical review of the manuscript, which resulted in a number of significant and worthwhile alterations.

To each and all, heartfelt thanks!

# Contents

# List of Illustrations

## *chapter one*

# Maximize Your Profits

- **Where the Magic Is**
- **To Trade or to Invest**
- **The Most Dollars in the Least Time**
- **How the Trading Interval Affects Profits**
- **Adding Magic By Compounding**
- **Maintaining 100% Investment**
- **Four Steps to Riches**

## WHERE THE MAGIC IS

### "Stock Prices Fluctuate"

This statement may describe the only stock price characteristic on which any two students of the market will unequivocally agree!

It's a mighty important truism, however—for on it rests a solid fact: More money *can* be made faster from these price fluctuations than in nearly any other way known to man—*provided you own a crystal ball which tells you when the fluctuations will occur.*

There is another truism which even tells one how to turn on the Golden Stream: "Buy low and sell high."—Or does it? How low is "low," and how high is "high"? Phrased differently: *when* is "low" and *when* is "high"?

It can be seen from the preponderance of "whens" in these all-important questions that the faucet handle is labeled "Timing."

### Very Real Magic Lies in Transaction Timing!

But—given timing capability—a whole new concept of profit maximization becomes possible, in which two other factors are nearly as potent. We shall be dealing in this chapter with the concepts of short-term yield and profit compounding, leaving the major problem of timing for the rest of the book.

## TO TRADE OR TO INVEST

The existence of exchanges and the resulting "liquidity" permit the phenomenon of price fluctuation. In the days of the Hudson's Bay Company–when there were no exchanges–stock price motion as we know it could not exist. Today, stock prices fluctuate by 10's and 100's of percent in value while dividend yields are measured in single digits.

Given zero ability to anticipate price turns, risk is primarily concerned with the cancellation of dividend benefits by capital loss. In such a case, long-term investment is the least-risk course of action, and freedom to select time of liquidation is limited.

Given 100% perfect ability to time transactions, trading risk becomes zero–and investing can no longer be contemplated. Such timing is, of course, unachievable, but our goal in what follows approaches 90%. Under these conditions, the first tenet of a profit-optimization philosophy is:

**We are in the market to trade–leaving dividends to help offset margin interest.**

## THE MOST DOLLARS IN THE LEAST TIME

The next question is: "How much is a lot?" Suppose we discuss a friend who bought 100 shares of stock at $20 and sold it at $40. He doubled his money, made $2000 on a $2000 investment. Not bad. But suppose also we found out that he was 20 when he bought it and 40 when he sold it. His yield was 5% per year, and he might as well have put his $2000 in the local bank!

Another friend bought a stock at 20 and sold it at 40 after holding it only one year. *He* made 100% per year on his invested capital. Better? But suppose also we found out that he couldn't find another stock that he liked during the next 19 years. He also made 5% per year over the 20-year period–and also should have stuck with the local bank.

To maximize profits an additional principle is needed:

> We must measure success in investing in terms of profit per unit time over the entire time of investment activity.
>
> To maximize this we must maximize percent per year return on each trade and approach 100% time usage of our funds as closely as possible.

We have now established the broad basis for a profit-maximization philosophy. We know that we must:

1. Trade–not invest.
2. Maximize percent per year yield on each trade.
3. Seek 100% time investment of capital.

All well and good in theory–but how to go about it?

## HOW THE TRADING INTERVAL AFFECTS PROFITS

We will now see that there are two vitally important parts that the concept of "trading" under the assumption of improved timing plays in achieving profit-optimization goals. Each of these has to do with the trading interval.

Turn your attention now to Figure I-1. Here is a typical "high-low" chart for Alloys Unlimited. The total range of the chart for about one year is from 12 to 49 3/4. Suppose you had $10,000 and were astute enough to pick up the stock in November 1966 at 12. Holding it through December 1967, you then sell it at 49 1/2 and sell short at the same price. You cover your short in March of '68 at 32 1/4. With this ideal transaction timing (never achievable in practice), you would net $44,780 in profit on a $10,000 investment in 70 weeks for a yield of 333% per year. As lovely as this sounds, let's try something else.

Look at Figure I-2. This is the same chart with a few curvy dotted lines and additional points on the chart emphasized by symbols. Looking at the curvy lines we see that during the time you held the stock for the previous transaction there was a number of price trend reversals. Each significant high and low is denoted by a letter on the chart, associated with the price of the stock at that time in points and eighths.

Now suppose that you bought the stock at A (at 12) then sold and sold short at F (39 3/8). You cover your short and buy again at G (30 5/8), then sell and sell short at J (49 3/4). Finally you cover your short sale at K (32 1/8). What happens to profits? Four transactions were required instead of two as before, but you netted $75,690 after all transaction costs, instead of $44,780. The yield is now 562% per year on your $10,000 initial investment.

Let's go a step further. Buy at A (12) then sell and sell short at B (23 5/8). Cover the short and buy at C (18 1/8), then sell and sell short at D (32 3/4). Cover this short and buy again at E (24 5/8), then sell and sell short at F (39 3/8). Continuing in this manner to K, you will find ten transactions to be completed. *But this time you net $290,000 for a yield of 2150% per year on your money!*

Let's summarize. Over the same total time span, trading in the same stock, assuming the same ground rules of perfect transaction timing (to permit comparison):

Two trades netted 333% per year
Four shorter trades netted 562% per year
Ten still shorter trades netted 2150% per year

Now we're getting close to the real reason why improvement in transaction timing is worth all the effort we can put into it. Even discounting the effect of the unrealistic assumption of perfect timing in the examples, the timing improvement that made the 10 trades possible is well worth striving for. And it all comes about because *improved timing permits shortened trades!*

The impact of trading interval is a dual phenomenon that holds true for all stocks. Assuming accuracy of transaction timing, you will always make more money by short

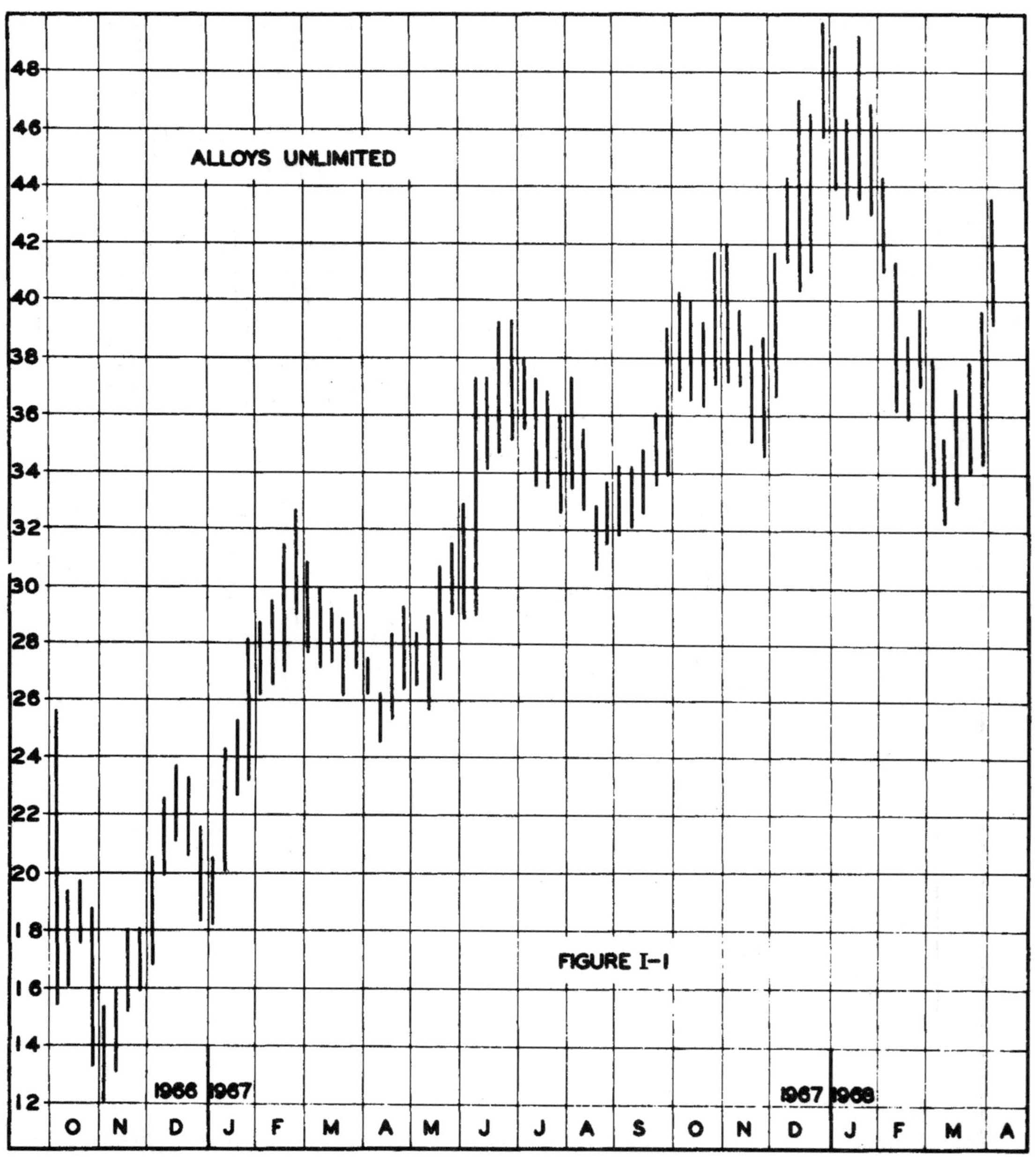


Typical Weekly "High-Low" Chart

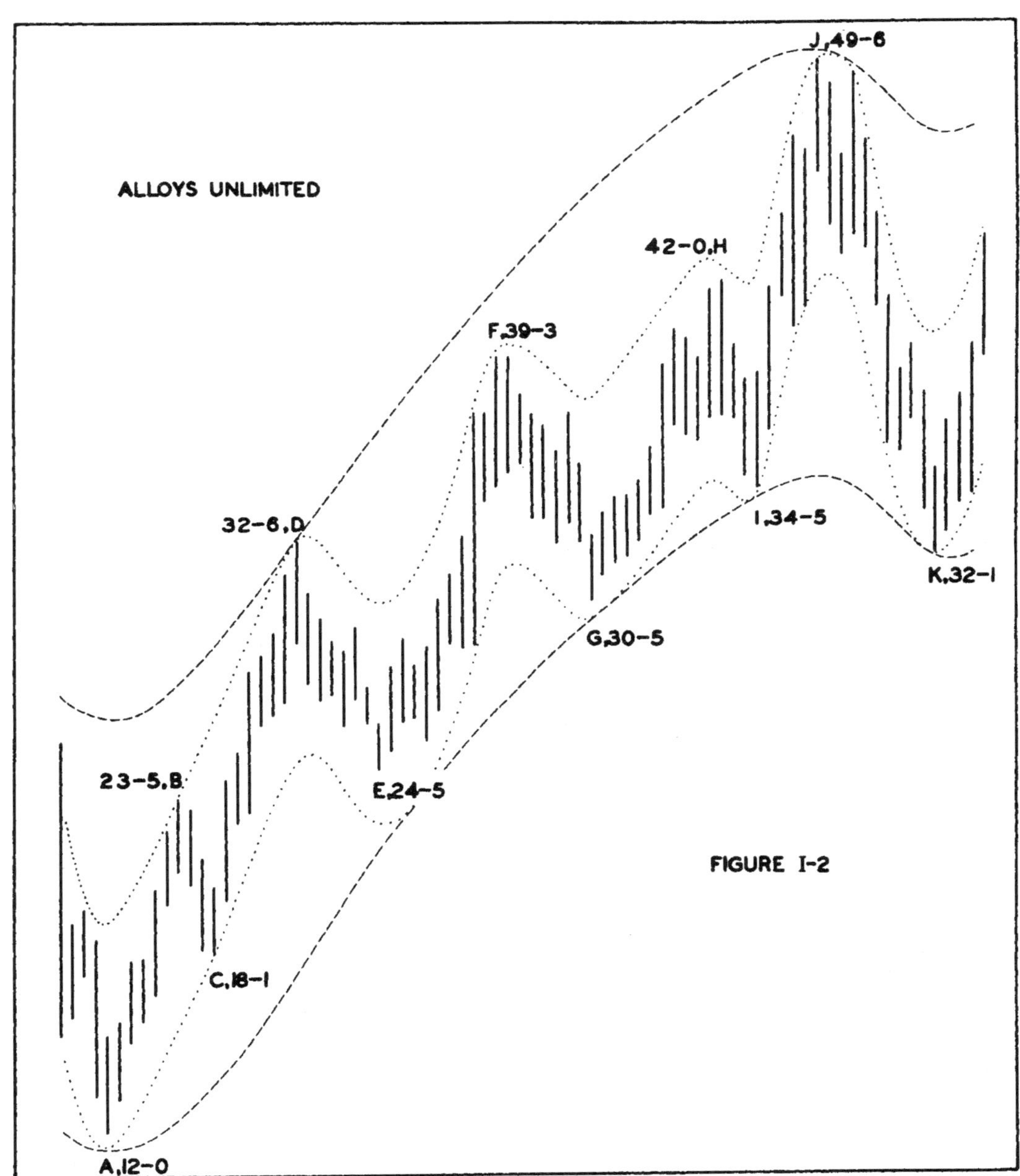


**Ideal Transaction Timing**

trades than by long ones. There are two reasons for this. One of these is intrinsic to the nature of stock price moves and will be understood after formulation of the price-motion model of the next chapter. The other is a case of:

## ADDING MAGIC BY COMPOUNDING

Far and away the most important factor in the overall profit-maximization picture is the influence of profit compounding. After each successful trade more funds are available for re-investment than before. Now the nature of the compound interest law is such that the overwhelming contributor to capital growth by this means is—you guessed it: *How often the compounding takes place. In short—how short the trades are!*

Let's see how this works by juggling some numbers. We'll start with the same $10,000 as before and assume a modest 10% profit (average) on each trade. Assume one trade per month. At the end of a year you will have $31,380 for a profit yield of 313% per year. Take the same $10,000, compound it at the same 10% but do it twice per month. At the end of a year you will have $109,150 or a profit yield of 1091% per year! At once per week, you have $1,410,000 at the end of a year, or 14,100%!

Now it is seen why trading is so important if accurate timing of transactions is consistently possible. Trading brings profit compounding into play—while sufficiently accurate timing to permit short-term trading drastically amplifies the compounding effect. This principle is so important to profit maximization that it deserves entry as the next basic tenet: Profit optimization requires short-term trading.

## MAINTAINING 100% INVESTMENT

All sounds pretty rosy so far—but how do we go about keeping funds working all the time if we're hopping in and out of trades every time we turn around? The answer is rapid selection and analysis. We already know that we must find a way to drastically improve transaction timing. We now know that we must do this in such a way that issue selection and timing analysis can proceed simply and fast. If we can do this, we can maintain a number of issues ready to go at all times—so that as one trade ends there will be a minimum lapse of time before the next starts. Like timing accuracy, this is a function of the rest of the book—and we make the assumption in this chapter that it can be done.

For psychological reasons the timing techniques to be developed must be such as to provide objective signals, created by actual price action. Such signals must be predetermined by analysis—after which stock prices must be tracked as signals are awaited.

## FOUR STEPS TO RICHES

The preceding discussions provide the bits and pieces. Now in pulling them all together, we find that we require:

1. A profit-optimizing investment philosophy, the elements of which include:
    - Trading—as opposed to investing
    - Maximization of percent per year yield on each trade
    - Maximization of percent of time invested
    - Minimization of the trading interval
    - Optimization of transaction timing.
2. Fast and simple issue selection
3. Fast and simple transaction-timing analysis
4. Accurate and timely stock price tracking

It is the purpose of the remainder of this book to weld these elements into a practical method of extracting the profit magic from stock transaction timing!

*chapter*
*two*

# Timing Is the Key

- Something New and Unconventional Is Required
- What Makes Prices Change
- The Impact of Historical Events
- The Source of Trends
- "X Motivation"—and What it Does to Stock Prices
- How Cyclicality Expresses Itself in the Market
- The Summation Principle
- The Commonality Principle
- The Variation Principle
- The Nominality Principle
- The Proportionality Principle
- And Now You Have a Price-Motion Model
- The Significance of Cyclicality
- How to Go About Observational Analysis
- Adding Envelope Visibility
- "Nesting" Envelopes Upward
- "Nesting" Down
- Using Expanded or Contracted Data
- Extracting Cyclic Model Elements
- Cyclicality in Individual Issues
- How Synchronization Is Expressed
- Summing It All Up

Timing is the key—and the price-motion model described in this chapter is the key to timing! Chapter One presented an investment philosophy which is practical, and capable of producing very large yields on invested capital—*provided* transaction-timing accuracies of very high order can be achieved. Such accuracies simply are not possible using traditional approaches to investing.

## SOMETHING NEW AND UNCONVENTIONAL IS REQUIRED

Only two basic reasons are advanced in traditional approaches for the price motion of stocks:

1. Random events causing individuals and groups to make buy and sell decisions at unpredictable times.
2. What investors think the impact of various "fundamental" factors may be on the price of a stock.

By their nature, random events *cannot* be of aid in the prediction of price changes. Foreseeable fundamental factors can theoretically help. In fact, researching these is the traditional approach. This whole field has been thoroughly plowed for many years by many competent people. It is highly unlikely that really significant transaction-timing improvement is achievable by going back over this well-trampled ground. If we are to achieve the needed help, it must come from another quarter entirely—and it will therefore be unconventional in nature.

This chapter supplies a third major reason for the price gyrations of stocks. For convenience we will call it "X motivation" for the present. It is the existence and nature of this factor upon which transaction-timing improvement depends, for it is the "something new and unconventional" that is required!

The material in this chapter does not constitute proof of the existence of the phenomena discussed. This will be developed bit by bit in later chapters in sufficient depth to satisfy most individuals. Where more rigorous evidence is needed, but would distract from the main theme (which is applications), references will be made to the Appendix at the appropriate times. With this in mind, let us state the objectives of the current chapter:

- To define the nature of price motion. The statements of fact then become an explanation or "model" of price change on which all specific timing methods will depend.
- To present simple graphical and visual demonstrations of key elements of the price-motion model. This is done for two reasons:
    1. To provide you with enough evidence of model credibility to permit acceptance of the existence and nature of "X motivation" effects so that you can make use of it without doubt or mental reservation.
    2. To demonstrate for you the first of several graphic and visual techniques that you must learn to use later for yourself.

It should be borne in mind that something vastly unusual is necessary for our purpose. Some of the conclusions reached will appear strange indeed to persons versed in the traditional approach to socio-economic world-of-finance type problems. Such readers are strongly urged to reserve judgment until the entire story is unfolded. "The proof of the pudding is in the eating," and you will find that the methods described work!

## WHAT MAKES PRICES CHANGE?

Decisions. Prices change because stock owners *decide* to buy or *decide* to sell at a specific time. Which way prices move when buyer and seller face each other (through exchange representatives) depends on how strongly the buyer feels about buying in relation to how strongly the seller feels about selling. But decisions in themselves are effects—not causes. Something *causes* an investor to decide to sell—and at a particular time at that.

The cause of decisions is "motivation." If a stockholder decides to sell for no other reason than to raise money to remodel the house, the motivation can be classed as random in nature. Millions of investors deciding to buy or sell for reasons unrelated to the current or possible future price of a stock cause price changes due to random motivation.

*The magnitude of all such "randomly-motivated" price motion amounts to no more than two %!* This statement is the first element of our price-motion model—and will appear incredible to many. Accept it for the moment, for it is a demonstrable fact. And it is one you must keep firmly in mind as you trade and prices vary in an apparently random manner.

## THE IMPACT OF HISTORICAL EVENTS

One of the major misconceptions that must be dispelled is the conviction that large-scale historical events dominate market activity. From all sides we are continually presented with this or that national or world event which is credited as the cause of current market behavior. In Chapter Nine it is shown that the facts just do not fit the conviction! And if you believe that they do, you are effectively prevented from applying a profit-optimized trading philosophy.

As a singular example, consider the case of the traumatic assassination of President Kennedy. It is to be hoped that you were not one of those who sold at a loss during the 15 minutes of panic following the announcement. Beginning immediately thereafter, the market (as measured by the Dow-Jones 30 Industrial Average) climbed in nearly unbroken manner from the region of 710 to that of 1000!

*The impact of wars, global financial crisis, and all other similar events on market price action is utterly negligible!* This statement is the second element of our price-motion model.

## THE SOURCE OF TRENDS

Historical events represent only one type of so-called "fundamental" motivation for the buying or selling of stocks. At least three other categories require consideration for our model:

- Events which can be anticipated and which influence the outlook for entire industry groups.
- Events which can be anticipated and which influence the outlook for a single issue.
- Events (usually associated with a specific company) which cannot be anticipated.

*Foreseeable fundamental events influencing investor thinking regarding industry groups and specific issues account for 75% of the price motion of stocks. The effect is long-term, smooth, and trend-like in nature.*

*Unforeseeable fundamental events influencing investor thinking principally with regard to single issues add "specific randomness" to stock price motion. The rate of occurrence is small, but the effect can be large and sudden.*

These two statements are the third and fourth elements of the price-motion model and can use amplification. Unlike historical events, investor motivation stemming from fundamental factors affecting group and individual issues *does* influence price-motion to a large extent. The effect is of the nature of an underlying trend which is relatively smooth and slow to change direction—if the factors involved are foreseeable. If not, the impact can be large and swift; this is the principal reason for the need of "profit-preservation" type action signals. Unfortunately, the underlying fundamental trend is of little use for our purpose, except to accentuate price moves due to "X motivation."

## "X MOTIVATION"—AND WHAT IT DOES TO STOCK PRICES

The forgoing price-motion elements must be understood and used in successful trading—but they have virtually nothing to do with specific transaction timing! The bulk of the remainder of this chapter will have to do with that price element which *does* have to do with timing—namely: "X motivation."

First of all, discard any reservations you may have regarding choice of names. The all-important effect to be described exists and can be used—regardless of what causes it, or what it is called. The choice of the classical symbol of the unknown, "X," is simply based on the fact that only theories exist regarding the cause. That the effect is present and useful is *not* theory—and can in fact be proven beyond all question!

*23% of all price motion is oscillatory in nature and semi-predictable!* This is the result of "X motivation"—and the statement constitutes the fifth tenet of our price-motion model. The oscillatory motion involved is not simple—in fact it is extremely complex. Fortunately for our purposes, a few outstanding traits characterize it sufficiently to establish utility. We must now state and fully understand the implications of these traits. The description of oscillatory or "cyclic" price action will be referred to as the "cyclic model"—which in turn is one element only (though a very important one) of the overall price-motion model.

It is absolutely essential to your further progress that you gain a complete and fundamental grasp of the cyclic nature of this 23% of all price action! The facts are straightforward and simple—but elemental in their significance.

## HOW CYCLICALITY EXPRESSES ITSELF IN THE MARKET

Let us first clarify what we mean by "oscillatory" or "cyclical." When a quantity starts low, rises smoothly and without interruption to a high—then descends in the same manner and in the same length of time to the low it started from, we will say it has completed one "cycle." If it repeats this action, completing the next cycle in the same length of time as before, we will call it both cyclic and periodic. The principal characteristic with which we will be concerned is the time required to complete one cycle, which we will call the "duration" of a cycle. The entire cyclic activity will be referred to as a "component."

Item A of Figure III-1 is a representation of an ideal periodic-cyclic motion. Variations from this ideal are possible and will be discussed as we go along.

## THE SUMMATION PRINCIPLE

*Cyclicality in price motion consists of the sum of a number of (non-ideal) periodic-cyclic components.* This is the first element of our cyclic "sub-model." Now. What do we mean by the "sum" of such fluctuations? Any desired number of such cyclic components, each of which differs from the other, can be visualized. But the differences must be found in one or more of three descriptive quantities:

- The magnitude or size of the motion (as measured from peak to trough).
- The length of time required to complete one cycle—or the duration.
- The relative positions in time of one motion with respect to another.

Two such waves (and a straight line), differing from each other in one or more of the three ways described, are shown in Figure III-2, where the two periodic-cyclic components are identified as A and C. Now at each point on the time scale, simply add the vertical size of the two waves (and the straight line) at that moment and plot the result. This is the shape of Figure III-3. You have accomplished the process of summing two cyclicalities and a straight line. Any number of such fluctuations may be so added together to get a new, composite wave form. You will be going through this process over and over again in the cyclic analysis of your stocks—and should become thoroughly familiar with it. This is the manner in which "X" motivated cyclicality combines in the price motion of stocks.

## THE COMMONALITY PRINCIPLE

Summed cyclicality is a common factor among all stocks. This is the second element of the cyclic model. Commonality of cyclic price motion is expressed in several ways:

- Cyclicality exists in the price motion of all stocks.
- The cyclic components in each issue have similar durations.
- The highs and lows of cyclic fluctuations are time synchronized.
- The relative magnitudes of cyclic components are similar in all issues.

These four statements are part of the principle of commonality.

## THE VARIATION PRINCIPLE

Price motion is different from issue to issue primarily because of differences in the 75% of underlying fundamentally inspired movement. However, a secondary source of differences arises from variations from commonality in the cyclic action. *Each cyclic component varies from the ideal in that magnitude varies slowly as time passes. As magnitude increases, duration also increases. As magnitude decreases, duration also decreases.* This concept of cyclic magnitude-duration fluctuation is the third element of the cyclic model.

In addition to this primary source of variation, deviations from commonality also contribute to differences from issue to issue. The most important such deviations are as follows:

- Relative magnitudes and durations of cyclic components differ slightly from issue to issue.
- Time synchronization is not perfect. A cyclic high or low in one issue will not necessarily occur at exactly the same time as in another.
- Several components may tend to dominate in a given issue at a given time, while others may dominate in other issues at the same time.

These statements are part of the third element of the cyclic model.

## THE NOMINALITY PRINCIPLE

The effect of the variation principle is to force the use of a nominal cyclic duration in the quantification of the cyclic model. These nominal durations are an element of commonality, and the deviations from these over a given range are the expression of the principle of variation. The nominal durations of the principal cyclic components are:

**Table II-1**

| | *Years* | *Months* | *Weeks* |
|---|---|---|---|
| | 18 | | |
| | 9 | | |
| | 4.5 | | |
| | 3.0 | | |
| | 1.5 | 18 | |
| | 1.0 | 12 | |
| | .75 | 9 | |
| * | .50 | 6 | 26 |
| * | .25 | 3 | 13 |
| | | 1.5 | 6.5 |
| | | .75 | 3.25 |
| | | .375 | 1.625 |

*The 26- and 13-week components often appear in data as a combined effect of 18-week nominal duration.

This tabulation is the fourth element of the cyclic model.

## THE PROPORTIONALITY PRINCIPLE

*The greater the duration of a cyclic component, the larger its magnitude.* The nominal relative relationship between these quantities is as shown in Figure II-1.

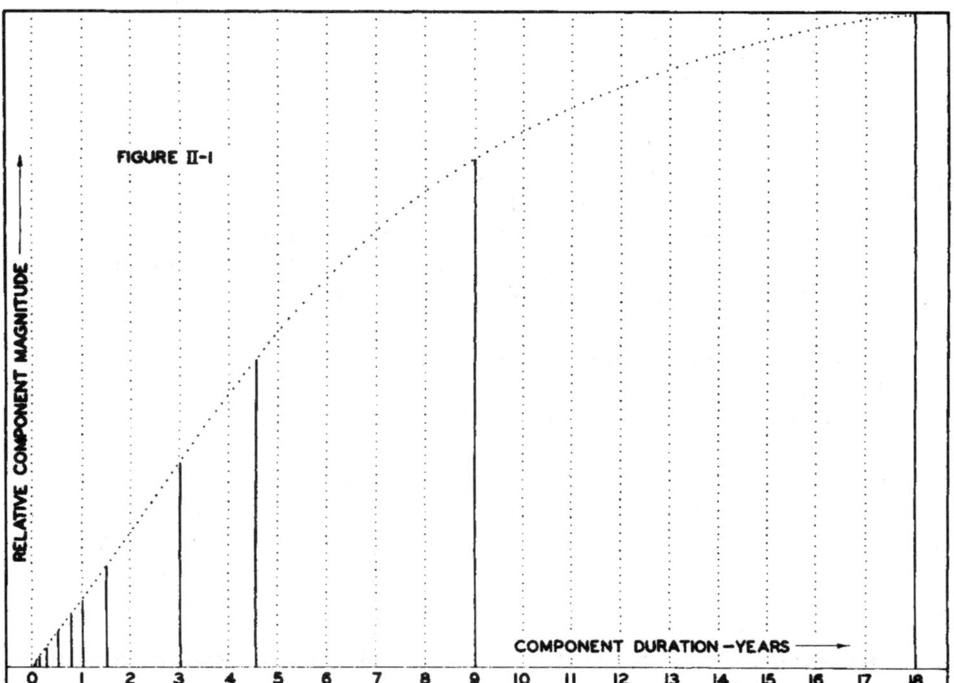


**The Magnitude-Duration Relationship**

This statement and chart constitute the fifth and final element of the cyclic model. *And now you have a price-motion model!*

You should read and re-read the features of this model until every aspect is burned deeply into memory. The more or less mechanical timing techniques to be presented based on this model will not in and of themselves be sufficient to assure successful trading operations. Your degree of attainment of results will hinge in large part on your ability to resolve ambiguities via your understanding of the elements of price motion!

For convenience, the elements of the price-motion model are compactly assembled as follows:

I. Random events account for only 2 percent of the price change of the overall market and of individual issues.

II. National and world historical events influence the market to a negligible degree.

III. Foreseeable fundamental events account for about 75% of all price motion. The effect is smooth and slow changing.

IV. Unforeseeable fundamental events influence price motion. They occur relatively seldom, but the effect can be large and must be guarded against.

V. Approximately 23% of all price motion is cyclic in nature and semi-predictable (basis of the "cyclic model").

VI. Cyclicality in price motion consists of the sum of a number of (non-ideal) periodic-cyclic "waves" or "fluctuations" (summation principle).

VII. Summed cyclicality is a common factor among all stocks (commonality principle). Cyclic commonality expresses as follows:

- Existence in all issues
- Similar durations
- Similar relative magnitudes
- Time synchronization

VIII. Cyclic component magnitude and duration fluctuate slowly with the passage of time. In the course of such fluctuations, the greater the magnitude, the longer the duration and vice-versa (variation principle). In addition, issue-to-issue variation expresses as deviation from commonality as follows:

- Deviations in relative magnitude and duration.
- Imperfect time synchronization.
- Differences in component dominance.

IX. Principle of nominality: an element of commonality from which variation is expected. Nominal cyclic component durations are shown in Table II-1.

X. The greater the nominal duration of a cyclic component, the larger the nominal magnitude (principle of proportionality). The relationship between the two is illustrated in Figure II-1.

The above ten statements constitute the formal, quantitative, price-motion model. Because of its importance, let us restate the model qualitatively in homely terms for additional clarity.

Visualize a general tendency to change slowly and smoothly because of basic fundamentals. Mix in occasionally a bit of short-term, sometimes quite sharp, price motion due to specific and unforeseen fundamental developments. Conceive of all of this so far as causing about 75% of all price change, but as still being a generally smooth situation (few fluctuations). Now stir in a little random action. Superimpose the sum of 12 cyclic motions totaling some 23% of all price change. Imagine the longer duration elements of this motion as being largest in size also. Cause each of these to fluctuate slowly in magnitude and duration. Now have the whole mix influence human decision-making processes, en masse. The resulting buy and sell decisions terminate in purchases and sales—which in turn reflect changing prices. And there you have it: A simplified explanation (or model) of stock price fluctuations—*with predictive implications!*

## THE SIGNIFICANCE OF CYCLICALITY

### "Stock Prices Fluctuate"

They certainly do- and we now know that they do so in a reasonably ordered manner!

### "Buy Low and Sell High"

The key to transaction timing is in knowing *when* is low and *when* is high. The price-motion model elements promise us this knowledge—as exact as our ability to untangle the 12 periodicities of the model as time goes along. This can never be done precisely. However, techniques will be developed in later chapters which convert the imperfect predictions possible into precise action signals. The expectations for being completely incorrect are about 10%, and even this error factor can be effectively prevented from causing significant loss. The remaining 90% of correct action signals is more than sufficient to bring into prominence the profit compounding principle of Chapter One.

## HOW TO GO ABOUT OBSERVATIONAL ANALYSIS

We will now go into the first and most elemental method of determining the status of cyclicality at any given time. This is an essential first step in "predicting" what is likely to occur in the future. This will be done by illustrating key points of the cyclic model. (The remaining elements of the price-motion model are discussed in Chapter Nine and the Appendix.) A dual purpose is served in this approach: you can see for the first time the elements of the model in operation, *and* the techniques used will be needed later as you analyze the market and individual issues for yourself.

Let's first of all take a look at cyclicality in the Dow-Jones 30 Industrial Average (DJIA). Figure II-2 is a weekly high-low chart of the DJIA from early 1965 through early 1969. Prices have certainly fluctuated during this period, ranging from a high of 1001.11 in February 1966 to a low of 735.74 in October of the same year. Our objective is to extract as much cyclic information as possible from this chart, using the expectations of the cyclic model as a guide.

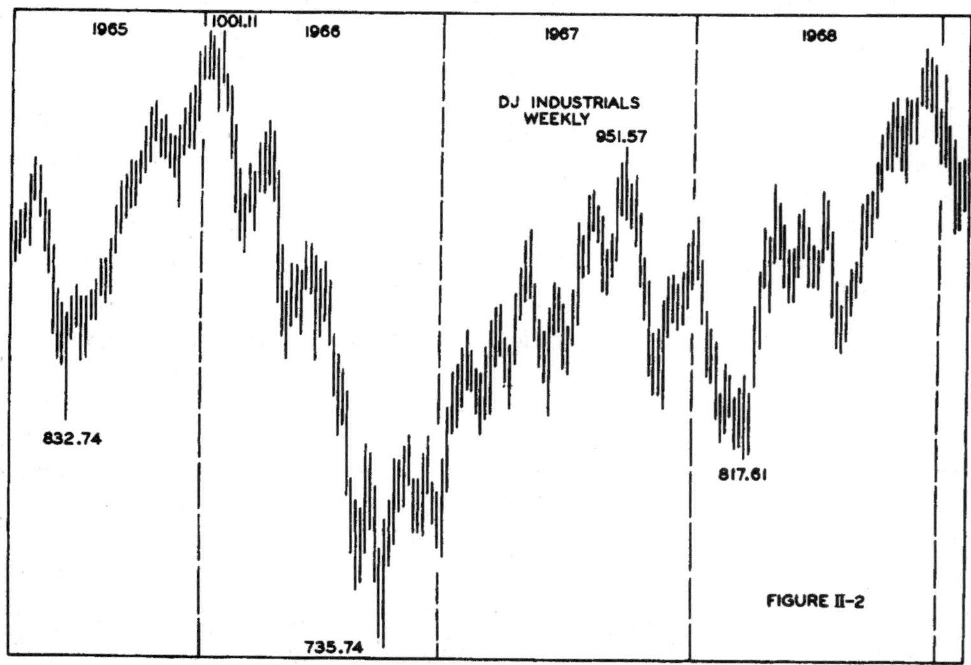


**Price Fluctuations In The Dow Average**

Now look at Figure II-3. This is the same chart except that a smooth envelope has been drawn surrounding the data. Do not be overly concerned just here about the mechanics of constructing this envelope. This will be covered in detail in Chapter Four. Suffice it to say that the envelope is unique and is constructed according to fixed rules. It encloses all of the data on the chart (with the exception of the peak of the action of one week in May 1968), and is uniformly and precisely the same vertical thickness over the entire span of time represented. You will be making much use of such envelopes later because *construction of such an envelope is always the starting point for observational cyclic analysis.*

Now notice that the envelope boundaries are contacted (or approached closely) by the data only in certain spots. These are identified in Figure II-3 by letters. In short, prices gallop back and forth within the envelope—and the points of actual or near contact represent highs and lows of *one* of the cyclic components we're interested in.

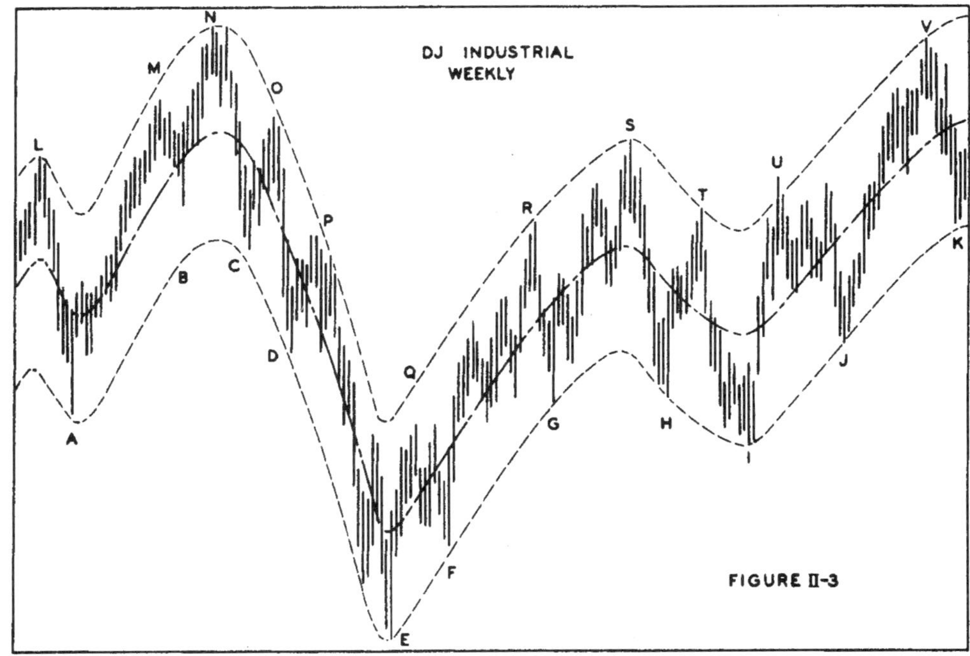


**A Constant-Width Envelope: The Starting Point In Observational Analysis**

Continue the analysis by counting the number of weeks between lettered lows. Lows are always preferable for this purpose since you will find them to be better defined than are the highs. The results can be tabulated as shown on the following page.

Notice the decline in duration between points B-C, C-D, and E-F. *These are examples of magnitude-duration fluctuation (the variation principle), as expected from the cyclic model.* Of the ten cyclic samples available, ignore the obvious variants—and average the remaining seven durations. The result is a nominal cyclic duration of 21.428 weeks. *This is the current time expression in the DJIA of the 26-week nominal duration cyclic component of the price-motion model.* Now record the variation from

| *Time Period* | *Duration (weeks)* |
|---|---|
| A-B | 23 |
| B-C | 14 |
| C-D | 9 |
| D-E | 21 |
| E-F | 12 |
| F-G | 22 |
| G-H | 24 |
| H-I | 17 |
| I-J | 20 |
| J-K | 23 |

average of the seven samples, which is +2.572 and −4.428 weeks. Average these limits to obtain ±3.5 weeks. In view of the relative inaccuracy of the method, round off decimals—and your expectation is for 21.4 ± 3.5-week cycles to continue to make an appearance in the near future in this indicator. These results must, of course, be subjected to continuous up-dating since the principle of variation is in constant operation. One final bit of very useful information can be obtained from this exercise by forming a center line mid-way between envelope bounds. The significance of this line is that it represents the *sum of all cyclic components of duration longer than 21.4 weeks—added to any fundamental trends existing at the time.*

## "NESTING" ENVELOPES UPWARD

Using the same data, let us now apply the same technique to extract information regarding the next longer duration cycle of the model.

Turning to Figure II-4, we see the same chart as before, but now a second envelope has been added. The characteristics of this one are exactly as before, except that they apply to the first envelope, rather than to the original data. It is immediately seen that the first envelope oscillates back and forth between the bounds of the second, establishing contact at the lettered intervals. Proceeding as before, count the weeks between lows. Two samples are available with durations of 67 and 75 weeks. Averaging these produces 71 ± 4 weeks as the nominal expected duration and extent of variation in the near future. The cyclic model calls for the presence of an 18-month cycle. Eighteen months is 78 weeks—and the 71 ± 4-week fluctuation noted is the counterpart of the 18-month component of the model for this period of time in the DJIA.

We now have a set of "nested" envelopes, and the process of constructing a second envelope about the first one we will call "nesting" upward. The mechanics of envelope construction does not permit the existence of envelopes containing fluctuations of duration between 21.4 and 71 weeks in this particular sample of DJIA data. Noting this, and referring back to the cyclic model, you will see that a 9- and 12-month component appear to be missing. They are, in truth, present—but of such small magnitude at this particular time as not to be "observationally significant." *This is an example of the "dominance" characteristic of the principle of variation in action.*

During this same period of time, the "missing" components can be found dominant in other indicators and specific issues. Once again, a center line can be drawn

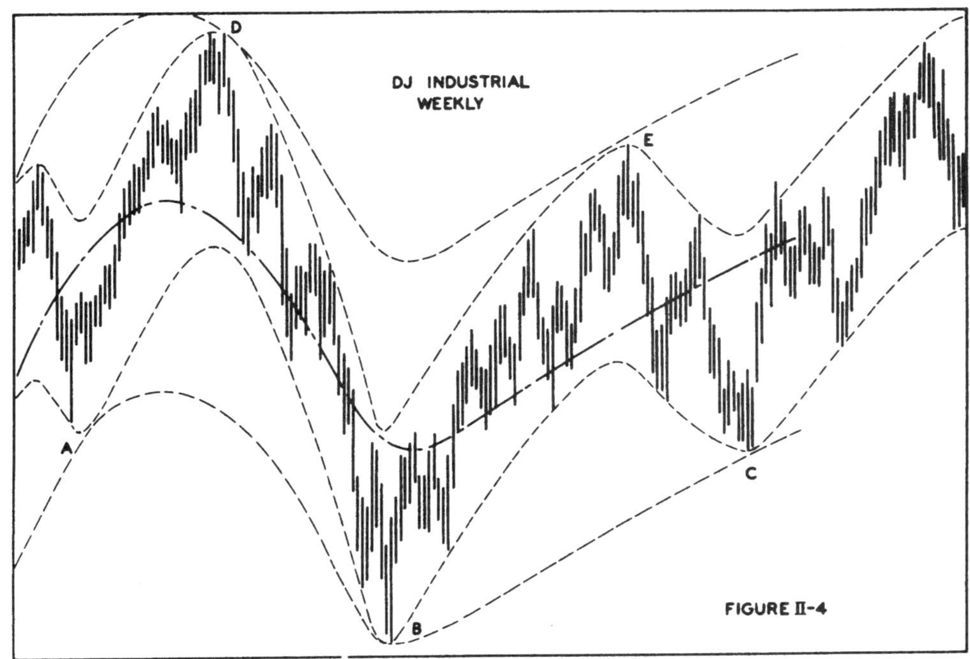


**Nesting Envelopes**

between the bounds of the second envelope. The significance, as before, is the representation of the sum of fundamental trends and all longer duration components (in this case longer than 71 weeks). This type of information will be put to good use in later chapters.

## "NESTING" DOWN

After nesting upwards to the point where you run out of cyclic samples (as in this case), the same data can be made to produce still more information by nesting down. However, you will find that envelope smoothness deteriorates steadily as enclosed cyclic durations decrease. Part of this is due to the use of weekly data, and can be overcome by shifting to daily plots. But the bulk of the problem is intrinsic to the expression of the principle of variation.

Accordingly, another technique is introduced that you will often find useful. Let's go back and re-examine Figure II-3. Observing the region of this figure between letters F and G (lows of the 21.4-week cycle), we note that prices did not move smoothly up and then down again, but did so in now familiar gallops. In fact, between F and G, three such gallops are seen. What about G and H? Again three. Between H and I the same occurs, except that the imagination is stretched a bit on gallops two and three. But, between I and J, once again three movements are clearly noted.

Now the average duration of the F-G, G-H, H-I, etc. type movements was previously established as 21.428 weeks. One third of this is 7.142 weeks. *This is the expression at this time in the DJIA of the (nominal) 6.5-week component of the cyclic model.*

A third technique can be employed to provide additional estimate accuracy.

- Form a new envelope between the letters E and J of Figure II-5 by carefully connecting each weekly low on the plot to its neighbor with short, straight lines to obtain the bottom of the envelope.
- Similarly, connect the weekly highs to form the envelope upper bound.

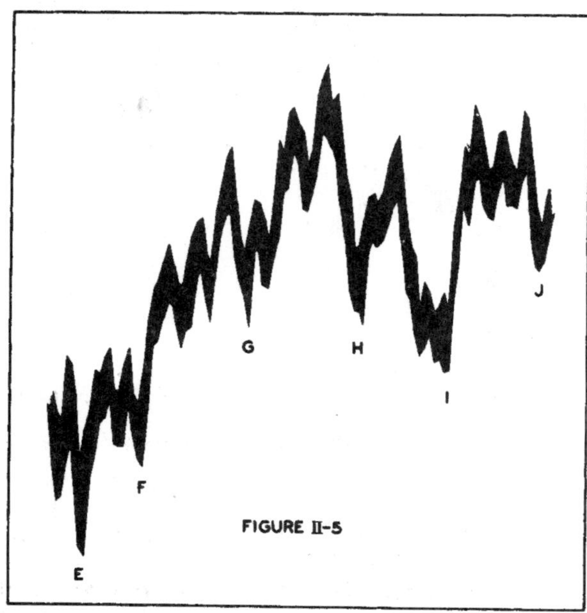


**Another Envelope Technique**

The result is seen in Figure II-5 with all extraneous information removed—and the fluctuations of interest are clearly seen. Now run a center line through this envelope as in Figure II-6 (where the lows of interest are numbered). Referring these back to a time scale, weeks between each can be counted and averaged. The outcome—15 samples with an average duration of 6.766 weeks. This is within 5.3% of the original estimate based on one-third of the 21.4-week cycle—and is considered more accurate. The average of the extremes of the deviation from nominality is ±.8 weeks.

## USING EXPANDED OR CONTRACTED DATA

All components of the cyclic model which are present in this sample of the DJIA between the nominal ones of 6.5 weeks and 18 months have now been identified. To proceed further, the price action must be presented in a different form.

To extract still shorter duration fluctuations, daily data must be used. Any time the price chart permits less than six or seven data points in the time span covered by the duration of one cycle of a given component, the display must be *expanded* by going to closer data spacing. To extract longer duration fluctuations, a longer time period

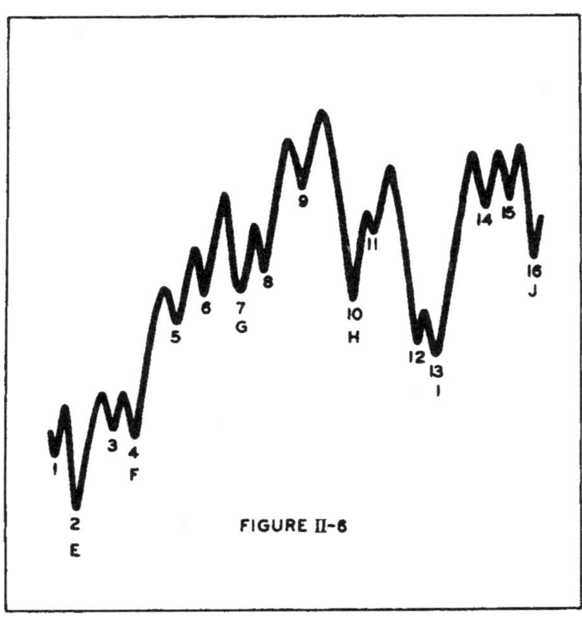


**An Example Of Short-Duration Cyclicality**

must be covered by the data. Effort can be minimized here by following the rule of a minimum of six or seven data points per cycle. Any time you run out of cyclic samples in your data, it is time to *contract* your display (if you desire information on longer duration cycles).

We will choose contraction for the purposes of further illustration. In Figure II-7, the DJIA is extended into the past to May 1949 on a monthly basis. This plot is constructed on a logarithmic rather than a linear scale. This device is useful whenever the sum of all trends and components longer in duration than the cycle of interest is extremely steep.

The same plot is reproduced as Figure II-8, with the familiar constant-width envelope added and distractions removed. *Over this 20-year time period, four samples of periodicity are present. The duration is 52 ± 1 months*. The cyclic model leads us to expect a component of 4.5 years' duration, or 54 months. We have obviously isolated this (nominal) model component in our example. We will not proceed further with this illustration of the cyclic model in action in the DJIA, since our purpose has been served.

The procedure in such preliminary analysis is now clear. And the purpose is to obtain dominant component identification (using the cyclic model as a guide); determine the near past nominal durations and expected variation; and pinpoint the location in time of the *last low of each component.*The ways of using this information to improve transaction timing will be made clear in subsequent chapters.

Before leaving the subject, two additional key features of the model require

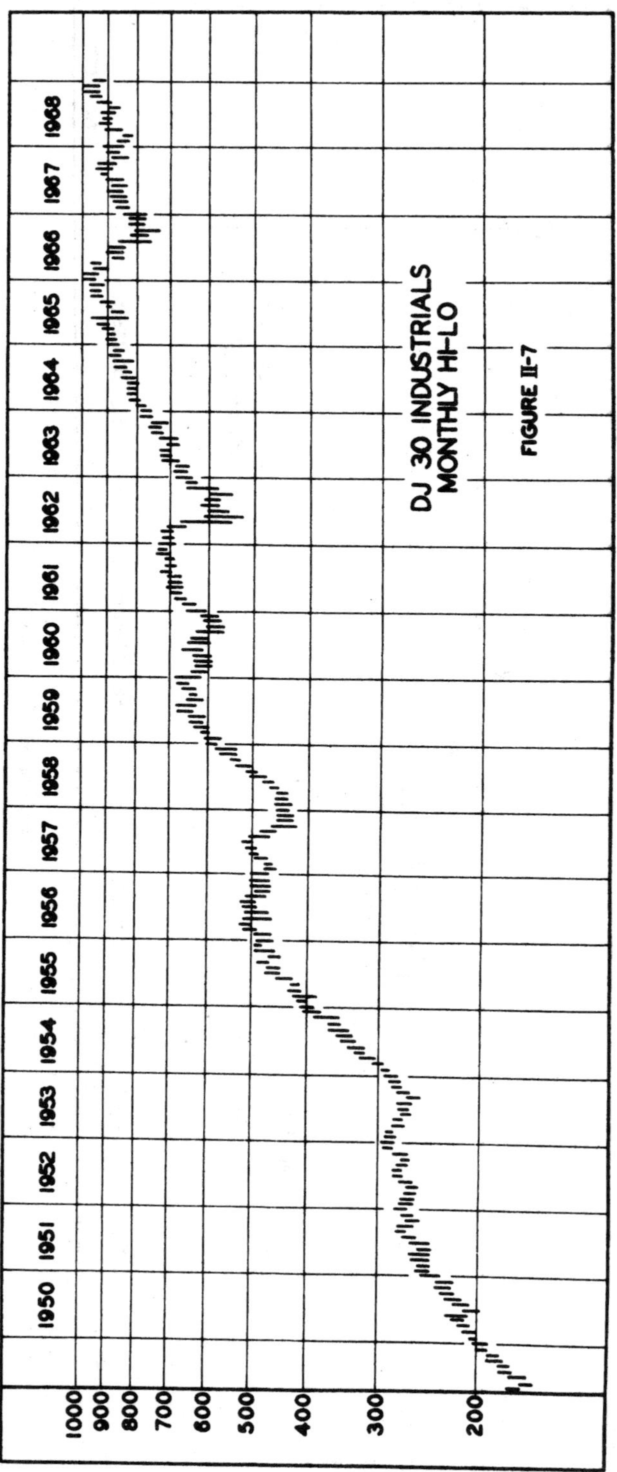


**The Longer Duration Cycles Require Monthly Data**

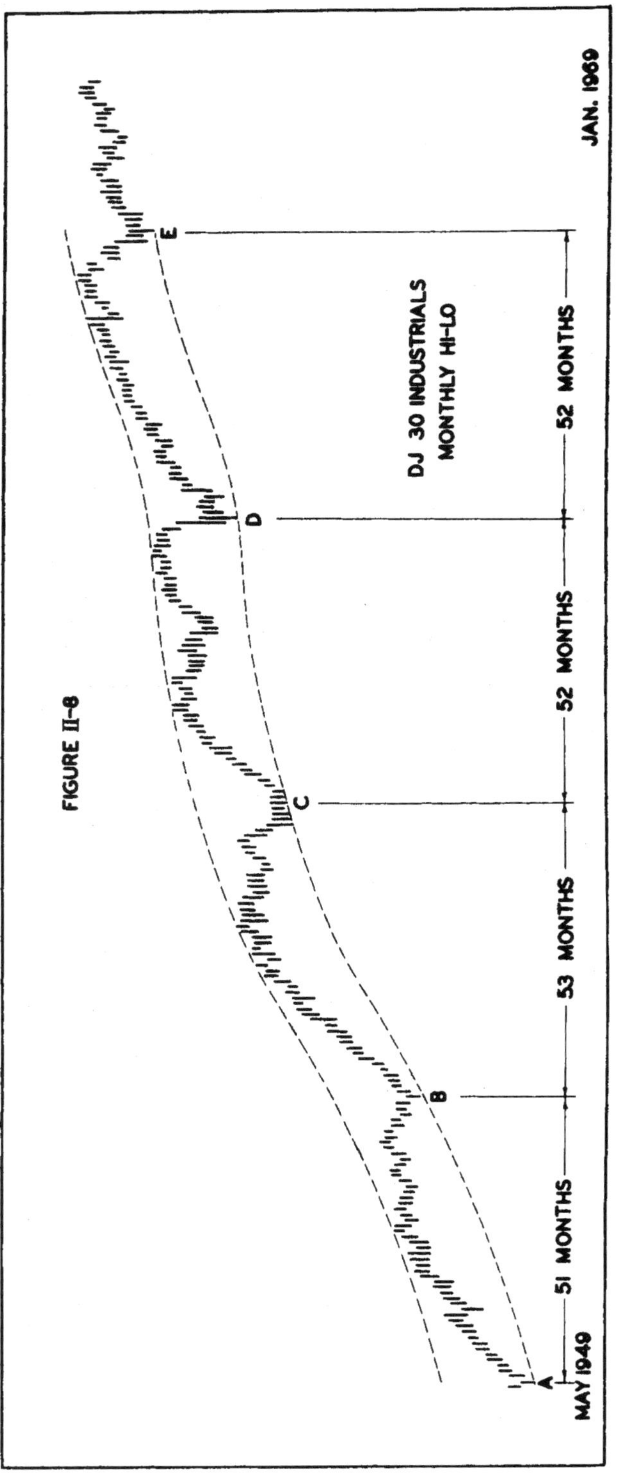


The Infamous "Bull-Bear" Cycle

demonstration. You should have a better idea of the characteristics of magnitude-duration fluctuation than can be gained via envelope analysis. The same is true for the expectations of the principle of commonality.

## EXTRACTING CYCLIC MODEL ELEMENTS

Envelope analysis is a simple and fast technique for determining present status of cyclic components, but leaves much to be desired in the way of detail. To progress further, the techniques of numerical analysis are required. You will never need to apply these time-consuming methods as you trade, but you should be aware of their existence and power. Chapter Eleven and the Appendix will make method and function clear.

Using such techniques, the plot of Figure II-9 was prepared. Here, the 18-month (nominal) cycle of the model has been cleanly extracted from the closing prices of the DJIA over the time-period January 4, 1935, to December 28, 1951. *Thirteen samples are present with an average duration of 68.3 weeks. This compares with the two samples previously seen in the 1965-1968 time period of 71-week duration.* This is an example of the principle of variation in operation over a long period of time.

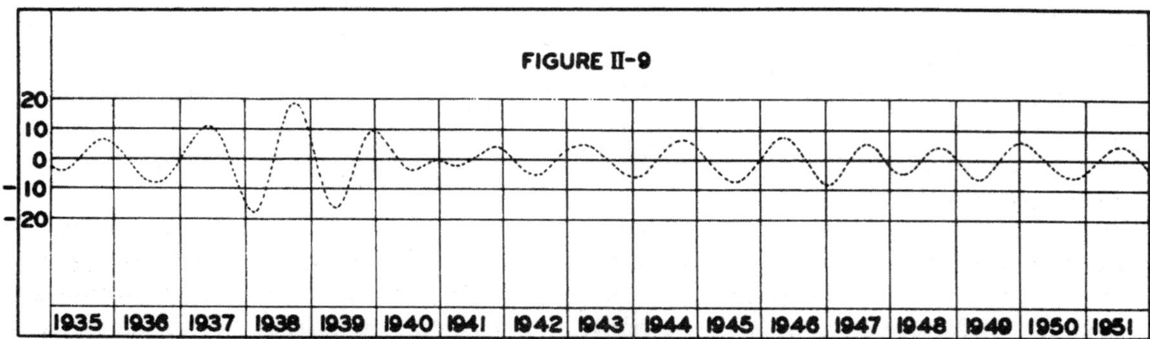


**The Time-Persistence Of Cyclicality**

Even more important, you can now get a much improved idea of the nature of the magnitude-duration fluctuation phenomenon. Using the envelope technique on this extracted fluctuation we arrive at the results of Figure II-10. It is seen that such fluctuation is slow and smooth. The rate of change is much slower than the individual oscillations that comprise the envelope. This is very important, for it means that near past nominal magnitudes, durations, and variations are unlikely to be much different in the near future.

## CYCLICALITY IN INDIVIDUAL ISSUES

Model element demonstration to this point has employed only the Dow-Jones Industrial Average. The principle of commonality assures us that the results hold essentially true for all stocks, but neither this nor the extent of expected variation from commonality has yet been illustrated.

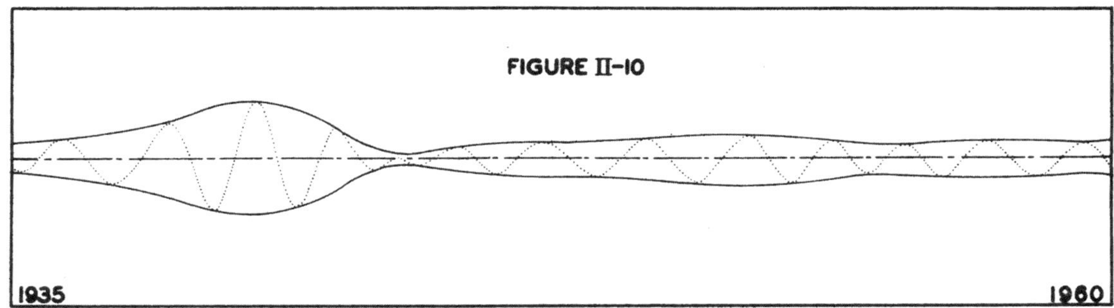


**The Principle Of Variation At Work**

For this purpose, turn to Figure II-11. This is a weekly plot of Warner Company (listed on the New York Stock Exchange) for the 1961-1963 time period. The cyclicality that has been extracted using numerical analysis techniques is clearly visible in the stock price as you compare the two. The following elements of commonality are noted:

1. Magnitude-duration fluctuation.
2. Five samples are present, the last of which is foreshortened per the principle of variation.
3. The remaining four average 18.5 weeks. This is the expression of the combined effects of the 13-and 26-week components noted in the model.

The principles of commonality and variation can also be demonstrated to some extent using envelope analysis. For example, Figure II-12 plots Standard Packaging (New York Stock Exchange) from 5 May 1967 through 10 January 1969. Noting a seeming regularity with two lows appearing in 1967 and three more in 1968, we apply the constant-width envelope technique. The result is shown in Figure II-13, sans all extraneous information. Four samples are present, averaging 18.75 weeks in duration—which we recognize as consistent with the cyclic model.

Noting again that progress of prices from low to peak of this component is not smooth, we form a new envelope by connecting weekly lows and highs. The result of passing a smooth curve through the center of this envelope is depicted in Figure II-14. This time 14 samples are present, with an average duration of 5.71 weeks. The ratio of 18.75 to 5.71 is 3.28, indicating once more the presence of approximately three of the shorter duration cycles within the span of the longer one. The 5.71-week duration compares favorably with the 6.766 number obtained for the DJIA in the same time period—and *demonstrates both the principles of commonality and variation for this particular issue.*

Contracting the data produces Figure II-15. Here Standard Packaging is shown from 9 April 1965 through 24 May 1968. The envelope technique reveals two samples of 70.0-week average duration. The two samples taken for the DJIA in the same time period averaged 71.0 weeks!

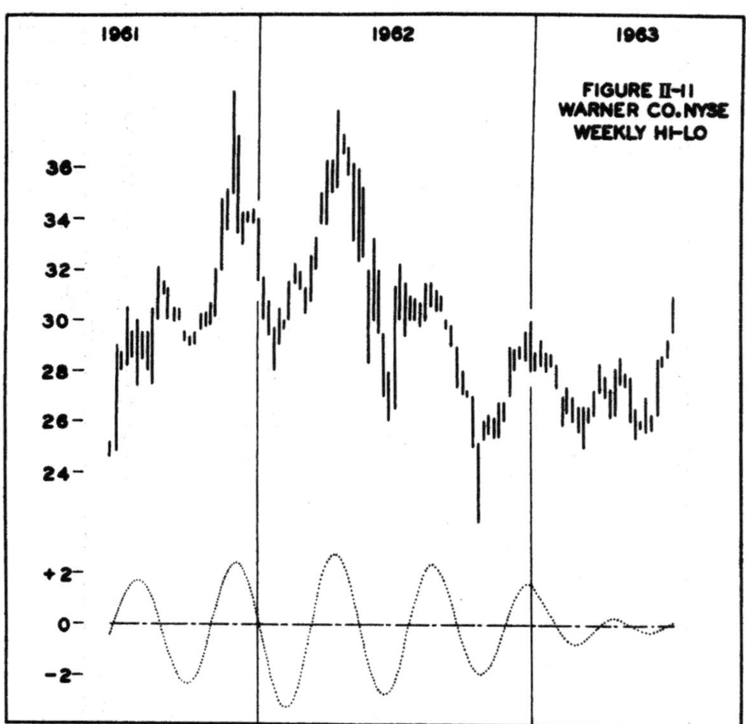


Cyclicality And Numerical Analysis

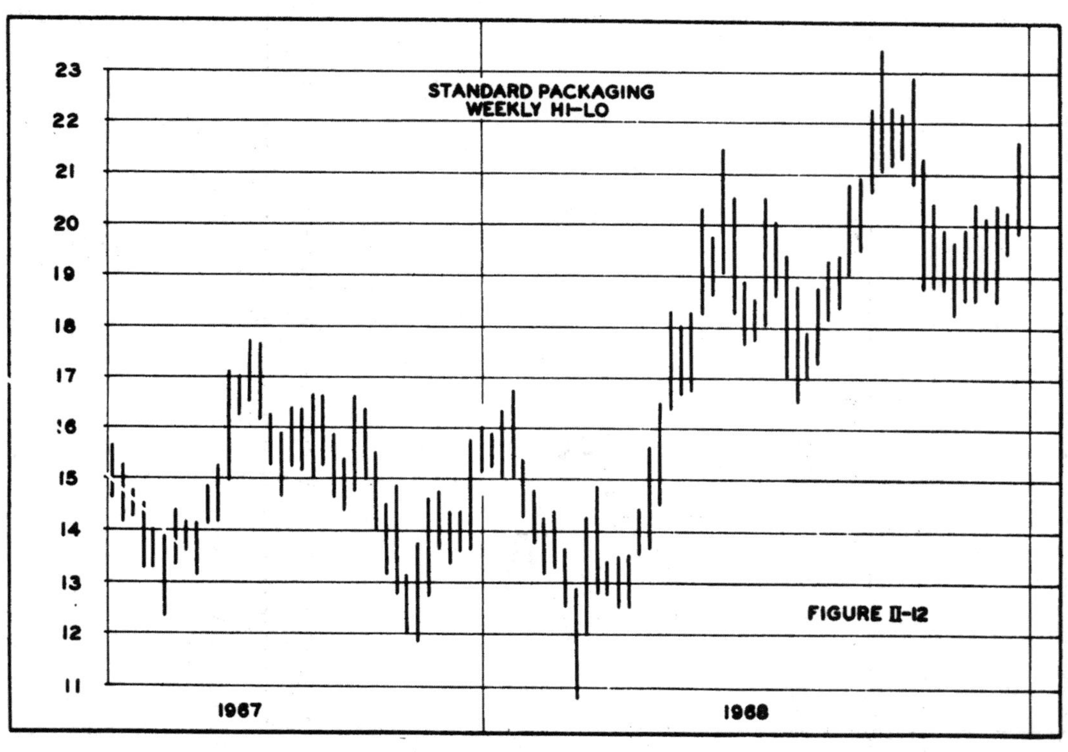


Before Envelope Analysis

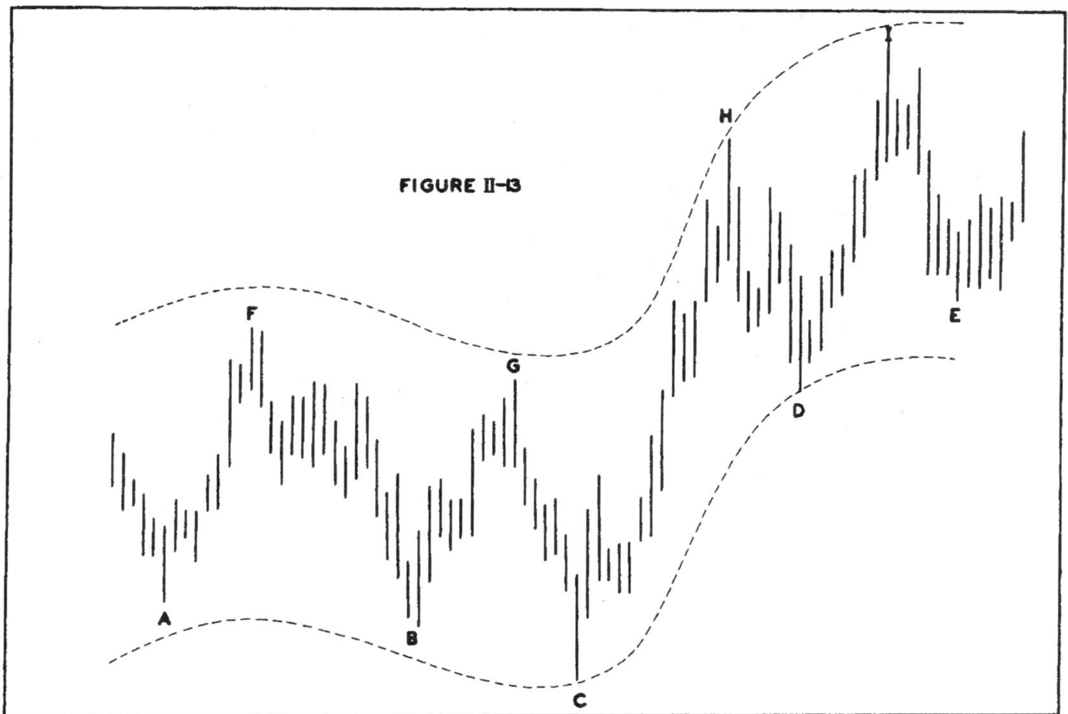


**Envelopes And Standard Packaging**

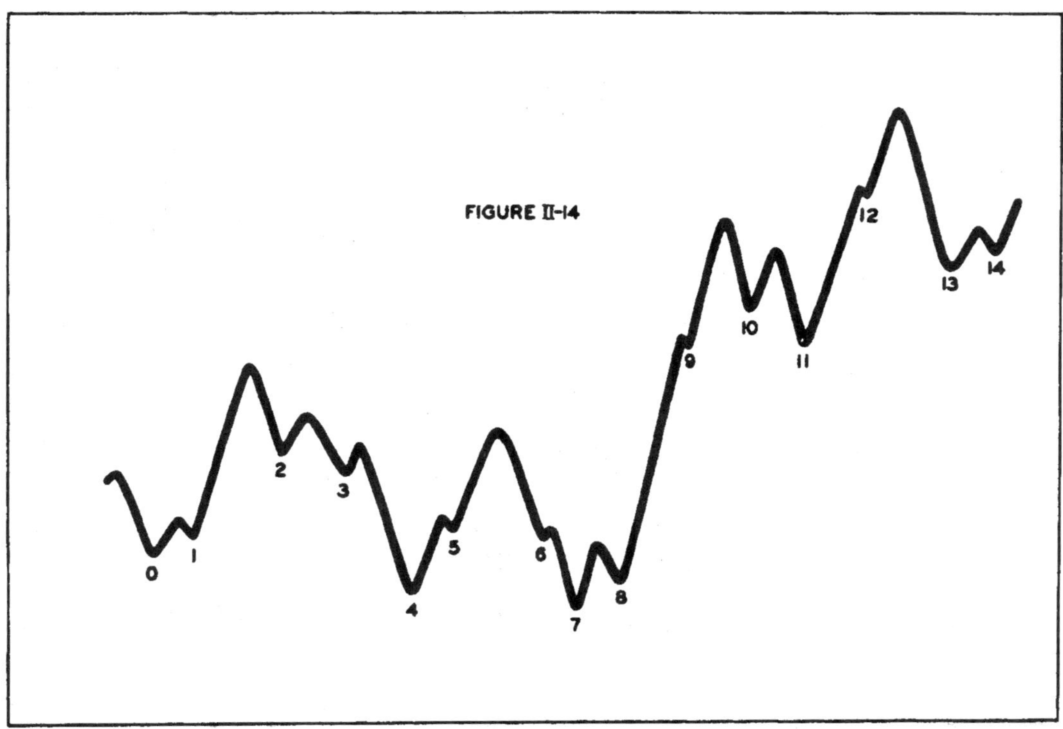


**Nesting Down**

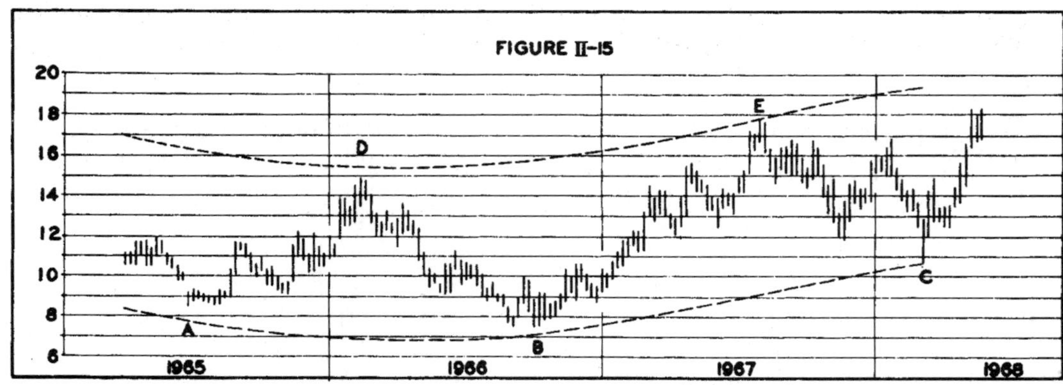


Nesting Up

## HOW SYNCHRONIZATION IS EXPRESSED

One of the characteristics of the principle of commonality is the manner in which cyclic component highs and lows occur at nearly the same time from issue to issue. We can use Standard Packaging again to demonstrate this aspect of the cyclic model.

In Figure II-16, Standard Packaging and the DJIA are plotted in a manner suited for price-turn comparison. The data have been proportionally adjusted in this figure so that the total price variation for each over this time period is identical. The timing of *all* fluctuations of *all* durations is seen to be virtually identical. In fact, "where goeth the Dow, there goeth Standard Packaging" would seem to describe the results with considerable accuracy!

In spite of this, the principle of variation is seen at work in the gentle divergence of the two price histories before and after the 65th week on the plot, even while time synchronization is firmly maintained. The commonality of synchronization is more broadly demonstrated in the Appendix.

## SUMMING IT ALL UP

- A large percentage of the price motion of all stocks consists of the sum of a number of periodic-cyclic "waves"
- The waves in each stock have many common characteristics, including duration, relative magnitude-duration relationships, and a strong tendency to be time synchronized. This feature can be expressed as a principle of commonality.
- Deviations from commonality are minor and can be expressed as a principle of variation.
- Very little of stock price change is random in nature.
- Smooth, underlying trends are caused by fundamental factors related to the growth of the economy and of specific industries and companies.
- Major historical events do not significantly influence the market.
- Relative independence of stock price fluctuations from random and historical events, plus the periodic and common nature of the cyclic components permit timing analysis on a purely "technical" basis.

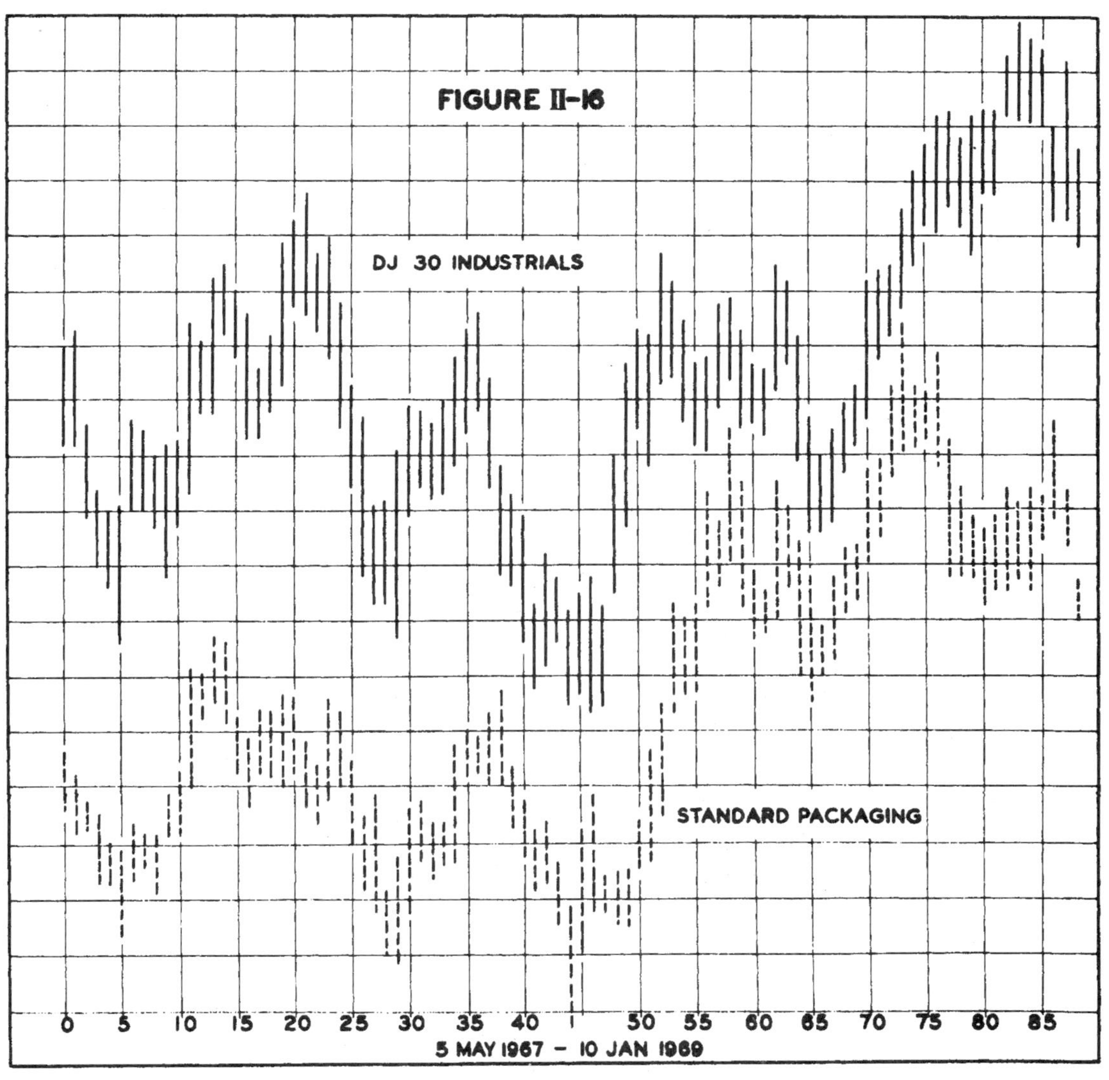


**Commonality And Standard Packaging**

- A model of price motion can be constructed as the basis for such analysis. The principles of summation, commonality, variation, nominality, and proportionality describe the most important aspects of this model.
- The graphical method of data enclosure by special "envelopes" is a useful method of roughly determining the status of cyclicality.
- The price-motion model permits the development of numerous techniques for refined transaction timing which are described in later chapters. A firm understanding of the nature and meaning of the price-motion elements of the model is essential to the proper application of these techniques.

# chapter three

## Verify Your Chart Patterns

- **Why Trend Lines and Channels Form and Repeat**
- **Where Head and Shoulder Patterns Come From**
- **About Double Tops and Bottoms**
- **The Significance of Triangles**
- **How to Tell in Advance If a Chart Pattern Will "Fail"**
- **Understanding Other Chart Patterns**
- **How Cyclicality Gives Meaning to Chart Patterns**
- **The Significance of Moving Averages**
- **Why Ten-and 30-Week Moving Averages Are Useful**
- **How to Plot and Interpret a Moving Average Properly**
- **How a Moving Average Can Aid Cyclic Analysis**
- **Summarizing Chart Patterns**

In Chapter Two you were introduced to an unconventional concept of stock price motion. Before applying the resulting price-motion model you must develop confidence in it—and that is part of the purpose of this chapter. If the "X motivation" concept is valid, it must be able to explain the existence and reoccurrence of common chart patterns—and why they impart information to the investor. Thus, reconciliation of the model with the precepts of charting is strong evidence of the *validity* of the model—which adds to confidence in usage.

The second purpose of the chapter is to show you how the price-motion model can be used to resolve chart patterns. Such patterns can be used to help determine the status of cyclic activity, and this in turn can be used to determine which way and when price motion will go at pattern termination. For those of you that are unfamiliar with chart patterns, reference is provided in the bibliography to several good books on the subject.

## WHY TREND LINES AND CHANNELS FORM – AND REPEAT

These are two of the very most basic tools of the chartist. The chartist will note two or more consecutive fluctuation lows, and if each one occurs at a higher price level, he will draw an "uptrend" line connecting or just below them. Similarly, he will draw a "downtrend" line connecting or just above two or more consecutive fluctuation highs when each successive high is at a lower price level. He will then draw upon the adage that "trends tend to persist," and expect the uptrend or downtrend to continue–until the trend line is broken.

Furthermore, our chartist will often note a situation where prices are generally trending in one direction or another, but appear to bounce back and forth between two imaginary, parallel lines. He will draw these lines in on the chart and call them a channel.

In Figure III-1 we have extracted the simplest possible set of elements from our model. One of our cyclic components (any one) is shown at "A." It is assumed that all longer duration components sum for the time being to the straight line at "B." At each point in time, the price values of "A" and "B" are added to get the resultant, "C." As a result of this highly simplified extraction from our model, both an uptrend line and an uptrending channel are formed!

Trend lines and channels have often been described in awe-filled tones, for it does sometimes seem like magic when stock prices consistently reverse themselves at channel or trend line boundaries almost as if these were very real constraints. At this point, however, we can see that there is no magic to it at all: *It is simply the natural result of the existence of "X" cyclicality!*

## WHERE HEAD AND SHOULDER PATTERNS COME FROM

Now we will add just a little more complexity to our simulated price action. In Figure III-2, we see two of the cyclic elements of our model at "A" and "C." The magnitude and duration relationships between these are approximately those that our model says should exist between the 18-week and 18-month periodicities. As before, we will not clutter up the picture with any other cyclic activity, and will assume that all regularities of longer than 18 months duration sum to the straight line at "B." Again we will add the value of all three together for each interval of time and show the results as Figure III-3. Quite a complex bit of price motion for such a simple beginning, isn't it? Imagine what it's like with all 12 periodicities at work–*and* with fluctuation of magnitude and duration added!

Now let's put a few of the chartist's favorite lines in place in Figure III-4.

### Pay Dirt!

Almost everywhere we look we see a chart pattern of traditional significance! An uptrend line and a downtrend line both appear. These are each parts of short up and down channels respectively. Both downside and upside breakouts from trend lines are present, and in each case forecast what the chartist says they should–a reversal of trend! Another charting favorite also strikes the eye. The head and shoulder pattern is

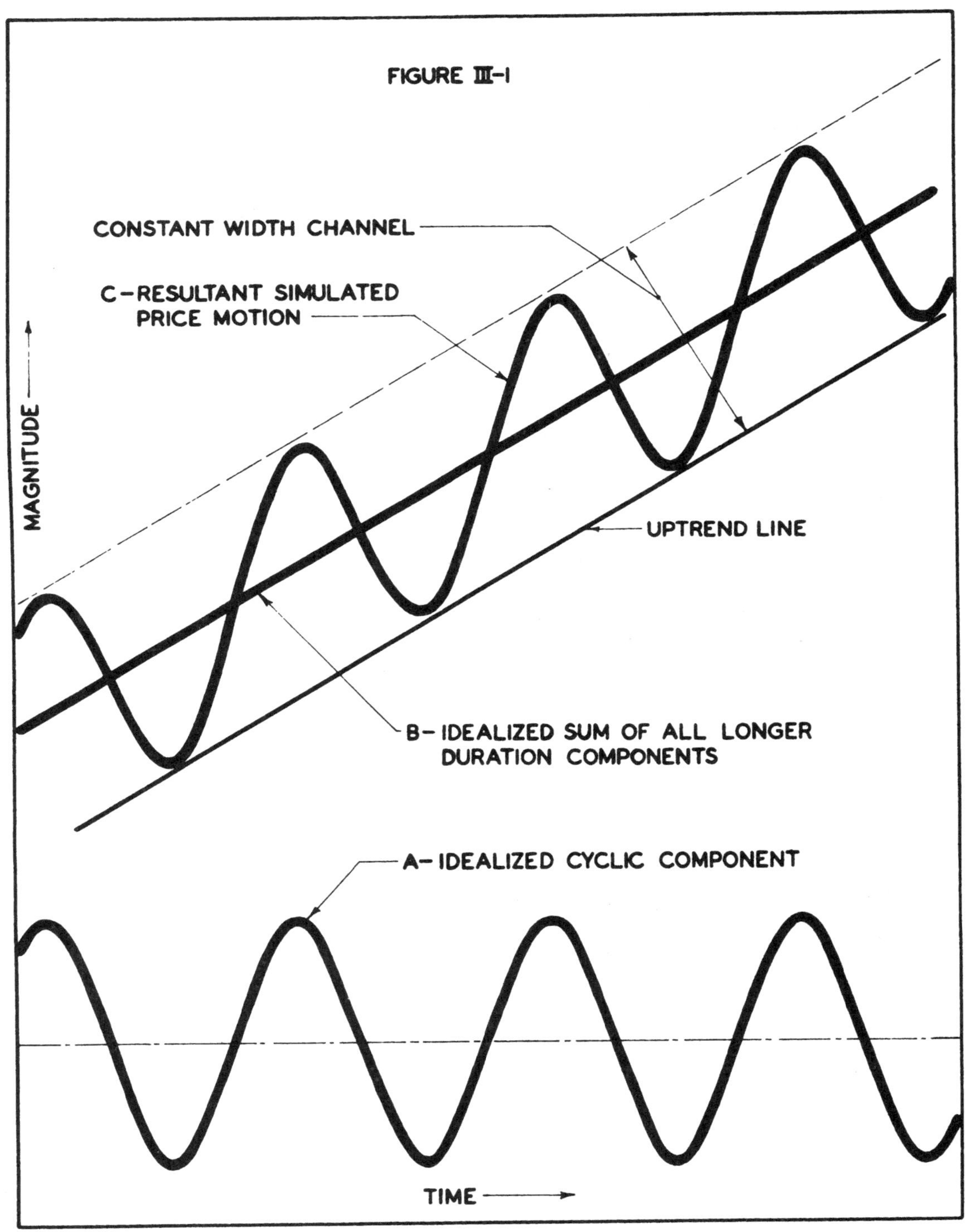


Channel Formation

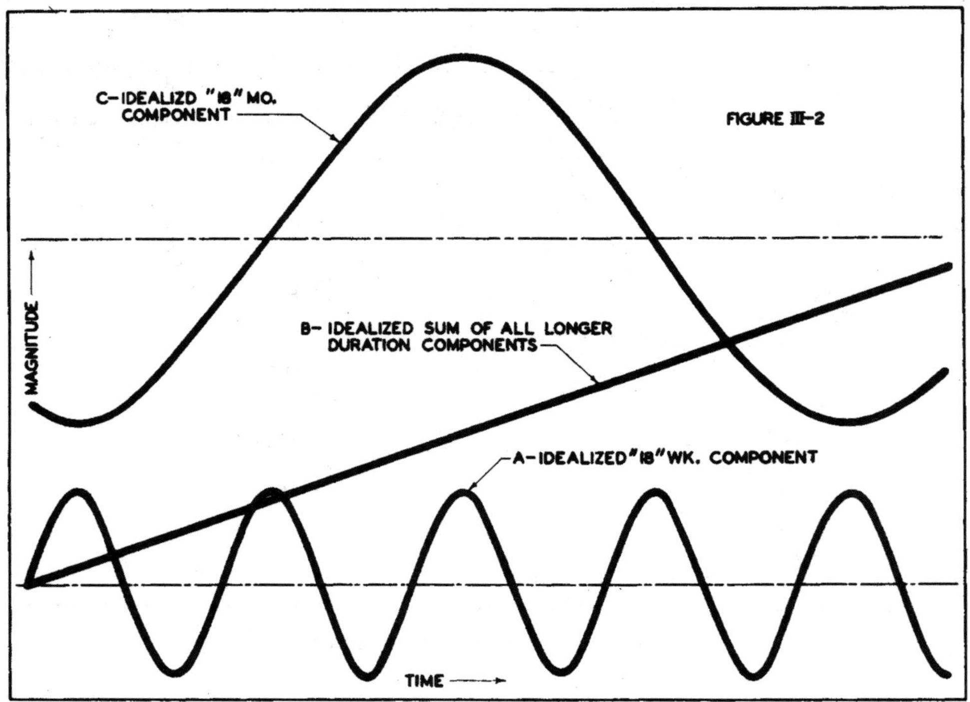


**Adding Another Component**

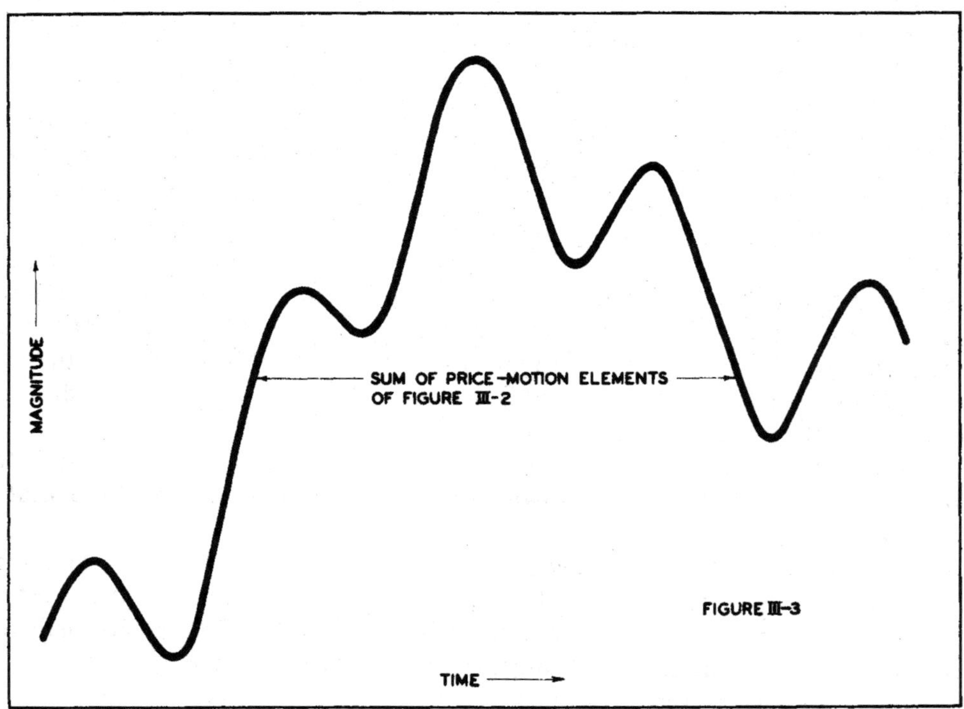


**The Summation Principle Applied**

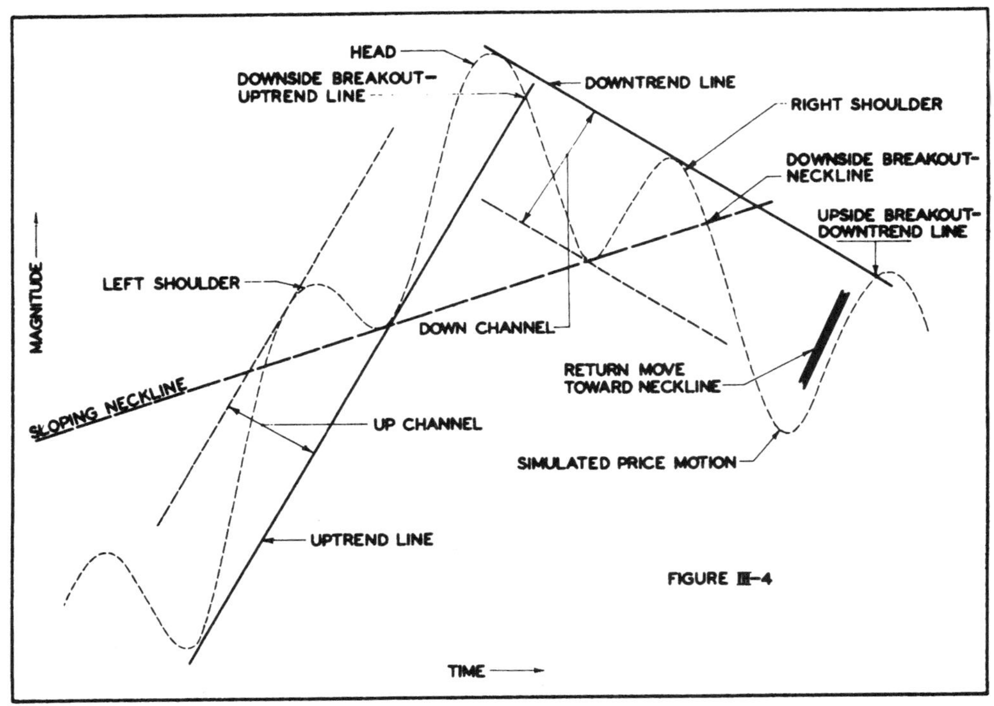


**How Head And Shoulder Patterns Form**

a classic one with a sloping neckline. The downside breakthrough confirms the trend reversal called by the previous breakthrough the uptrend line, and calls for further downside activity. The oft-noted "return move" to or near the neckline is present, followed (as per tradition) by further downside activity. All of this from an almost ridiculously simplified version of our price-action model!

Let's pause a moment and discuss what we've seen happen. Direct your attention to Figure III-5. The simulated price motion of Figure III-3 is reproduced here, but this time with our constant-width envelope of earlier chapters added. The constant-width envelope phenomenon is seen to be a *mandatory* outgrowth of the cyclic model! Obviously, when all fluctuations completely fill such an envelope over any given period of time, the magnitude-duration fluctuations for the intra-channel cyclic component must be nil for this time period. And indeed, this is exactly what Figure III-5 shows, and exactly the way the simulated price motion was formed in this case! Furthermore, when the fluctuations do *not* fill such an envelope, we are warned that such magnitude-duration fluctuations are forming up.

Now note the overlay in Figure III-5 of the previously remarked up and down trend lines and associated up and down channels. It is easy to see here that the chartist's trend lines and channels are simply straightened-out segments of our constant-width envelope boundaries, which actually are curved! Clearly, when a longer duration cycle than the one contained within the channel begins to turn over, our curvilinear channel turns also, and prices quickly "break" through the chartist's trend lines and channel boundaries. His assumption, therefore, that this indicates a major price reversal is founded on the facts that:

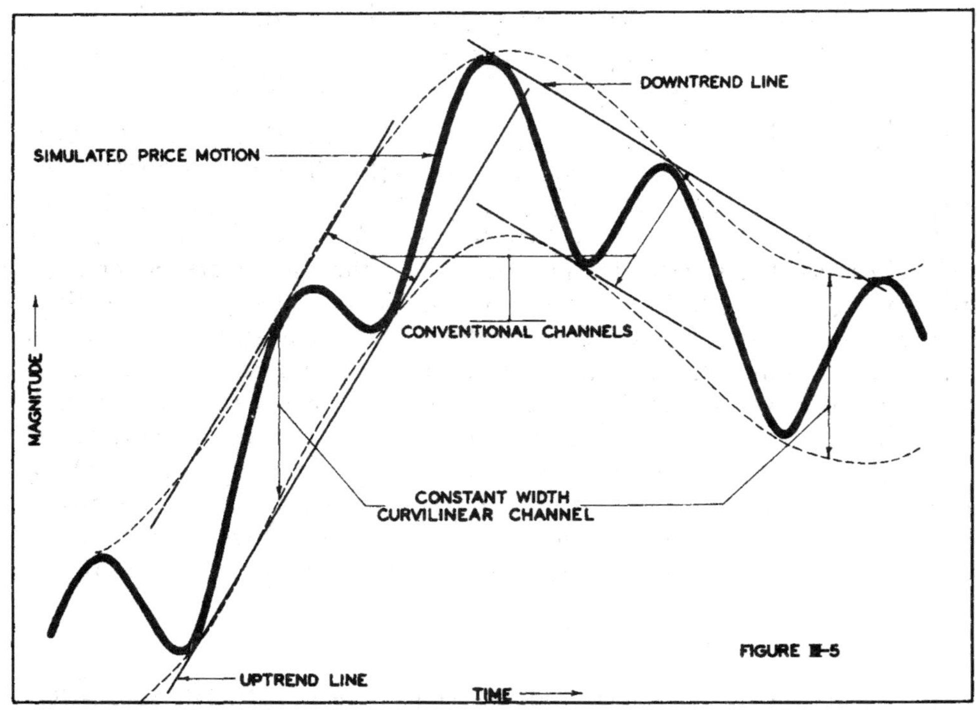


**True Channels Are Curvilinear**

1. A *long* duration cycle has caused the effect, hence it will be quite *long* before the previous trend is resumed!
2. A long duration cycle has *large* magnitude associated with it, hence the amount of price motion in the reversal is apt to be quite *large*!

Over the years, chartists have noted that such breakthroughs are usually followed by a significant reversal: this information has been obtained empirically. Through the application of our model, we now have shown how and why it happens from a purely theoretical standpoint. Our results and the chartist's observations are quite in agreement!

The case is similar for a head and shoulder formation. We can readily see (Figure III-4) that the neckline the chartist draws is in this case simply a second uptrend line. The preceding uptrend line connected the first two cyclic lows in this figure. When this trend line was broken on the downside, followed by a third cyclic low, then the second and third lows formed a new trend line, with sharply reduced upward slope. This is merely a rather crude way of causing the straight-line segments of the chartist to conform to the curving channel that we now know exists! In fact, a head and shoulder pattern *must* be formed as a consequence of our price-motion model as price motion is turned by a longer duration component, *so long as the time relationship of the two components in question is similar to that shown in Figure III-2,* from which Figure III-4 was derived!

## ABOUT DOUBLE TOPS AND BOTTOMS

But what, we ask, about a case where prices reverse *without* the formation of such a pattern? Figure III-6 shows the segment of Figure III-2 which contributed to the formation of the head and shoulder pattern. Now note the dotted cyclicality in this figure which is in every way identical to the one marked "A" except that the position of each low is shifted slightly in time relative to the "A" cycle. Summing these as before, we get Figure III-7. The result of this simple change is a double top, yet another charting favorite! It becomes clear that whether a head and shoulder pattern or a double top forms—or indeed, whether a head and shoulder pattern has an up-sloping, horizontal, or down-sloping neckline—is dependent only upon the time relationship between two cyclic components. It is also apparent that the same reasoning holds true for inverted head and shoulders patterns, and for double bottoms! In each case, the chartist notes the patterns and the most probable following action. We now know why such patterns form (and regularly!) and what causes them. We will see later how we can put this added knowledge to good use in transaction timing.

## THE SIGNIFICANCE OF TRIANGLES

Let us now call into play one more element of the cyclic model. In Figure III-8, the sum of all components from Figure III-2 that formed the left shoulder of Figure

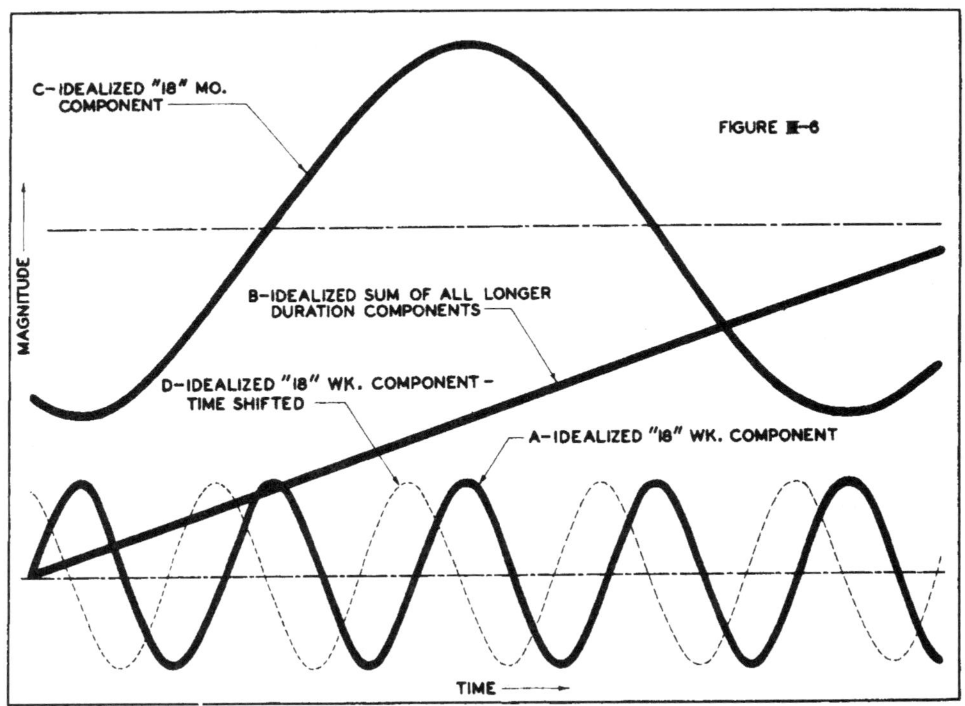


**The Effect Of Cycle Timing Change**

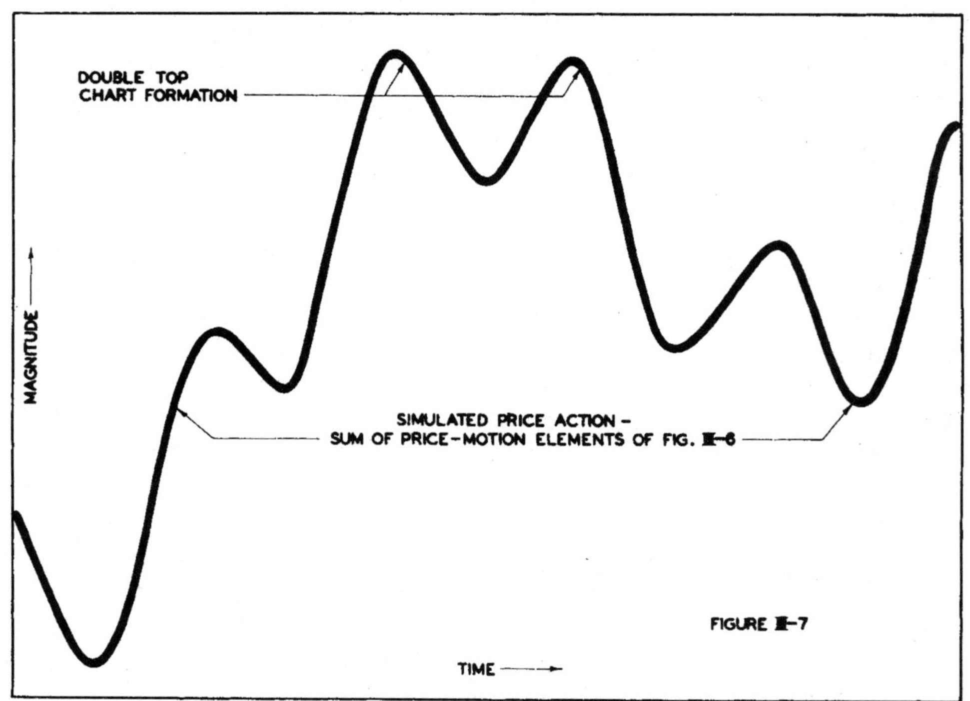


**How Double Tops (And Bottoms) Are Formed**

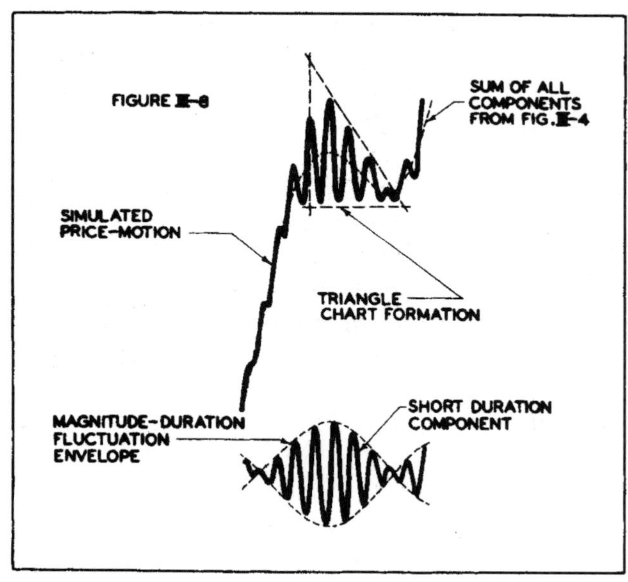


**How Triangles Come About**

III-4 is shown as a dotted line. To this we will now add one more component – of still shorter duration and, of course, of correspondingly smaller amplitude. For the first time we will also assume the magnitude-duration fluctuation to be expected from the price-motion model. Therefore, to the elements that formed Figure III-4, we have added two additional ingredients:

1. A third cyclic component.
2. Magnitude-duration fluctuation–thus getting the simulation a little closer to agreement with our more complex model.

Once more we sum up each of the elements proposed to get the result at the top of Figure III-8. This time we have a pattern which abounds on all charts. The chartist variously refers to this type of formation as a "coil," "triangle," "flag," "pennant," "box," "diamond" or "wedge." All are formed from cyclic elements in the same manner. The differences are dependent upon the state of magnitude-duration fluctuation of a short duration component at the time when the sum of all longer duration components is pausing due to cyclicality. In each case, the rules of charting which impute probabilistic follow-on to such patterns are based soundly upon the existence and behavior of the cyclic elements of our model.

## HOW TO TELL IN ADVANCE IF A CHART PATTERN WILL "FAIL"

Triangles may be formed also in much the same manner as double tops and head-shoulder patterns. Let's examine in some detail a specific case which is reported in a popular book on charting. The stock is Perkin Elmer and the time period is March through September 1961. This time a daily high-low chart is used so that we can see the impact of shorter duration periodicities. Two triangles were shown in the book on charting in which this example appeared, and these are reproduced in Figure III-9.

Now we must examine this chart carefully in the light of our model. Two samples of a periodicity are shown with lows at A, B, and C. The average duration of these is 13.9 weeks, which we note is satisfyingly close to the 13-week nominal duration cycle of our model. Each of these is seen to consist of three shorter duration elements, the lows of which are shown on the figure as points 1 through 7. Six samples are present, averaging 4.6 weeks. This is the 1961 time period equivalent of the nominal 3.25-week component of our model. Each of these consists of two shorter duration regularities. Twelve samples are present with an average duration of 2.3 weeks, again the 1961 equivalent of the 1.625-week nominal component of our model. This situation is a good example of the deviations from model nominality that can be expected in individual issues and for varying periods of time. Each of the 2.3-week durations also shows a one-half duration cycle of 1.15 weeks average. This periodicity has not been mentioned in our model as yet, except for the statement that such shorter duration regularities exist.

Now inspect the small triangle at the top of the figure closely. *It consists of three cycles of the 1.15-week periodicity!* Magnitude variation is clearly evident here, with the result being more properly described as the chartist's "flag." The breakout on the downside denoted *trouble* to the chartist–as well it should! Let's see what the cyclic situation was at this point in time:

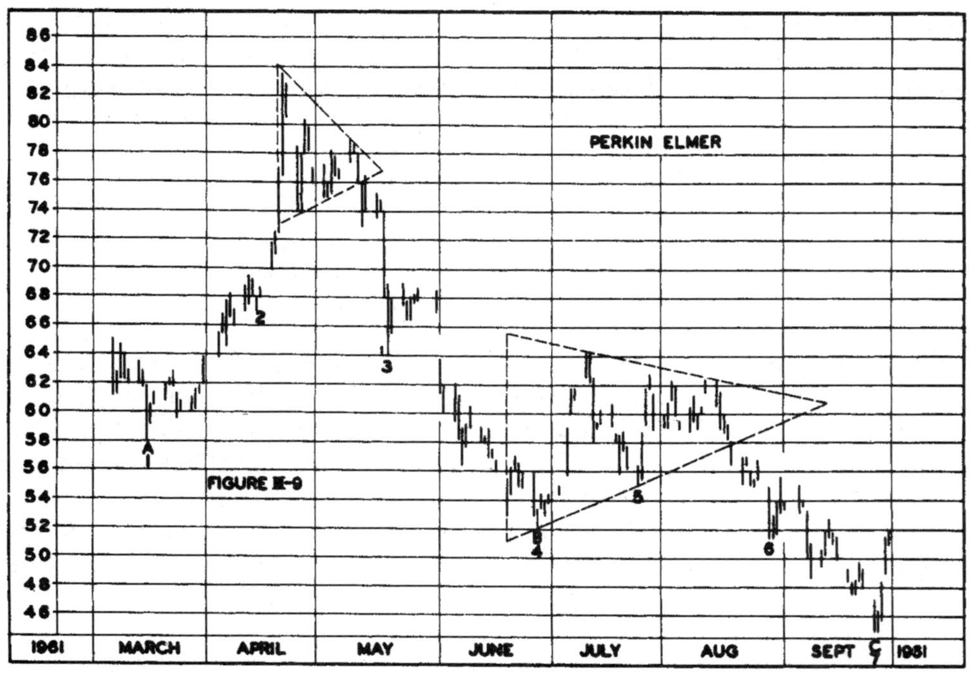


**Triangle Analysis In Perkin-Elmer**

| | |
|---|---|
| 1. 13.9-week cycle | 8 weeks along–*hard down* |
| 2. 4.6-week cycle | 3.8 weeks along–*hard down* |
| 3. 2.3-week cycle | 1.3 weeks along–and *hard down* |
| 4. 1.15-week cycle | 1.1 weeks along–and *hard down* |

Is it any wonder that a downside breakout of the triangle occurred?

Actually, something else of interest should also be noted here. The charting rule for such triangles is: The probabilities favor the continuation of the trend that preceded the triangle formation. As pointed out in the book from which this example was taken, this triangle represented a failure of charting expectations. No reasons for such failures are usually postulated, but we can easily see how our new knowledge of cyclicality allowed us to forecast this failure from a triangle! Such a capability adds immensely to the utility of such chart patterns. Not only can we understand how and why they are formed (so they are no longer a mystery to us), but we can often read much more into them than can the conventional chartist!

Now let's look at the large triangle to the right of the chart. This one is formed in a completely different way than the preceding one. The triangle is composed of one and most of a second cycle of our 4.6-week periodicity. The 13.9-week cycle is going over a top, and the same formation mechanics occur as in the case of double tops and head-shoulder formations. It is only the particular combination of magnitude-dominant cyclic durations, the time relationships between these, and the particular rate at which the sum of all longer duration components is moving that make the formation appear as it is.

If we were watching this triangle form, how would we analyze the situation? The chartist would apply his probabilistic rule and say he expects a downside breakout – and he would be right. Would we come up with the same conclusion?

| | |
|---|---|
| 1. 13.9-week cycle | 7.4 weeks along–*hard down* |
| 2. 4.6-week cycle | 3.6 weeks along–*hard down* |
| 3. 2.3-week cycle | 1.3 weeks along–*hard down* |
| 4. 1.15-week cycle | bottoming out–*flat to up* |

In addition to this we note that the preceding 13.9-week cycle has formed a lower low. This tells us that the sum of all components with durations in *excess* of 13.9 weeks is also hard down. Under such circumstances we would positively predict a downside breakout, and again be right! We see that our cyclic model has enabled us not only to agree with the chartist when he is probabilistically correct, but also to (correctly) disagree with him when he is wrong. In short, we can explain why such patterns form, why they provide more right answers than wrong ones, and in addition, reduce the number of times in which a wrong decision is made! We begin to see some of the utility of our "X motivation" model.

The chartist's patterns and our price model work hand-in-hand. The chart patterns are an aid in calling our attention to specific cyclic activity. The chartist's expectations for the pattern may then be verified or repudiated, based upon cyclic considerations.

## UNDERSTANDING OTHER CHART PATTERNS

To carry our comparisons further, let us now consider "V" top and bottom patterns. These occur when an intermediate duration cycle tops or bottoms out in perfect time synchronization with the next longer duration component. The "V" is further accentuated when the next *shorter* duration cycle also tops or bottoms simultaneously. In cases where four or five of these behave in this manner, the "V" can be very exaggerated and sharp indeed!

Saucer formations, measured moves, gaps, islands, one-day reversals, and all other well known chart patterns are as completely identifiable and explainable by cyclic theory as are the patterns discussed. It would be a very good exercise for you, the reader, to go through each of these situations, and prove this statement for yourself.

## HOW CYCLICALITY GIVES MEANING TO CHART PATTERNS

But let's move on to other areas of interest. One of the biggest difficulties in charting to date consists of the inability of the chartist to answer the following question: "How do you know *which* fluctuations (separated by how much time) to use in setting up your chart patterns?"

We have already seen in preceding chapters that an envelope may be drawn about any and all of our cyclic components. Just so, when a chartist draws a straight segment of a channel or trend line (representing part of our cyclic channel), we may always find other fluctuation lows or highs which define other channels or trend lines during the same time period and for the same issue. *Which of these has valid meaning?* Certainly, at any given time we can find trend lines which are both up and down. Refer back to Figure III-5 for example. We know from the manner in which this chart was constructed that if the chart were continued longer than shown we could draw another channel using the peaks and lows of component "C" of Figure III-2. This channel is strictly an *upside* channel, and the bottom bound of it forms strictly an *uptrend* line—*during the precise time period when the trend lines of Figure III-5 are both up and down!*

### So Which of These Has What Meaning?

Exactly the same is true of all other chart patterns. We will often find, for example, that the left shoulder (or head, or right shoulder) of a clearly visible head and shoulder pattern will exhibit a head and shoulder pattern of its own. This is, of course, caused by shorter-term cyclic fluctuations than those which formed the larger pattern. But again, the chartist usually sees only one of these, and appears at a loss to explain the significance of more than one when they appear.

### On What Basis Does He Attach Significance to One and Not to the Other?

Triangles, flags, etc., marked by a chartist may also be seen to form only a part of a larger triangle or flag. Why did the chartist single out the one he did for detailed consideration? This is all considered to be a part of the "arty" aspect of charting. Actually, the missing link is knowledge of cyclicality. The trouble is that there is no reference time period on which to base a selection. And even if there were, this reference time period would have to be different depending on whether daily, weekly, monthly, or yearly charts were considered!

Our cyclic model neatly solves this dilemma. For the facts are that *all* such patterns within patterns are significant. The cyclic model, by providing the explanation for chart pattern formation and the relationship between magnitude and duration of components, essentially quantifies the significance of each chart pattern that forms. This is what we are evaluating in effect by our tables which show the up-down-sidewise status of each observable periodicity. We not only see when members of these are working together to produce price motion in either direction, but we can predict when the pressures of each are likely to let up. In cases of nip and tuck, we can then call into play our knowledge as to how much more potent any one component is than, say, two others that may be opposing it—based upon our knowledge of magnitude vs. duration. We can further refine our estimates as to what is likely to happen by noting signs of magnitude-duration fluctuation in each component by observing the formation of flags, failure to fill constant-width envelopes, etc. By adding knowledge of cyclicality to charting techniques we take a major step in reducing the "art" of charting to the "science" of prediction!

## THE SIGNIFICANCE OF MOVING AVERAGES

Now let's discuss an artificial chart pattern. As we have seen, the price motion of stocks forms repeating patterns for perfectly valid cyclic reasons. However, the chartist has still more in the way of tricks up his sleeve. As you observe chart services, you will often note the addition of curving lines to the chart which appear to be somewhat related to price motion, but are not a part of it. These are "moving average" lines, which have come into popular usage quite recently. Why are these added to the chart and of what significance are they? Each of these has been tested by usage and found to convey more information than if price action alone were displayed. In short, they were derived empirically (which means stumbled upon more or less by accident!), and found to be of some use.

In order to understand why these are useful, we must probe deeply into what the characteristics of a moving average consist of. This is done in the Appendix, and only the significant results are presented here.

1. A moving average is a "smoother." It is a numerical process applied to a sequence of numbers (such as the time sequence of closing prices of a stock). The result is an elimination or reduction in magnitude of short-term fluctuations, while leaving the longer-term fluctuations modified little if at all. The net result is a *smoother* time sequence of numbers than the sequence to which it is applied.
2. But there is a variable involved in the use of a moving average. For example, the most commonly used ones are a ten-week and a 30-week moving average. This simply means that in each case the average is formed over a ten-week time span, or over a 30-week time span. By inspection of the results it can be seen at once that they are different (Figure III-10). Yet they operate upon the same numbers, namely the closing prices of a stock. Obviously, *the time span of the average used alters its characteristics.*

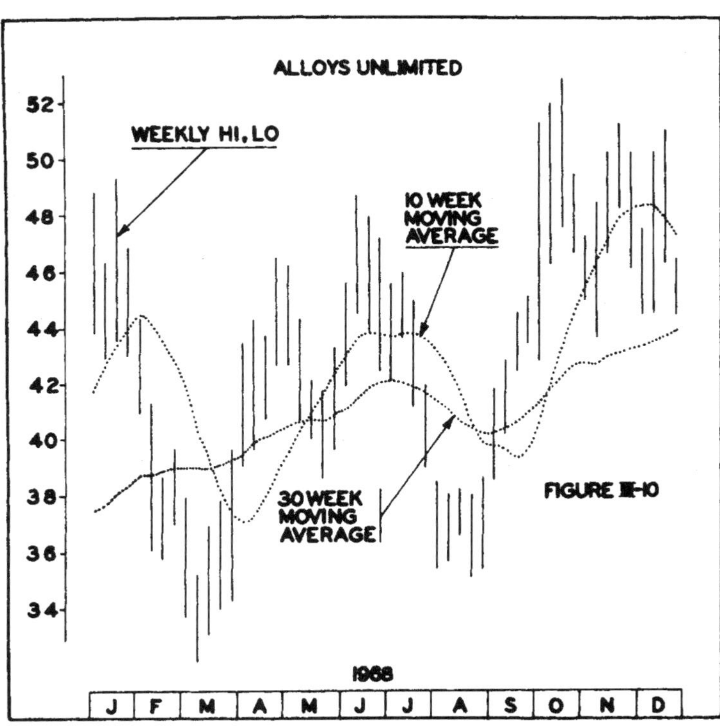


Moving Averages Versus Time-Span

3. These alterations in characteristics can be completely quantified and predicted (as in the Appendix). The following general results are found to be true:
   a) A moving average of any given time span exactly reduces the magnitude of fluctuations of duration equal to that time span to zero.
   b) The same moving average also greatly reduces (but does not necessarily eliminate) the magnitude of all fluctuations of duration less than the time span of the moving average.
   c) All fluctuations of greater than the time span of the average "come through," or are also present in the resulting moving average line. Those with durations just a little greater than the span of the average are greatly reduced in magnitude, but this effect lessens as periodicity duration increases. Very long duration periodicities come through nearly unscathed.
4. Notice that the "cutoff" point, or point where a given duration periodicity is completely eliminated (duration equal to the span of the average), is a controllable variable. By choosing the span of a moving average correctly, we can control this cutoff point, thus controlling what duration periodicities we want to suppress, or want to allow to come through for observation!

From the above description of a moving average it is seen right away that the user, while not necessarily possessing knowledge of cyclicality in price motion, nevertheless is employing a tool which is only useful in accentuating or diminishing visibility of cyclicality. That the result does indeed produce enough useful results to warrant a great deal of extra computational effort in stock charting is a tribute and testimony to the significance of cyclic phenomena in stock price motion!

## WHY TEN-AND 30-WEEK MOVING AVERAGES ARE USEFUL

Now then. Why should empirical results have shown the ten-week and 30-week moving averages to be exceptionally useful? Is this explainable in terms of our model?

Refer back now to our cyclic model component tabulation of Chapter Two. Remembering the significance of the moving average time span in setting a smoothing "cutoff" point in fluctuation duration, we note that a ten-week span moving average will set a cutoff point almost exactly midway between our 6.5- and 13.0-week duration components. This means that all components of 13.0 weeks' duration and more will show up in the moving average results, while the components of 6.5 weeks and less will be drastically reduced in magnitude (or "smoothed" out). Well! We find that a ten-week moving average is useful because it calls our attention only to cyclic fluctuations of 13 weeks and longer, allowing us to ignore the "distracting" shorter duration oscillations.

What about a 30-week moving average? The cutoff this time is found to be between the 26-week and nine-month (39-week) components of our model. This time, all cyclic phenomena of nine months or longer duration are allowed to "come through" while components of duration 26 weeks and less are ignored or smoothed! In other words, if we had set up these smoothing objectives in advance with full knowledge of the importance of our cyclic model in mind we could not have chosen the proper "cutoff" points much better—right smack in between the nominal durations of several of our most interesting and dominant cyclic components! It seems that once again our chartists are very observant people. Without full awareness of cyclic phenomena, they nevertheless used trial and error methods to good avail and came up with the right answers.

## HOW TO PLOT AND INTERPRET A MOVING AVERAGE PROPERLY

There is, however, one small but important characteristic of a moving average which they did overlook. This is demonstrated in the Appendix, and described here.

> A moving average is an effective smoother of fluctuating time sequences of data. However, the time relationship between the moving average and the data it smoothes is *not* the one that is always shown on stock price charts. In fact, the moving average data point plotted in association with the last price datum should be associated with a price datum one-half the time span of the average in the past!

Let's make this clearer with an example. Suppose we're computing the latest possible moving average data point for a ten-week moving average of the weekly closing price of a stock. The procedure used is to add up the last ten weekly closing prices, then divide the sum by ten. Now on stock price charts, the resulting value of the ten-week moving average is always plotted at the time of the *last* price data point used in computing the average. *This is incorrect!*

The proper time relationship between the computed moving average and the stock price data it is smoothing is obtained by plotting the value computed above at a time half-way between the fifth and the sixth *previous* price data points. This falls in the middle of the week of a weekly chart, and hence is associated with *no* value for the weekly close of the stock. For this reason, it is always better to use an odd number of data points in preparing a moving average, so that there is always a stock price to be associated with each average datum computed.

## HOW A MOVING AVERAGE CAN AID CYCLIC ANALYSIS

What does all of this mean? Well, it can be important. Take a look at Figure III-11. The weekly data for Alloys Unlimited (as used in Figure III-10) is presented. On this chart the ten-week moving average of Figure III-10 has been shifted five and a half weeks into the past as it should properly be plotted. *It is now apparent that this line represents a smoothing of actual price fluctuations.* In fact, it is found to move almost precisely down the center of one of our now familiar constant-width channels!

What is happening? Remember that the ten-week moving average is suppressing all fluctuations of less than ten weeks' duration while allowing longer duration periodicities to "show through." In this case, the ten-week moving average is an imperfect (but not bad) representation of the sum of the 13-week and all longer duration periodicities! The 13-week cycle here just barely comes through (note the dip in the moving average at the top of the peak in May-June). However, the longer 24-week component (equivalent of the 18- to 20-week cycle of the model), and all longer duration fluctuations are tracked to perfection. Note the difference in visibility achieved by this means as you compare Figures III-10 and III-11!

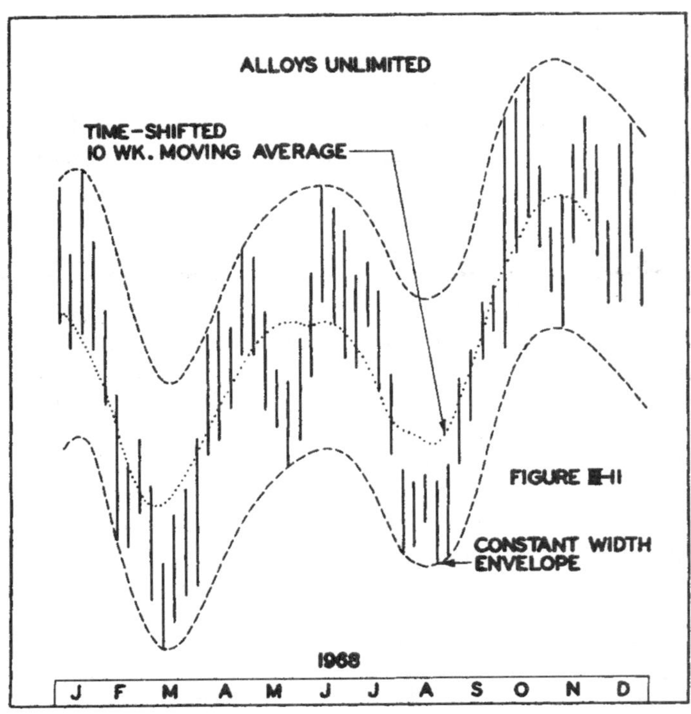


"Centering" A Moving Average

When plotted in this correct manner, two immediate uses for a moving average come to mind:

1. It can be used to help isolate any desired component. By selecting the span of the average properly, the stock price can be caused to oscillate about the moving average in sympathy with the shortest duration component that the average does not suppress! With this added visibility, we can often then place the correct envelope about cyclicality, unambiguously selecting the proper highs and lows.
2. Since the moving average (plotted in this manner) only fails to be "up-to-date" by about one-half the duration of the component isolated above, we can usually estimate quite accurately (from the remaining stock price motion) what the average will later be shown to be doing—hence the envelope also.

These techniques can be of considerable help in the case of some stocks where, for one reason or another, cyclicality is not readily apparent.

Here is a case then, of an artificial price motion pattern which the chartist has found from experience to be useful. Its utility is seen to be directly explainable in terms of the "X motivation" model. Even more important, understanding of the model *and* of the characteristics of moving averages allows us to utilize the moving average properly, and in ways not yet exploited by chartists at all!

## SUMMARIZING CHART PATTERNS

It is time to sum up the results of this chapter. We could go on and on comparing the expectations of the cyclic model with chartist observations—and this has been done in extensive detail. In every case the model is shown not to be in conflict with charting principles. Instead, it explains chart pattern existence and formation, and provides the applicant with interpretation and information not otherwise available.

As you continue reading, you should keep in mind at all times the following relationships between cyclic analysis and chart patterns:

1. Chart patterns form and repeat because of the repetitive nature of cyclic price action.
2. Trend lines and channels are a mandatory outgrowth of the price-motion model.
3. Head and shoulder, double tops and bottoms, and "V" chart patterns are all caused by the same cyclic action. Whether one or the other results is completely dependent on the time relationships of the cyclic components that cause the pattern.
4. Triangles, diamonds, wedges, flags, and pennants are formed by the same type of cyclic action. In these patterns, the magnitude-duration fluctuation aspect of the price-motion model is dominant. Triangles may also be formed by a similar process to that which produces head and shoulder type patterns. It is essential for you to be able to differentiate between the two formative causes.
5. Cyclic analysis provides the means of telling in advance in which direction prices will go when a pattern terminates.
6. The price-motion model provides the reference times without which chart pattern analysis remains an "art."
7. Moving averages are smoothers.
8. The "span" of a moving average is the design variable that permits the use of such averages to improve cyclic visibility.
9. The price-motion model explains the significance of the empirically derived ten- and 30-week moving averages.
10. A moving average becomes a great deal more useful if properly plotted. To do so, the theoretical time lag of such an average must be taken into account.
11. Moving averages can be of aid in cyclic analysis. They can be used to establish the trend of summed long-duration cyclic components, and to identify unambiguously lows and highs about which curvilinear channels should be formed.

*chapter*

*four*

# Timing Your Buys With Graphics

- Prediction by Graphics
- How to Construct Curvilinear Envelopes
- Prediction of Price Turns Using Envelopes
- Use This Example as Your Channel Prediction Guide
- Constructing the Dominant Channel
- Finding the Outer Envelope
- Setting Up Price-Turn Predictions
- The Kind of Results You Can Achieve
- How to Generate Graphic "Buy" Signals
- What to Look For
- Recognizing the "Valid Trend Line"
- "Edge-Band" Transaction Timing
- "Mid-Band" Transaction Timing
- Points to Remember Regarding Graphic "Buy" Signals

## PREDICTION BY GRAPHICS

You have seen what is required to maximize investment profits. Transaction timing is the golden key—and the price-motion model implies a way. However, concepts of the price-motion model must now be applied in a practical manner to generate objective investment decisions. Of all the methods available to do this, graphical techniques are by far the fastest and easiest to apply. This chapter will tell you how to form and interpret curvilinear envelopes, and how to combine price-motion model concepts with conventional chart patterns to provide definitive "wait," "buy," and "hold" signals.

The first and most basic step is the identification of the dominant cyclic components present in a particular stock, and the status of these components at the present time. The objective is what we might call "first-order" prediction. That is, we want to derive transaction timing benefits from the price-motion model by giving ourselves a high statistical probability of correctly estimating when a set of cyclic components will form a low (or a high). We must use knowledge of cyclicality coupled with past price action in order to form an opinion of probable price turning points in the future—and we wish to do this using simple and fast graphical techniques.

## HOW TO CONSTRUCT CURVILINEAR ENVELOPES

The constant-width envelope that you were introduced to briefly in Chapter Two is a powerful tool for the accomplishment of this task. You have seen several examples of such envelope analysis now. In each case data on the stock of interest was presented in a figure *before* addition of envelope bounds. This was done to provide a feeling for the large increase in visibility afforded by the technique. Charting a stock tells you much more at a glance than looking at tabulated data. Similarly, addition of constant-width envelopes brings out and stresses the cyclic price-time relationships on the chart. It would be a good idea at this point for you to return to and study the pairs of such figures presented in previous chapters.

To start, you must construct or procure a weekly high-low chart of the issue you are interested in. The time period covered by the chart should be at least long enough to include one and a half cycles of the periodicity that is *next longer in duration* than the one you are interested in trading on. If practical, it is even desirable to include the *second* longer duration component in your data. Remember that these long-term regularities have much larger magnitudes than your trading cycle, and can therefore be very influential in determining where the price of the stock goes, regardless of what your trading cycle is doing!

By observation of your weekly chart, you will always find that some one cyclic component is most clearly discernible. This will usually be some variation of the 13- or 26-week (nominal) periodicity of the model. Keep the general outline of this price motion in mind while you look for a narrow band of prices which will essentially enclose the data, and will fluctuate with the dominant movement.

Start by lightly sketching in upper and lower bounds to this band (an overlay of tissue or vellum is of help here). Now use a piece of scratch paper to measure the channel height vertically at several points. Choose an average of these and correct your embryonic envelope to constancy of width. If any data points cannot be included in this channel, widen the envelope until *all* price motion is accounted for.

Now repeat the process while decreasing the width of the band. You will normally find a minimum-width envelope which contains all of the data except two or three stray points which will be obvious by virtue of being the only data in the space between the two envelopes you've drawn. Erase the wider of the two envelopes, for it has now served its purpose.

The final envelope will now enable you to make a more accurate estimate of the duration of the dominant periodicity by clearly demarking locations of highs and lows, free from distortion caused by the presence of fluctuations of shorter duration. Tabulate your estimate.

Now look *within* the envelope you've drawn. Note where the data touches or comes close to envelope bounds. Price motion will tend to sweep back and forth between these limits—somewhat regularly. Pick the most clear-cut such movement and measure between the lows, again using marks on scratch paper. Look now for other lows both forward and backward in time from the first one. Knowing in this way the approximate location at which you should find such additional lows, it is usually apparent where they are, even when duration-magnitude fluctuation is present. As each one is located, mark it on the chart. Note the duration of each sample found, and average these. This is your best estimate of the expected duration of the component contained within your first envelope. A second envelope can sometimes be constructed about this component—but more often than not you will find it to be too irregular to be of much help.

Go back to your original channel and examine it closely. If you have charted sufficient data you will have at least two highs and two lows of the dominant component shown. These peaks and valleys constitute points on a second envelope which contains the dominant component. Sketch this one in, using the same techniques as for the first. *You have now identified three of the cyclic components dominant in the specific issue you have chosen!*

With this much accomplished, you can normally spot still shorter duration periodicities within your narrowest channel. These will typically display too much variation in duration and will be too near the next longer duration component in size to allow identification using other envelopes. However, you *can* mark the lows involved with a check or something similar.

## PREDICTION OF PRICE TURNS USING ENVELOPES

Prepare yourself a table showing the condition of each of the identified components just prior to each major up or down move on your chart. Do this by using the average durations you have obtained for the samples present of each cyclicality. Then count weeks from the last low preceding the point of interest. Remember, any given periodicity reaches a peak and starts back down one-half of the average duration from the last low. You will find that, if you have properly drawn your channels, the resulting tabulations will completely explain every fluctuation you see in the stock price!

Now, repeat your tabulation of cyclic condition for the last data point on your chart. What you are looking for, of course, is the case where two or more cyclic components are due to bottom out in the very near future, at the same time, and the sum of all longer duration components is hard up. Once found, you are ready to track the issue closely, determined to buy the moment price action tells you the process you expect has started! If you use your average cyclic durations and measure from the last visible low of each cycle into the future, you will have a pretty fair idea as to just how soon your ideal buy point may occur.

A few comments on the above. You may wish at this time to change your mind with regard to your preselected trading interval. From the above work, you can see clearly which of the components found is most regular and altogether dominant. You can also determine roughly the percentage move to be expected. Naturally, you will want to trade on a component move that provides plenty of room to clear transaction costs, and to make the size profit you desire. Do not forget to take into account the fact that you will probably be unable to buy at the very bottom and sell at the extreme top.

It is helpful to note whether or not a given whole number (usually two or three) of shorter components exists in the duration span of the trading cycle you select. The behavior of these can be used to sharpen up your get in and get out points. Oftentimes, several of these shorter duration cycles can be used, each telling you something about the status of the next longer duration one.

It is a good idea also to make or procure a daily chart for your stock. This does not need to cover as long a time period as the weekly one, but it should show at least one and a half cycles of the trading component. Transfer the appropriate channels from the weekly to the daily chart. You will usually find that several more periodicities (of very short duration) are identifiable here. Usually the variability of these prohibits use of more channels, but the successive lows can be identified. These may be used as a very fine vernier on your transaction timing.

If you find (as you occasionally will) that you cannot make "cyclic sense" from the stock you have selected, it is a good idea to forget it as an investment vehicle and find another. After all, there are literally thousands to choose from. Why take chances with one you cannot understand?

As you practice making these envelopes, note the following: the envelope is valid, past-history, and will never need changing from the last well defined high or low backward in time. Since this point can never be much more than half a cycle duration from present time, the maximum time lag of channel validity is one-half cycle of the enclosed fluctuation. Of course, you should always draw in lightly your best estimate of what the channel is doing in this period–changing channel bounds as price action makes this necessary until you reach a new high or low. *At this point in time, the time lag is zero and your channel is valid up to current time.* This means uncertainty is at a minimum and the situation represents a particularly low-risk decision point. Even before this time you will often note that a single day's price motion will alert you to a change of conditions by moving outside the estimated channel position. This tells you either that fundamentals are changing, or that you have previously misestimated the status of the sum of all longer duration components. In either case, appropriate action can be taken.

The above discussion provides the overall considerations to be kept in mind when using channel analysis. Some of these procedures will be valid and useful for some stocks while other aspects of the analysis may be better for others.

## USE THIS EXAMPLE AS YOUR CHANNEL PREDICTION GUIDE

Assume that some one has provided you with the data tabulated below. All you have are the highs and lows for some issue (say "Z" Corp.) for a series of weeks as of the close each Friday:

| *Week Ending* | *High* | *Low* |
|---|---|---|
| 8-18-67 | 10-6 | 9-4 |
| 8-25-67 | 10-2 | 9-4 |
| 9-1-67 | 12-1 | 9-5 |
| 9-8-67 | 12-2 | 10-6 |
| 9-15-67 | 10-7 | 9-0 |
| 9-22-67 | 10-3 | 9-1 |
| 9-29-67 | 10-1 | 9-0 |
| 10-2-67 | 9-2 | 8-0 |
| 10-13-67 | 8-7 | 8-0 |
| 10-20-67 | 8-6 | 7-6 |
| 10-27-67 | 8-2 | 7-3 |
| 11-3-67 | 7-6 | 7-1 |
| 11-10-67 | 7-2 | 6-6 |
| 11-17-67 | 7-2 | 6-4 |
| 11-24-67 | 6-4 | 6-1 |
| 12-1-67 | 7-1 | 6-4 |
| 12-8-67 | 7-1 | 6-5 |
| 12-15-67 | 9-0 | 6-5 |
| 12-22-67 | 8-5 | 7-5 |
| 12-29-67 | 8-4 | 7-4 |
| 1-5-68 | 8-1 | 7-5 |
| 1-12-68 | 9-1 | 7-6 |
| 1-19-68 | 9-0 | 8-1 |
| 1-26-68 | 8-5 | 7-6 |
| 2-2-68 | 7-7 | 7-1 |
| 2-9-68 | 7-4 | 6-6 |
| 2-16-68 | 7-2 | 6-4 |
| 2-23-68 | 7-0 | 6-4 |
| 3-1-68 | 7-0 | 6-4 |
| 3-8-68 | 6-5 | 5-6 |
| 3-15-68 | 6-4 | 5-7 |
| 3-22-68 | 6-3 | 5-6 |
| 3-29-68 | 6-7 | 5-7 |
| 4-5-68 | 7-0 | 6-2 |
| 4-12-68 | 6-4 | 5-7 |
| 4-19-68 | 7-0 | 6-1 |
| 4-26-68 | 7-2 | 6-2 |
| 5-3-68 | 7-7 | 6-5 |
| 5-10-68 | 7-5 | 7-1 |
| 5-17-68 | 7-7 | 7-0 |
| 5-24-68 | 7-3 | 6-4 |
| 5-31-68 | 8-5 | 7-1 |
| 6-7-68 | 8-3 | 7-5 |
| 6-14-68 | 9-6 | 7-6 |
| 6-21-68 | 8-6 | 8-2 |
| 6-28-68 | 8-5 | 8-0 |
| 7-5-68 | 8-5 | 8-1 |
| 7-12-68 | 9-6 | 8-1 |
| 7-19-68 | 9-5 | 8-5 |

Now try something. Run your eyes down this tabulation and study it well. Just from this scan of data alone, infer just as much as you can about the future price action of the stock. Write down your conclusions before continuing this chapter. If you are like most of us, you will gain very little from this exercise regarding action you should take in order to trade profitably in the stock. Is the stock a buy? If so, now? Later? How much later? Should it be sold short? When?

Now turn to Figure IV-1. From this conventional plot of the data, you should *immediately* obtain a much improved feel for what the issue is doing. *Just the act of plotting the data has added visibility.* Once again, write down your impressions of what you should do with this stock. Is it likely to make you money if you get in it? If so, how much? Is it going down from here—or will it continue the current uptrend? *What should you do with it, and when should you do it?* At this point in the analysis, you will probably experience difficulty in answering such questions. Remember, you don't even know the name of the stock. You know nothing about the company that issued it or their products. You don't know whether dividends are paid or whether the earnings situation is improving or deteriorating. You are not even aware of what the market as a whole is doing! *Can channel analysis help?*

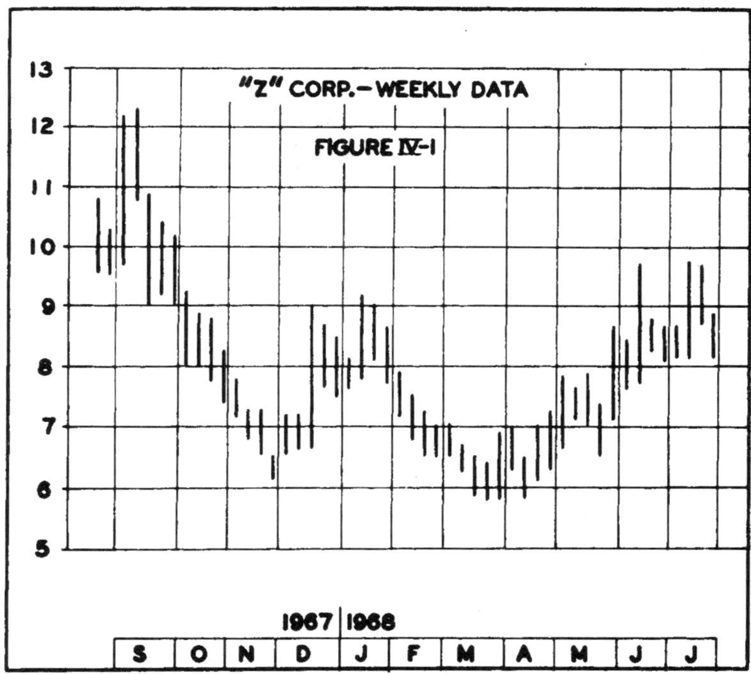


**Plotting Helps—But Not Enough**

## CONSTRUCTING THE DOMINANT CHANNEL

Turn your attention to Figure IV-2. Here is the same data, but with a first envelope drawn about it using the techniques described earlier. Notice that the channel is constructed to enclose a component for which eight samples are present of about

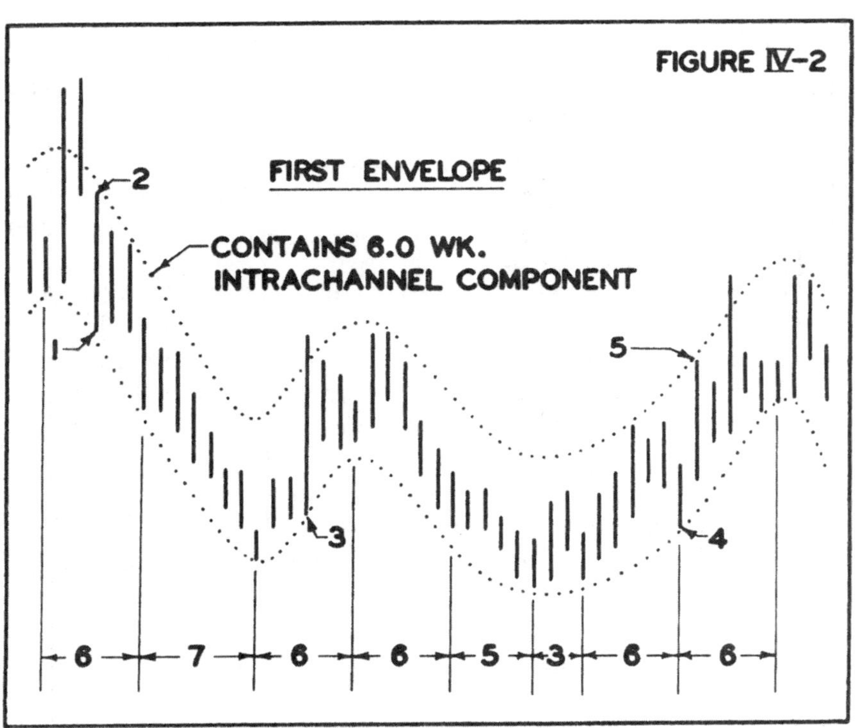


A First Envelope Adds Visibility

five to seven weeks in duration. One sample is only three weeks long. This one is a result of magnitude-duration fluctuation, and is to be ignored. The average duration of the remaining seven samples is 6.0 weeks.

Furthermore, it is seen that prices in three places exceed envelope bounds. This is not unusual. Envelopes should be constructed so that nearly all the data is enclosed, but a second criterion calls for minimum envelope width. Quite often a compromise is necessary. Notice that in each case of envelope overrun, the envelope could not have been drawn in any other manner without considerable widening. The overrun of the third and fourth weeks was dictated by the full channel width of the price action of the fifth week (points 1 and 2). Points 3, 4, and 5 (weekly lows and highs just prior to or just following channel overruns) *forced* channel bounds, showing clearly that the overruns were exceptions. The final downward hook to the channel is forced by point 5, the lows of the third, fourth, and fifth weeks before the end of data, and the highs of the second and third weeks before data end.

We have now added a small amount of additional visibility. We know that the trend of prices is *down* for the immediate future. We don't know how far or for how long, but we expect about three more weeks at least on the downside (the last six-week cycle is now three weeks along). We conclude that we wouldn't want to buy the stock right now.

## FINDING THE OUTER ENVELOPE

Now turn to Figure IV-3. Figure IV-2 clearly displayed a cycle of duration longer than six weeks. Again the techniques of channel construction are employed to draw a

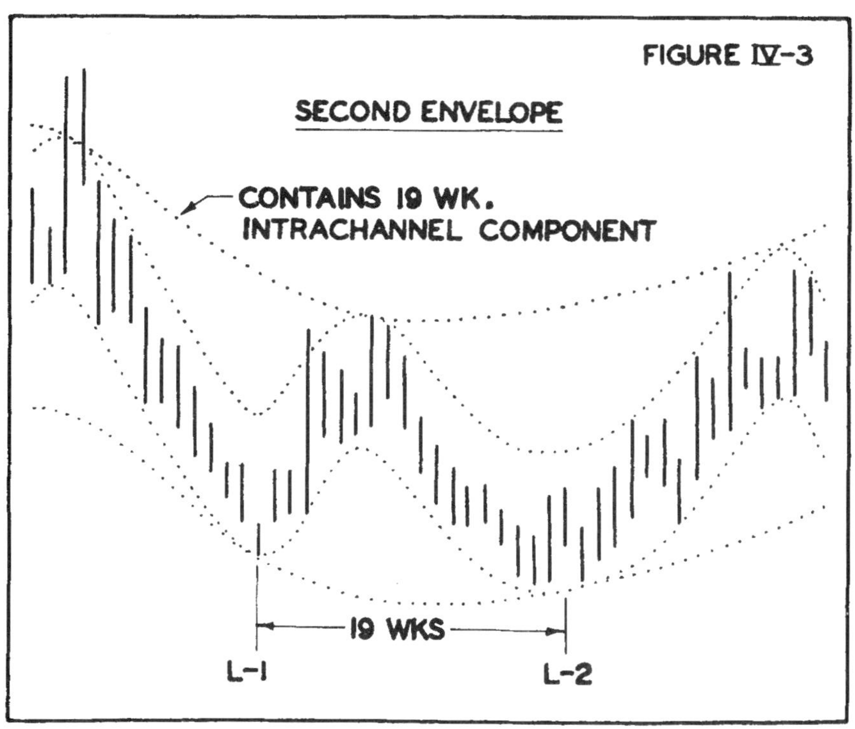


**A Second Envelope Clarifies The Picture Further**

second channel. Only one full cycle of this periodicity is present and it spans 19 weeks. Suddenly, a great deal of additional visibility is ours!

We notice that the sum of all periodicities of duration longer than 19 weeks (represented by the center line of the second channel) has rounded a bottom and is now *up.* We see also that we are about 16 weeks along on a 19-week (nominal duration) cycle. This means the 19-week cycle is due to low-out in about three weeks. We recall that the six-week cycle low is also expected in three weeks. Our interest stirs! Here is a case where long-term, large-magnitude cycles are boosting the price higher. We certainly don't want to short this issue. On the other hand, we don't want to buy it for two to three weeks yet as we suspect it will be moving sideways to down in that interval.

## SETTING UP PRICE-TURN PREDICTIONS

In Figure IV-4 everything we've learned about the stock so far is presented on one chart. We've gone further and sketched in an estimated continuation of each channel for the next five months. The outer envelope is simply extended at the same rate of curvature. L-3 timing is based on the three-weeks-to-a-low estimate previously formed, while the price level at that same time is determined by the lower bound of the outer envelope. L-4 is located an additional 19 weeks from L-3. The high in October is pretty much of a guess at this point, except that we know it is likely to occur more than halfway from L-3 to L-4 because of the uptrend of the outer channel.

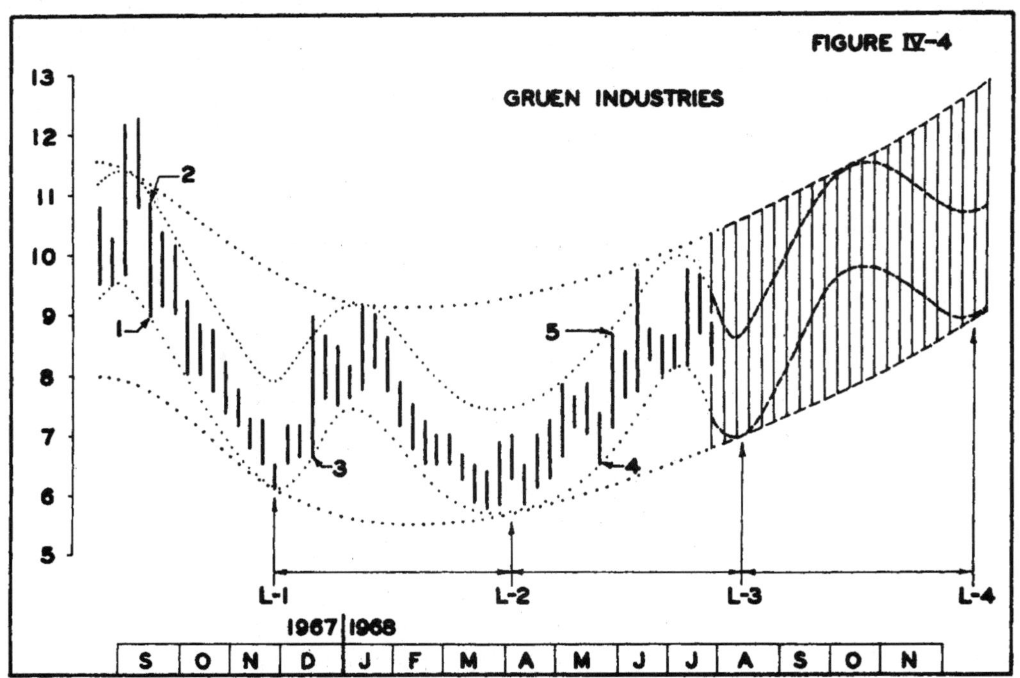


**Rough Prediction Using Envelopes**

## THE KIND OF RESULTS YOU CAN ACHIEVE

We started with a data tabulation which told us nearly nothing about the future actions of the stock. A conventional stock price chart was made which added a little, but still did not tell us *what* to do. We continued with envelope analysis and application of the concepts of the price-motion model. The result?

- The stock should be bought, not sold short.
- In about three weeks we should be able to get into it at around 7¼.
- We would expect an increase in price over the next eight to ten weeks to the region of 11¼. This would represent a 55% gain in two months, or an equivalent per year yield rate of 330%. Well worthwhile!

*But—is this what the stock will actually do?* Now you ask your data source for the name of the company—Gruen Industries. If you wish, check out the fundamentals; you've got several weeks of waiting anyway. If the stock moves to the vicinity of 7¼ to 7½ at about the time you expect it to, you buy it.

Figure IV-5 shows what happens. The time of turns and the amount of moves were very close to being correct over a five-month period into the future! You were able to purchase the stock at 7½ in the third week—and could have sold at your target price of 11¼ in just four weeks instead of the estimated eight to ten. Moreover, you would not have been idle all this time. Each week you would have rerun your analysis. As early as

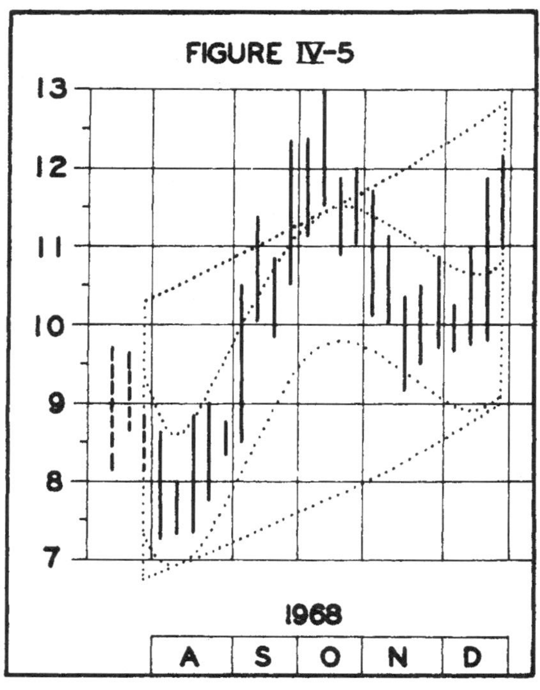


**How Results Compare With Prediction**

the third week after purchase, you had an indication that the stock was going to do even better than anticipated (puncture of the inner envelope on the upside and prematurely). The next week the outer envelope was also violated. Since it was *far* too early for a peak of the 19-week cycle, you would have re-estimated channel bounds at this point. Your new selling target would have become 12½ on this basis. Your net return on the transaction is 62% in eight weeks or an equivalent compounded yield of 2313% per year. And *remember*—you arrived at the conclusions necessary to do this *without any knowledge whatsoever of fundamentals—in fact, without even knowing the name of the issue.* You should be able to gain a good feeling for the power of the technique by comparing final analysis conclusions with the opinions you wrote down for yourself during the early part of the example.

## HOW TO GENERATE GRAPHIC "BUY" SIGNALS

The identification and analysis of status of cyclic components are basic to the generation and interpretation of specific action signals. You must practice the curvilinear envelope techniques diligently until you have mastered and thoroughly understand all of the variations from nominality to be expected from individual issues. While cyclic status is an essential first step on the road to improved transaction timing, it should be noted that by itself this type of analysis provides only crude timing information. We will now see how knowledge of the price-motion model, cyclic status analysis, and conventional chart patterns can be combined to refine timing criteria—all by use of graphical methods.

## WHAT TO LOOK FOR

Let us consider the characteristics we desire in a "buy" signal.

- A buy signal must be capable of being set up in advance of actual price action. We must be able to say: "For these logical reasons, if the stock behaves in the future in a certain, specific manner, this action will be interpreted as a signal to buy."
- Having caused us to buy the stock, the buy signal must have the characteristic of assuring us the highest possible probability that the stock will immediately proceed to make us the largest possible profit in the shortest possible length of time.

Envelope analysis meets some of these requirements, but not all. To improve the situation, we recall how the price-motion model explains the regular and periodic formation of common chart patterns. It has been noted that cyclic analysis can often remove the doubt from chart pattern interpretation. Such chart patterns serve a very definite purpose in calling attention to specific cyclic conditions. When combined with the predictive capabilities of envelope analysis, some of these patterns can provide accurate and totally objective transaction timing signals. The two that are the most useful for this purpose are the triangle and the trend line. Now let us add the concept of a "valid trend line" to our bag of techniques and methods!

## RECOGNIZING THE "VALID TREND LINE"

Remember in Chapter Three how it was shown that several trend lines can be in existence and force at the same time in the same stock? It was shown there that these were simply straightened-out segments of curvilinear channels, several of which always exist simultaneously. The nature of these channels is always such that those enclosing shorter duration cyclic components move both upward and downward more steeply than those enclosing longer duration periodicities. Therefore the straightened-out segments that we know as "trend lines" become increasingly steep as the component duration enclosed within the associated channel shortens.

Keeping this in mind, recall now the results of envelope analysis on Gruen Industries. We knew *approximately* when and where prices were going to stop going down and start upward. We knew that components of several different durations were going to bottom out—about three weeks from the time of the analysis.

- Each such component has a real or theoretical channel which can enclose it.
- Each such channel has an associated downtrend line.
- Each such downtrend line gets steeper as component duration diminishes.
- The valid downtrend line is the steepest one formed which leads into the time period in which a multiplicity of cyclic lows is expected!

Now let's stop and examine what's just been said. Envelope analysis tells us approximately when and where to expect price turns of the magnitude on which we wish to trade. But we do not wish simply to buy at about this time and price for several reasons. The stock may take off sooner than we expect and leave us uninvested (after all there *is* a variation of fluctuation duration to contend with). Or, we may have mis-analyzed and find our error only after having made a purchase. Again, fundamentals may enter the picture to the detriment of profit. For these reasons we would like the stock to demonstrate to us that what we expect to happen has started before we commit hard-earned dollars. Still, we do not wish to wait too late and find ourselves "chasing" the stock. So we need an accurate, sensitive, positive indication in the way of a buy signal that assures us that the right time is *now.*

The valid trend line accomplishes these objectives for us. General cyclic analysis plus the envelope capability to predict turns allow us to select that one of all possible trend lines through which a break is a valid indication that one or more of the expected lows has been formed—and that the time is right to buy!

Why is this a particularly low-risk buy point? Remember that you have already picked a particularly propitious time to buy. The stock has been going down—and *no* stock goes down forever. Buying always occurs somewhere along the line with an attendant price rise. You have carefully analyzed the issue and find that a number of cyclic lows should occur in a certain time interval. The result of all these lows forming more or less simultaneously is going to turn the sum of all components of duration longer than your trading cycle upward. It is even going to cause the price of the stock to fluctuate above this by the sum of your trading cycle move plus that of all components of still shorter duration! You are now using trend lines as a means of tracking the activity of each component as it nears a low. As each low is reached, by definition, the associated trend line must be broken—and the first one to do so will be that which is part of the channel enclosing the shortest significant component. But this one cannot break the trend line until the next longer duration component has rounded its low, etc. All of this is probabilistic, of course, but you are beginning to get a lot of the odds in your favor at this point!

## "EDGE-BAND" TRANSACTION TIMING

Let's start where we left off with Gruen Industries. In Figure IV-6 the results of the channel analysis are shown. This time the plot is of daily data, with the envelopes developed on the weekly plots superimposed. The shaded area represents a spread of uncertainty over time and price as to when we expect prices to turn up. The center lines in this area represent a time and price target—essentially our best estimate of each. Now start looking at the price motion for peaks along which to draw trend lines. The first peak of the current downtrend occurred two and a half weeks ago. This will be one point on one downtrend line. A second peak appears to be in the making as of two days ago. However, it is not certain as yet since a lower low has not followed. So at this point in time we cannot draw any downtrend line with confidence.

Now let two more days pass as in Figure IV-7. Two solid peaks are now evident, and an initial downtrend line is drawn which leads directly into the heart of our price turn zone. If no other trend lines form before, we determine that we will buy the stock as soon as we're within the time boundaries of the turn zone and prices break through this trend line on the upside.

Two more days pass, putting us into the time region of interest. As shown in Figure IV-8, a still shorter duration peak has formed, establishing a second and steeper downtrend line. If no other trend lines form before, we will now buy the stock at any

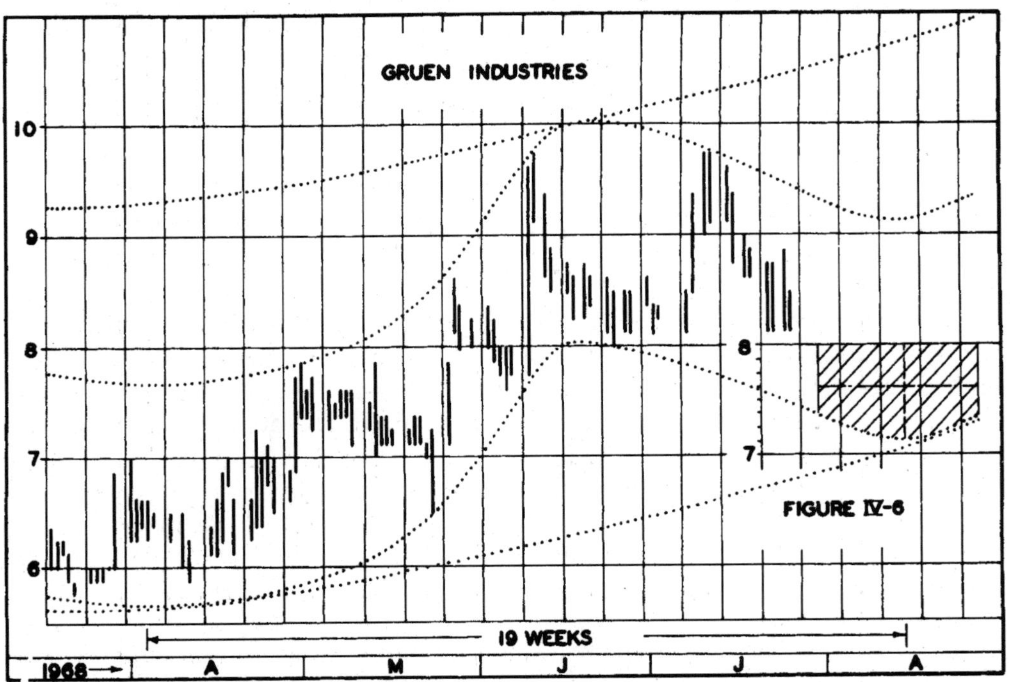


**Refining Predictions–By Going To Daily Data**

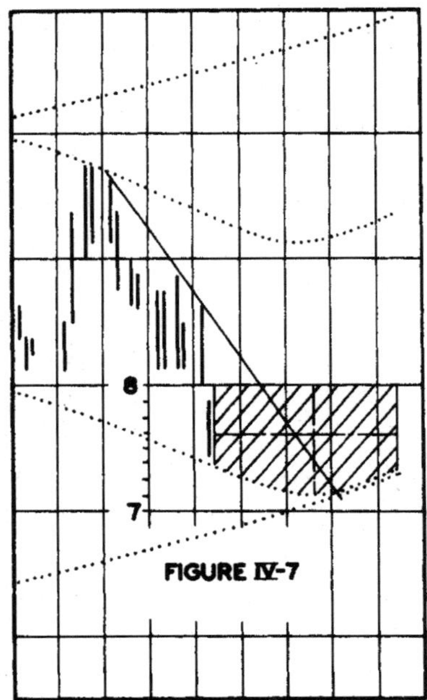


**The First Valid Downtrend Line**

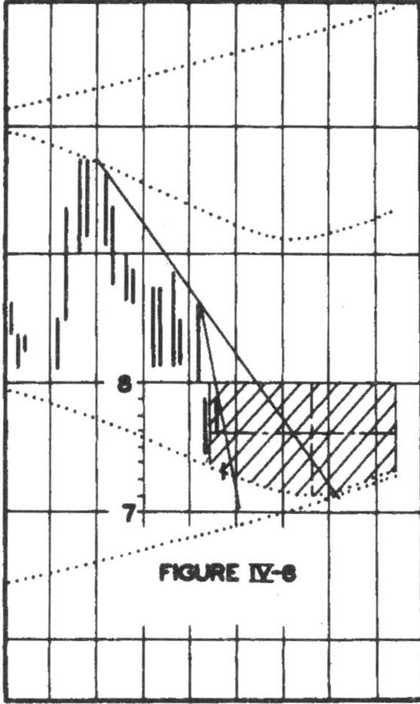


**The Second Valid Downtrend Line**

moment it breaks this trend line on the upside—provided time has not passed so that we've exited the time zone on the far side. Needless to say, our envelope analysis should not show violation either. Everything looks ripe and A-OK. Channel analysis predicted prices would be about here at about this time. A series of steepening trend lines has formed. We should be at or very near the bottom of all the multiplicity of channels that can be drawn. We should expect to have all the probabilities on our side if we use a break in this trend line as a valid buy signal.

*The very next day prices traded completely above our valid trend line* (see Figure IV-9). This means that the stock *opened* at a price which was above the trend line. This was our signal to place an immediate order to buy at market! Let's say we got our order executed at mid-range for the day, or 7½. The subsequent rise in price to 13 in the next 65 days is quite dramatic, isn't it?

This is an example of "edge-band" transaction timing. We utilized all the information the price-motion model provides to establish an objective and rational buy signal that put us in the stock at the lower edge of our cyclic channels. This method can be generally counted on to provide a maximum of room for upside price motion for the trading cycle selected. Notice that the same technique could have been used on any cyclic component. The investor with large amounts of capital who wishes to operate on a longer term basis would, of course, apply the same methods to longer duration cycles.

We are *not,* however, assured of maximum profits in terms of yield per unit time when using the edge-band technique. Let's see how this works.

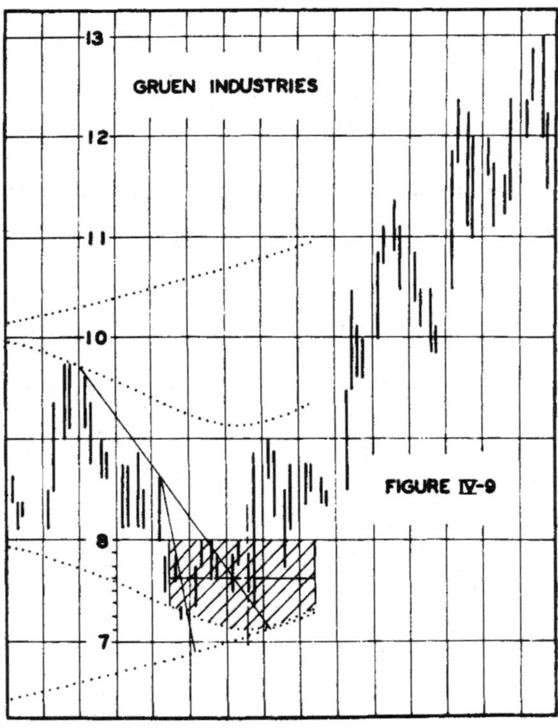


**The Buy Signal—And Profits In The Pocket!**

## "MID-BAND" TRANSACTION TIMING

Notice the fact (from Figure IV-9) that the price of the stock idled more or less in the purchase area for nearly two weeks before making an appreciable move upward. In terms of yield, this was wasted time. Then, within two days' time, the price moved nicely to 9, only to idle between 7-3/4 and 9 for an additional two weeks before moving on. Remember our investment philosophy which calls for maximum time rate of profit. *Those idle weeks represent time in which we could have had our investment dollars at work elsewhere.*

Why did prices tend to move out rather slowly, then gather momentum as time went along? We were buying in at the first indication that cyclic lows had been formed. Naturally, the first such indications came from the shortest duration periodicities, which top out and reverse themselves just as quickly. The longer term components forming lows at about the same time make their turn more slowly (by definition). In fact, *no* component provides maximum time rate of change of price until it is halfway between a low and a high (or high and a low as the case may be). Thus the large magnitude, long duration components that contribute the most to price motion are scarcely in motion on the upside when our first indication of a short term oscillation turn becomes apparent.

This brings us to a second type of buy signal which we may term a "mid-band" buy. The logic behind this is simply that we will wait *after* the "edge-band" buy point until a slightly longer duration cyclicality causes prices to pause. Then we will utilize the same type of valid trend line technique to set up a buy signal closer to mid-channel–hence closer to the point of maximum rate of price increase. We won't expect to make as much per trade, but we hope to make a higher percent per unit time yield, and to compound our profits more often. Remembering our trading philosophy, it is the compounding effect that produces profits more quickly than any other single factor. Of course, we must pay for this gain through added labor; i.e., having complete analysis ready and available on a number of issues at once so that we are given sufficient buying opportunities to maintain near 100% time investment of capital.

Let's see how mid-band timing would work out in the case of Gruen. Figure IV-10 shows the required analysis. It is assumed that all previous analysis has been completed and the stock was being tracked. The edge-band buy signal was given and

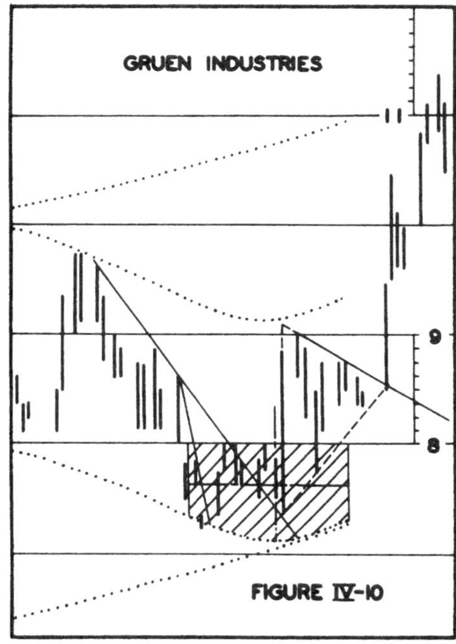


**Triangle Resolution–And A Mid-Channel Buy Signal**

noted without action, since we have predetermined on a mid-band buy. The moves to 9 and back to 7 3/4, then to 8 3/4 and back to 8 3/8 were seen. *On this exact day, two important things are noticed that immediately cause us to take action:*

1. We note that we are approaching a low on a component of roughly four weeks' duration (two samples present).
2. A triangle is forming composed of two one-week cycles.

We are ready to set up our mid-band buy criteria! First, let us analyze the triangle.

| | |
|---|---|
| 1. Sum of all components longer in duration than 19 weeks (represented by center line of 19-week cycle channel) | HARD UP |
| 2. 19-week component | 3½ weeks along–hard up |
| 3. 4-week component | Bottoming out to turn up |
| 4. 2-week component | Bottoming out to turn up |
| 5. 1-week component | Bottoming out to turn up |

We predict all odds in favor of an upside resolution of the triangle–and very soon! The upper boundary of the triangle is also the valid trend line at this point in time. It is validated by two peaks of the one-week cycle. No steeper trend lines have formed as yet. It trends right into the heart of the time when upside resolution of the triangle should take place. We draw in the valid trend line and conclude that an upside breakout is a valid mid-band buy signal.

The next day immediately provided this signal. Now notice several things:

1. You would have had to employ special intra-day tracking procedures to have handled the mid-band buy signal without chasing the price. This can be done, and techniques are described in later chapters. But again, more time and effort are involved.
2. Assume for the sake of comparison that you were able in both the edge-and mid-band cases to sell at the top–at 13. Your gross profits on the edge-band transaction would be 73.5% in 65 calendar days or an equivalent per unit time yield of 418% per year. The mid-band transaction grossed only 53%, *but it did it in 36 days.* The resulting equivalent per unit time yield is 539% per year!

As usual, the shorter time interval of trading produced the highest profit yield, not to mention the effect on profit compounding which is even more impressive. However, the price exacted is increased time, effort and attention.

In this example a triangle formed at the precise mid-band buy point. This was a fortunate happenstance that will not always occur. The two important points to remember are these:

1. Always watch for triangles of all sizes and shapes. This chart pattern, when analyzed for resolution using price-motion model concepts, always provides extremely valuable timing information. *Never pass up the opportunity to analyze a triangle!*
2. If a triangle does not form at the mid-channel buy point–simply utilize the valid downtrend line concept applied to the shortest duration component present. Be sure to complete a cycle status analysis as each new high and low (either daily or weekly) becomes available. This will assure you of the continuing validity of the downtrend lines you are using.

## POINTS TO REMEMBER REGARDING GRAPHIC "BUY" SIGNALS

- As many envelopes should be formed as the amount of data available permits. At least one and preferably two components of duration longer than the one you wish to trade on should be identified by envelopes.
- If sufficient care is used in the construction of these, estimates to current time of probable envelope continuation from the last identifiable low (or high) can provide advance warning of change or analysis error.
- Estimates of cyclic duration variation may be formed by direct measurement (on scratch paper), or you may count weeks from low-to-low and average. In either case, envelopes provide enough visibility to give a fair estimate as to when cyclic lows are likely to occur in the future.
- An ideal buy point is approached as several cyclic components approach lows simultaneously, with the sum of all longer duration components being on the upside. (A center line through the middle of a channel is a good representation of the sum of all components of duration longer than the one contained by the channel.)
- Use of daily charts in conjunction with weekly ones provides additional information on the status of very short duration components. These normally occur in groups of two or three per some longer duration one. They can therefore be used as verniers on transaction timing decisions.
- Envelope analysis does not provide clear-cut, objective buy and sell signals, but it does lay the groundwork for prediction, and is the basis of all more definitive techniques.
- Triangles and trend lines when used in conjunction with channel analysis price-turn prediction can provide precise and objective buy signals.
- Downtrend lines must always be formed from clear-cut peaks of recognizable cyclic highs. (Uptrend lines are formed similarly from clear-cut lows of recognizable cyclic fluctuations.)
- As stock prices near a multiplicity of cyclic lows, multiple trend lines form corresponding to cyclic channels. Each trend line formed is steeper than the last.
- This steepening of trend lines occurs all along a channel, as various components low-out. It is only of significance when the time for a multiplicity of lows is approached as indicated by channel analysis.
- The steepest such downtrend line which is broken on the upside during the time zone of an expected multiplicity of cyclic lows is a valid downtrend line.
- The upside breakout from a valid downtrend line is a valid buy signal.
- If this occurs in the price-turn zone, it is an edge-band buy signal.
- If it occurs at or near the center of the channel enclosing the trading cycle, it is a mid-band buy signal.
- Mid-band buy signals are more lucrative than edge-band signals in terms of yield on investment capital, but compound the work and effort involved.
- Cyclic analysis of triangle formation and resolution provides strong additional evidence of buy signal validity.

*chapter*

*five*

# You've Made Some Money — How to Keep It

- **Use of Logical Cut-Loss Criteria**
- **Extension to Trailing "Sell" Signals**
- **How to Construct Selling Analogs**
- **How to Make and Use Non-Real Time Envelopes**
- **Selling Short**
- **Selling Rules to Remember**

Let's assume you've made a buy using any of the techniques of Chapter Four. You have done so knowing that the odds are very good that your timing was correct, and that you stand to make a profit on your transaction. But some small odds *still* favor an incorrect decision. How do you protect yourself against these small chances of transaction failure? You *could* pick an arbitrary amount of loss you are willing to risk in return for the long-odds profit potential you have set up for yourself. This is the usual route to go, and may be implemented either by a stop-loss order, or by a self-imposed level at which you will sell out by calling your broker. This approach is generally unsatisfactory, however. You always know in the background of your mind that the level you have chosen is arbitrary. With no particularly logical reason behind the choice, human psychology is such that it is a very strong temptation to "wait just a little longer" in the hopes that your buy decision will be vindicated. This usually results in the process known as "letting your losses run"!

## USE OF LOGICAL CUT-LOSS CRITERIA

There is a much better way, based solidly on the price-motion model. Once again, what is desired is a decision *made in advance* that if the price of the stock behaves in a certain way in the future, an automatic signal to cut losses short is given. This signal must not be arbitrary in nature; in fact, it should be so firmly based on cyclic precepts that minimum temptation will exist to ignore it!

Let's go back to our valid downtrend line concept. This is a straightened-out upper bound of a curvilinear channel enclosing the shortest duration cyclic component observable on the daily chart. But, by definition, a channel always has *two* bounds–upper and lower. Locate and sketch in the corresponding lower bound (it does not need to be accurately done). Now note the lowest low of the cyclic component enclosed by this channel just prior to the time when the valid downtrend line was broken. Draw a horizontal line on your chart at this price level, and either enter a stop-loss order at this value at the time of your purchase or vow vehemently to sell instantly on its violation!

Let's talk about the rationale behind this procedure. First of all you didn't make the purchase at all until the time was cyclically right and the stock price told you that the cyclic lows anticipated had been passed. Under these circumstances, you expect the stock to move no way but *up* after your purchase, buoyed in this direction by the summed rates of price motion of several cyclic fluctuations. In no circumstance do you expect the price to get lower than the bottom of the channel enclosing the shortest duration fluctuation present. If it should do so, the channel would still be on the downside, indicating that the sum of all longer duration components is still downside. This would mean that the expected multiplicity of lows has not yet occurred–and a low probability transaction timing error has caught up with you. Either this is true, or an unforeseen change has taken place. In either event–you want nothing but out until the situation resolves itself.

Set up in this manner, you will find that the resulting loss is seldom more than twice in-out commission costs. Best of all, you now have a solidly rational reason for cutting your losses short, with an attendant increase in likelihood that you will do so! Your reasons for selling at this point are at all times as good as the reasons for the purchase in the first place. If you have developed confidence enough to buy on cyclic criteria, you should also have enough confidence to cut losses short on the same criteria.

Let's try this procedure on for size in the case of the Gruen Industry buy signals. Turning to Figure V-1, we see the now familiar edge- and mid-band buy points for Gruen. The first buy level is at about 7½ when the edge-band valid downtrend line was violated. The lower channel bound (of which this trend line was an upper bound) is shown dotted. The breakthrough told us that this tiny section of channel had curved sharply upward. This could only occur if the sum of all components of duration longer than the one enclosed by the channel has turned upward. In this case, the intra-channel component has a duration of about one-half week, and the components which have turned up sharply are the one-week, two-week and four-week ones. We mark the low from which prices pulled away on the breakout as TLL 1 (Trailing Loss Level No. 1).

If our analysis has been correct, and if cyclic action is not overridden by fundamentals, the stock price should not see this level again until our profit objectives are reached. If it does, something is wrong, and the stock should be sold without delay.

It is noticed that the stock did not violate this level, but continued to behave per expectation. But suppose that it *had.* What would have been the nature of our loss? We would have bought at 7½ and sold at 7 1/8. The percentage loss due to decreased stock price is 5% and we are charged another 4% in in-out commissions. This is just about

**A Triangle Resolution "Hold" Signal**

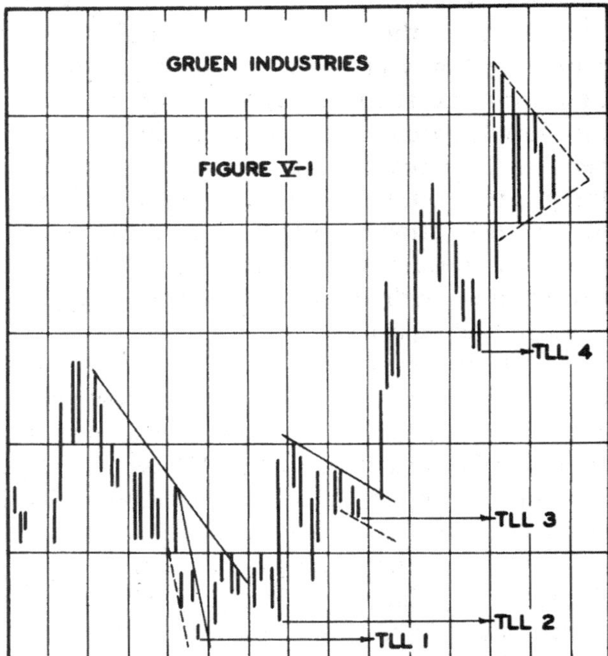


twice commission costs–a loss of 9% which we have risked against a precalculated potential for a 55% gain. Coupled with the fact that we have prestacked the deck heavily in favor of the large gain (as opposed to the small loss if we are wrong), the prospects for this transaction are too good to pass up! It will be found in practice that this method of setting up stop-loss levels, predetermined at the time of the buy, will average about 10% as the stop-transaction loss factor. Best of all, you have a solid reason for believing that you should take the loss–and a correspondingly better chance of doing so rather than let losses run because of emotion and pride. At this point you should reason through for yourself the use of the price level marked TLL 3 in Figure V-1 as the initial stop-loss level for the mid-band buy signal.

## EXTENSION TO TRAILING "SELL" SIGNALS

A fairly common trading practice is to use so-called trailing stop-loss orders (or price levels) to protect profits on a transaction, the theory being that as paper profits mount, you keep raising the level at which you will sell out if prices start to drop–thus always assuring retention of some portion of the maximum possible profits on a transaction. This scheme is good, but the same difficulties are encountered as in the setting of an arbitrary cut-loss level. If you trail prices too closely, a small dip may sell you out causing you to miss a much larger rise. If you trail too far behind prices, you salvage less and less of your paper profits if a dip turns out to be a major turn-around.

The concept for cutting losses short based upon the price-motion model points up an excellent way of getting around this difficulty. The initial cut-loss level, of course, serves as the first stage of the trailing profit preservation process. Since you are presumably in the stock just as it is pulling away from a multiplicity of cyclic lows, the very next low you expect to see is that of the shortest duration component present. Following the stock by cyclic analysis you should fairly well know in advance *when* this should occur. As soon as it does come about–and you know it has happened because the price has then pulled away again on the upside–mark the new low (above the previous one) as a new sell-out level. If your trading cycle is the one which is next longer in duration than this shortest observable one, you may continue in this manner until you are automatically sold out. Normally, this will not be so. There will be several periodicities with durations between those of the shortest duration one and your selected trading cycle.

Where this is true, you should maintain your original trailing loss level until you experience a low of the component next shorter in duration than your trading cycle. Then, as prices pull away confirming this low, a new level may be marked. Continue cyclic analysis as time passes. Always keep updating your estimate of when the next low will occur for all components–but especially for the trading cycle and the next shorter duration component.

Suppose the trading cycle normally contains three of the next shorter duration fluctuations. When the first low of this cycle is reached (and confirmed by prices pulling away from it again), mark *this* low as an emergency sell-out point. At this time, your sell level should assure you of a fair amount of profit retention. *Notice this:* if you had continued to use the lows of the shortest duration cycle to establish these sell levels, you would probably have been sold out at the just-reached low of the component next shorter in duration than your trading cycle!

Now note the position of prices within your best estimate of where the trading cycle envelope is. You should be approximately halfway to the upper bound. If you are close to the upper bound, shift immediately to use of the sell levels created by the shortest duration component. If about midway, you should continue to use the level set by the last low of the component just shorter than the trading cycle. All through the process, use your envelope as a guide. Remember, for months in the past your stock price motion has oscillated within this envelope. It is highly unlikely that it is going to go screaming out the top of it just because you're in it. Any time prices approach the upper bound and cyclic analysis indicates you've got the channel drawn correctly, you should be using the shortest duration component as a means of setting emergency sell levels. In fact, as you approach upper bounds, it is best to shift to a series of uptrend lines, using the valid one to provide a take-profit signal. No matter what happens–as long as your emergency sell levels and valid uptrend lines are not violated, the signal is "hold." You never know, you may get caught in one of those short-sharp fundamental things that override cyclicality and drive prices sharply upward and you'd hate to miss the ride! And if it happens to occur on the downside, your sell signal criteria should still preserve profits for you–or at least prevent loss.

Applying these concepts to Gruen, return your attention to Figure V-1. The trading cycle selected for both edge- and mid-band buys was the 19-week one. (All shorter duration components were used only as verniers in setting up precise buy timing.) The next shorter duration component is the four-week one and it is the demonstrated lows of this cycle that should be used to establish trailing loss levels until the time for profit-taking draws close. The successive lows of this periodicity are shown in the figure as TLL 1, 3, and 4 respectively. The use of an in-between level in this case (TLL 2) is predicated on the size of the pull-away move from the first two-week low. With this kind of price action we *know* we've timed our transaction well. Accordingly, we do not expect the next two-week low to see the one marked TLL 2 again, and we can validly "up" our loss level a small amount.

## HOW TO CONSTRUCT SELLING ANALOGS

To this point, we have discussed sell signals which prevent excessive transaction loss or preserve profits in case our price objectives are not reached for some reason. However, as time passes, we must reach a peak of our trading cycle somewhere along the line. We could use our trailing sell signals to tell us when to get out, but doing so will sacrifice a goodly part of the maximum gain potential. Therefore, we would like a bag of tricks which provides us with definitive, *in advance* signals that it is time to take profits. In most cases such sell signals are analogs of the ones used to buy.

Continued envelope analysis is, of course, a requirement. Triangle analysis is always helpful when applicable. Let's study Figure V-1 again closely. We've made either an edge- or mid-band purchase. Trailing loss levels have been set up continuously as time passes. The data shown in this figure is up to date through the eighth week of the 19-week cycle. We know the time to take profits is not too far away. Should the stock be sold at this point?

On this precise day a fourth point on the boundary of a well-defined triangle has been formed. Immediately we set up a cyclic analysis of the probable direction of resolution.

| | |
|---|---|
| 1. Sum of components longer in duration than 19 weeks (center line of envelope enclosing 19-week component) | Hard up. |
| 2. 19-week component | 9 weeks along. Topping out. |
| 3. 4-week component | 2½ weeks along. Hard down. |
| 4. 2-week component | Bottoming out to go up. |
| 5. 1-week component | Bottoming out to go up. |

Our signals are mixed as expected this far along in the trading cycle. However, we expect immediate strength from two components, about one and a half weeks of bottoming-out activity on a third, sideways push from a fourth and a general push-up by the sum of the long duration ones. We would conclude that an upside resolution is imminent but that the upside motion to be expected is limited. We are immediately put on guard that profit-taking sell signals are to be watched for closely.

At this point we *reverse* our valid trend line buy signal methods. Figure V-2 shows the resulting uptrend lines formed since the buy. The spot at which price has

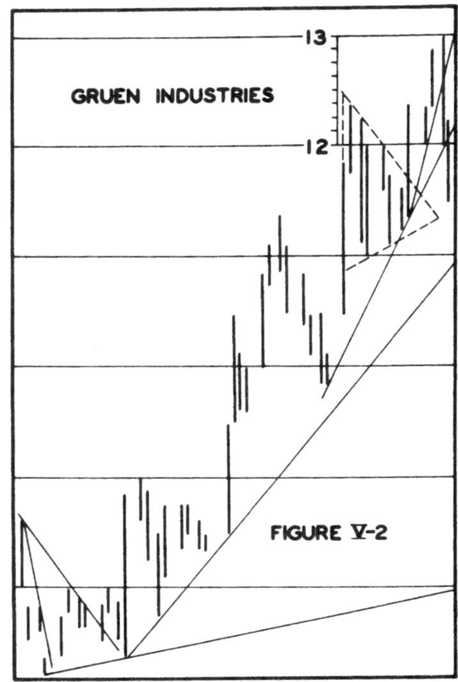


**Valid Uptrend Lines–And A "Sell" Signal**

pulled away from each successive trailing loss level establishes a new point on a generally upcurving trend line series. At the triangle apex, we shift to trend lines based upon shorter and shorter duration cycles. The day after the triangle analysis, price did indeed break out on the upside, providing an opportunity to steepen our trend line from one based on a four-week component to one based on a two-week cycle. Our triangle analysis has assured us that the breakout will be short-lived, in fact we expect a four-week cycle low in about one and a half weeks. We would anticipate this to be a lower low than the last one, and desire to take profits before then if this should come about. On the other hand if prices should continue to rise rapidly, we would like to remain invested.

Figure V-2 shows what happened. The first day's trading following triangle resolution stalled prices at our latest trend line. The next day pulled nicely away again. There has been no opportunity to set up a steeper uptrend line, so we live by the one drawn. The next day the trend line was broken at 12½, providing the desired sell signal–and a tidy profit! The validity of our decision is indicated by the fact that the price of Gruen declined from this point steadily (though cyclically!) to 9 over the next five weeks!

## HOW TO MAKE AND USE NON-REAL TIME ENVELOPES

You now have available simple graphical techniques to provide all of the needed investment action signals. However, the trading philosophy developed in Chapter One places great emphasis on risk reduction and profit maximization. It never does any harm to have an extra ace or two up your sleeve for this purpose.

Another case in point: suppose that Gruen had not formed a price-move termination triangle as it did. Are there any other criteria that could have been used to detect approach to the trading cycle peak? A much more generally applicable technique is needed, and is provided by the concept of *non-real time envelopes.*

The channel envelopes used so far are constructed in calendar or "real" time. But we know that cycle durations vary over a range. This variation coupled with inability to graphically separate components with accuracy sometimes leads to a situation where all of the information inherent in cycle presence is not displayed to us through channel construction. This effect can be minimized by forming channels from cyclic highs and lows that are artificially placed equidistant from one another on a pseudo-real time scale. The detailed significance of time is thereby lost, but information is often gained that is very valuable. Here's how such channels are made:

- Go back over your chart and tabulate the successive prices of the stock at all intra-day highs and lows associated with any component that you wish to plot in non-real time.
- Use a separate sheet of graph paper on which to plot these.
- Plot the first low on the stock chart on the far left vertical of your new plot. *On the very next vertical* plot the next high. On the next vertical, plot the following low.
- Proceed in this manner until the data is exhausted.
- Form a smooth, constant, and minimum-width envelope through your data points. Adjust width until all points are as closely related to the resulting channel as possible.

Now what has been accomplished? Horizontal distances on your new chart still represent time, but equal distances between points no longer necessarily mean equal times have elapsed. In fact, component duration changes from any cause whatsoever are completely eliminated. This envelope will not differ very much from the envelope on your stock price chart–unless cycle duration change becomes significant. But at that point, *the non-real time envelope will give you a much clearer picture of what is happening than will the one plotted in real time.*

Now try something else with your non-real time channel. On the lower channel bound and on the same vertical line as each "high" that is plotted, place a distinctive mark such as an asterisk. Do the same on the upper bound opposite each plotted low. Now, your last data point on the chart will be either a high or a low plot, depending upon whether the stock has last defined a cyclic high or low. Put an asterisk below or above this point, and spaced just the channel width from it. Now you can draw your non-real time channel, full width and right up to date. Note the slope and curvature (either up or down) of the channel at this point, and extend both channel bounds two vertical lines on your chart into the future. *The points of intersection of the extended channel bounds with the next two vertical chart lines represent a best estimate of the next high and low (or low and high) of the stock price at the times these should occur per cyclic criteria.*

Now go back to your stock price chart. For the component in question, average sample durations and mark on your chart the predicted time locations of the next high and low. Use the sample variation from average to show a time spread into which you expect these points to fall. Read the predicted stock prices for these times from your non-real time chart, add a reasonable plus and minus tolerance to these and plot the result on your stock chart as two "boxes." To the best of your ability you have now located the price and time regions into which the stock will move next. Continually update this estimate by cyclic analysis as time passes and the stock price changes. You will be surprised at how often the stock behaves per prediction!

There is another advantage in this type of graphical analysis. Occasionally the inevitable band of uncertainty connected with a real time envelope will mask the significance of a single day's price action which actually portends a non-cyclic change in the situation. The non-real time envelope will often catch such a situation, making you aware of it in time to take appropriate action.

Needless to say, this technique may be combined with the sell signal criteria of previous paragraphs to sharpen up your selling (or short covering) transaction timing. In fact, let's see how it would have worked in the case of Gruen. Figure V-3 shows Gruen again up to and including the day of termination triangle resolution. Our question on this day is how much further upside motion can we expect on this trading cycle move?

At this point in time, we do not know for sure whether or not point I on the chart is a low of the four-week cycle. However, assumption that it is will provide us with a conservative answer to our question, which is to be desired. We proceed to label each successive four-week high-low as A, B, C, D, E, F, G, H and our tentative I. The four-week cycle was chosen for this purpose because it is the component of next shorter duration than our trading cycle. Using the technique described above, the non-real time envelope for this case is drawn on the right, with corresponding peak and valley labeling.

Now note the effect of the low at I! To get to this point from the low corresponding to the high at H, the non-real time envelope must curve over sharply. We further note that if we are wrong about I being a four-week cycle low, the envelope would still be required to curve over unless this low were as high as 14! Since this is highly unlikely in view of the cyclic condition of things at this time, we are alerted that major components are indeed in the process of topping out, and we should be preparing to take profits. Note that this conclusion is identical with that derived from the triangle resolution analysis–but this time there is no dependency upon the triangle forming (in many cases it will not). We can go a little further. Continuing the turnover from I through the next two verticals on the non-real time chart establishes a conservative estimate of 12 3/4 for the next peak and 11 for the next low. With this information in hand the actual top-out at 13 and valid trend line sell signal at 12½ come as no surprise, and lend credibility to your decision to take profits on the sell signal. It is interesting to note that the real time envelope to the same point in time provides no hint of a turnover for nearly another week–too late to act as the desired confirmation of the sell signal. This is typical of the use and value of the non-real time envelope technique.

## SELLING SHORT

In Chapter Four and so far in Chapter Five objective signals based upon the price-motion model have been developed for "wait," "buy," "hold," "sell," and "protect-loss" situations. Only two more are needed to round out our armory. These

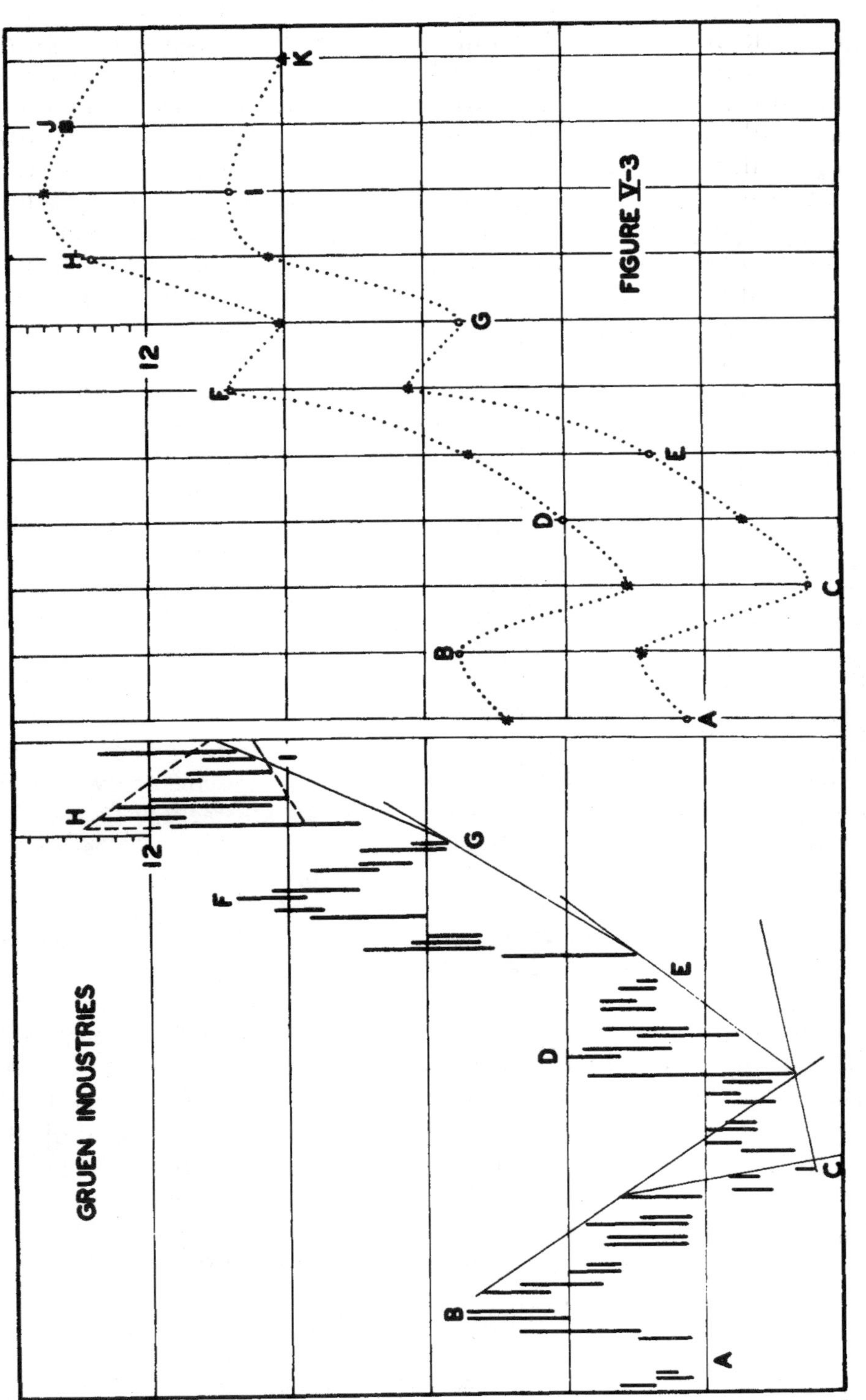


Non-Real Time Envelopes

are, of course, "sell-short" and "cover short sale" signals. By the nature of the development so far, it is clear that nothing really new is needed here. In fact, whenever a sell signal is noted, an automatic sell-short signal is implied. However, it is very important to keep one additional aspect of the situation firmly in mind: *It is seldom advisable to sell the same stock short that you have just profited in by making a buy!*

Why is this true? Hark back now to our investment philosophy–which is aimed at maximizing yield per unit time. Remember also that smooth, long-term fundamental factors account for 75% of the price motion of a stock. In selecting a stock to buy, you picked one in which the sum of all components of duration longer than your trading cycle was trending *up.* This meant that you had the impetus of the fundamental trend also in your favor. In selling the same stock short, you are bucking this trend–which cannot lead to yield maximization.

The correct procedure then is to select another issue in which the sum of all components longer in duration than your trading cycle is *down.* Analyze this stock as time goes along, just as if you had purchased it. When the trading cycle tops out sending up a sell flare, the simultaneous sell-short signal is valid.

Similarly, all of the techniques for buying into a stock are applied while you are short the stock. As time passes, these techniques will eventually establish a buy signal, *at which time you cover your short sale!* Cyclic analysis, real time and non-real time envelopes, triangle resolution, valid trend lines and trailing "protect-profit" techniques must all be applied as before while you hold your short position.

Now a word as to why you should ever prefer to sell short. Note the illustration regarding the degree of time-synchronization of cyclicality in the Appendix. The implication here is that as the DJ 30 (or S&P "500") Average tops out on your trading cycle (regardless of which one you have chosen), most individual issues are also near a top-out on this cycle. It is true that synchronization is not perfect by a matter of days (or even weeks for some of the longer duration components). Nevertheless, it is real suicide to attempt to trade on cyclicality on the long side when the overall market as measured by the averages is on a cyclic downside. On the other hand, if you simply step aside at this point you are violating the principle of profit maximization regarding 100% time investment of your capital.

What you must do is this: *Always treat the Averages just like a stock.* Keep a running cyclic analysis going on the averages just as if it were possible (and you intended) to buy them. As long as your analysis here is "buy" or "hold," trade long in individual issues. As your preselected trading cycle gets close to a top-out in the averages, start to liquidate your long positions in issues (as sell signals are given), and begin the search for suitable "short" candidates. The same applies in reverse as your analysis of the averages indicates a bottoming of the trading cycle.

## SELLING RULES TO REMEMBER

Now for a summary of our bag of sell tricks.

- Valid trend lines can be completed into short channel segments. The very short duration component intra to this channel is the basis for an effective cut-loss criterion based on the price-motion model.

- Trailing stop-loss levels can be based on confirmed lows of each cycle of duration next shorter than the trading cycle.
- Triangle resolution should be used all along the line in connection with cyclic analysis to provide insight into further price action.
- Non-real time envelopes can be used to help determine when to switch from trailing loss levels to short-term sell signal constructions.
- The concept of valid uptrend lines is an effective way of providing a sensitive "take-profit" sell signal.
- Sell-short signals are reverse analogs of buy signals. Selling short can significantly improve your percentage time invested.

# *chapter six*

# Compute Your Way to Increased Profits

- **Why You Need Computational Aids**
- **How to Construct and Use Half-Span Moving Averages**
- **Other Uses For Half- and Full-Span Moving Averages**
- **Now Turn Your Averages Inside Out**
- **Use the Inverse Half-Span Average to Improve Your Timing**
- **Try the Inverse Average in Other Ways**

## WHY YOU NEED COMPUTATIONAL AIDS

The graphic techniques for making use of the price-motion model presented in Chapters Four and Five are sufficient to vastly improve your timing. They may be utilized as is, with no additional aid from computation, and will suffice to make the investment philosophy of Chapter One work for you. However, decision confidence can be greatly increased and the types of stocks in which you can work enlarged, if you don't mind adding some arithmetic. Admittedly, this requires more time and effort, but the results can be extremely worthwhile.

Many, many computational approaches are possible. This chapter is intended to introduce you to several of the simplest and fastest of these. When you learn to apply the techniques given here, you will soon find yourself generating variations and whole new methods. Just as long as these are soundly based on the model, they can be considered valid. Further, the more elements of the model on which the technique depends, the more powerful you will find the aid to be.

## HOW TO CONSTRUCT AND USE HALF-SPAN MOVING AVERAGES

Valuable information is available each time a moving average with span equal to one-half the duration of the trading cycle changes direction! Let us examine this characteristic of moving averages in connection with the nature of the price-motion model to see why this is so.

From Chapter Three and from the Appendix, the characteristics of moving averages are summarized as follows:

- The span of a moving average is the length of time over which data is summed to obtain the moving average. For example, a 30-week moving average consists of 1/30th of the sum of the weekly closing prices of a stock for the last 30 consecutive weeks. The span of this average is therefore 30 weeks.
- A moving average "lags" the data it smooths by one-half of its span. This means that if the average is to represent a time-synchronized, smooth version of the data, the last computed point of the average must be plotted one-half span behind the last available data point. Thus, the last available point of a 30-week moving average is plotted between the 15th and 16th weeks behind the last closing price of the stock.
- A moving average reduces precisely to zero the presence and magnitude of any cyclic component with duration exactly equal to the span of the average.
- All shorter duration components are drastically reduced, but may show some sign of their presence.
- All longer duration components are definitely present. The longer the duration, the more completely the full magnitude of the component comes through.

Now assume we have a stock in which a dominant component has been identified with an average duration of 20 weeks. A moving average with a span of one-half of this, or ten weeks, is constructed. The lag of this average is one-half of its span or five weeks. Thus, when this average "tops out" and turns down, the 20-week trading cycle has signalled a turnover at this point, *but the price of the stock itself has been going down for five weeks already!* Remembering that it is the 20-week component that caused both the ten-week average and the stock price to top out, it is seen that the total downward move due to this component is just one-half complete at this time.

All of this occurs because the ten-week average will kill all price fluctuations of exactly ten weeks in duration and drastically reduce all shorter ones. Since the 20-week motion will come through at nearly full strength, the ten-week average will only change direction when the 20-week cycle causes it to do so. Then the five-week lag is precisely the time required for the 20-week cycle to drive prices half as far as the 20-week cycle is going to carry them. Similarly, when the ten-week moving average bottoms out, the stock has already been rising for five weeks—and is half as far up as the 20-week cycle is going to drive it.

This quality of a half-span moving average can only work, of course, if the price-motion model is a correct representation of stock price fluctuations. That it *does* work—time after time—is very powerful evidence indeed for the validity of the model. Let's list in order what must be done to make use of this timing aid:

- Use a quick and rough envelope analysis to establish the average duration of a dominant cyclic component on which you wish to trade.
- Construct a moving average of the closing prices of the stock which has a span equal to half the average duration of the trading cycle. If this comes out to be a fraction, round it off to the nearest whole number.
- Plot the moving average on the same chart used for the stock, taking care to lag the average one-half its span behind the stock data.
- When the average reverses its direction to the downside note the price of the stock and

how much it has already moved down. You may expect the downtrend to continue until the stock has moved down this much more.

- Reverse this process for moving average reversals to the upside to establish how much further up the stock will go.

The accuracy of this process can be further improved by the use of *two* moving averages. Proceed as before but compute and plot not only the half-span average, but the moving average whose span is equal to the average duration of the trading cycle as well. For the example used above, the trading cycle duration is 20 weeks. The half-span moving average is a ten-week one. The full-span moving average is a 20-week one. Now let's see why this is of aid.

The half-span average tops out when the stock price has dropped 50% of the 20-week fluctuation amount. This means that the stock price is right in the middle of the channel enclosing the 20-week cycle at this particular time. On the other hand, the 20-week moving average is *always* in the middle of the 20-week channel (theoretically). Remember, the 20-week average reduces the 20-week cycle to zero. Thus the 20-week average represents the sum of all components of duration longer than 20 weeks, which is exactly the import of the center line of the 20-week channel! The 20-week average also drastically reduces the size of all shorter duration components, allowing only small percentages of these to "leak" through—and these are easily recognizable and graphically smoothed.

Now when your ten-week average tops out, you can extrapolate both the ten- and 20-week averages through their lag periods up to current time. This is quite simply accomplished for the 20-week average especially, since it is so "smooth." Note the price level at which the stock, the ten-week moving average extrapolation, and the 20-week moving average extrapolation meet. Subtract this from the previous peak of the current move down. *This is your estimate of how much further down the stock will go.* A tolerance of ±10% should be allowed for the *total* move estimate.

As with all of the techniques discussed in this book, you should never rely on this estimate alone. But combined with the others, this method provides powerful confirmation of the validity of action signals. Let's see how it works by example.

Figure VI-1 is a partial replot of the data on Alloys Unlimited used as an example in Chapter One. This stock displays a dominant component in this time period that ranges from 17 to 22 weeks in duration. For the sake of computational simplicity we will assign it (as our trading cycle) an average duration of 20 weeks. We need therefore a ten-week (half-span) and a 20-week (full-span) moving average. The plot is presented just as a decision point is reached—the ten-week moving average has just bottomed out. We note and smooth a remnant of a 12-week component from the 20-week moving average. The result is shown in the plot as a dashed line.

We extrapolate both the ten- and 20-week averages to current time. These meet the stock price at 41. The stock has already moved up from 32, a total of 9 points. We expect it to continue another 9 points from 41—to 50. The total move predicted is 18 points. The tolerance is ±10% of this amount, or approximately 2 points. We therefore predict that this 20-week cycle will carry prices to between 48 and 52! If we had purchased the stock on this type of criteria, coupled with any or all of the forms of graphical analysis we now know about, the resultant conclusion is that we should hold the

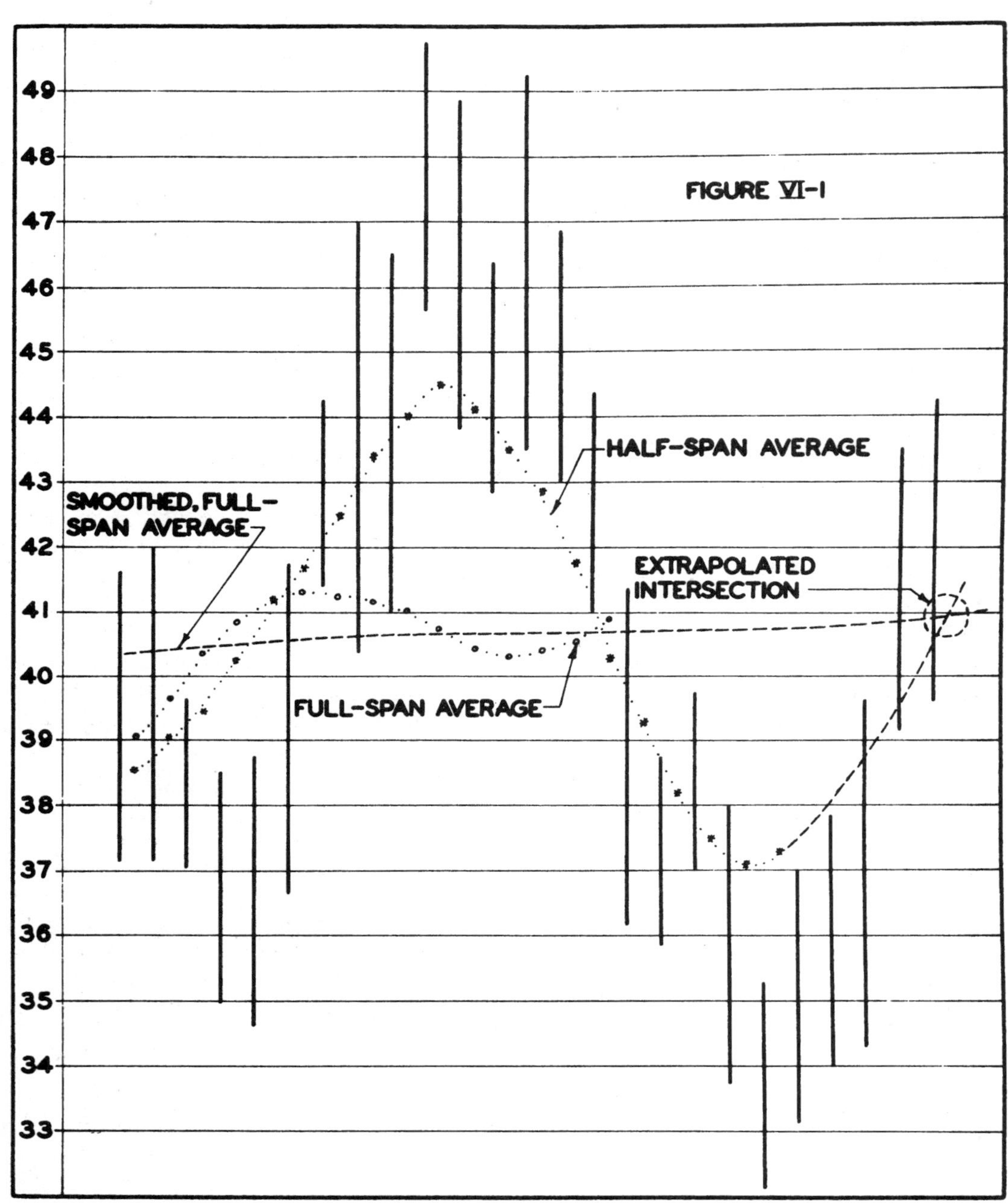


Using The Half-Span Average To Predict

stock for a move of about 9 more points. Further, any time the stock enters our prediction area, we are alerted that we should be setting up and using terminal sell signal procedures!

Figure VI-2 shows what the stock did. It entered the tolerance zone eight weeks later and topped out at 48 3/4! The sell signal generated here would also constitute a sell-short signal. With the 20-week moving average trending upward in this issue, better vehicles could be found for a short transaction. However, just to follow along with our new technique, suppose we both sold and sold-short Alloys Unlimited at this point around 47 or 48. How would we have fared?

Figure VI-3 shows the same stock three weeks later. Prices have declined to the neighborhood of 42 and we have a 5- to 8-point profit. Should we take our profit here?

Well, we note also that the ten-week moving average has just topped out. Let's estimate how low we expect the stock to go. Extrapolating both the ten- and 20-week averages results in an intersection with stock prices at 42. The stock topped out at 48 3/4 or 7 points higher. We expect it to go 7 points lower, to about 35. The total move anticipated is 14 points, providing a tolerance of about ±1 1/2 points. We predict the stock will continue to drop to the region of 33 1/2 to 36 1/2. The signal we've generated is "hold!"

Figure VI-4 shows what the stock did. The price entered the prediction zone four weeks later, and bottomed out at 35 1/8! Once again we could use our cover-short signal at these levels as a buy signal. Let us assume that we did so, covering our short sale and buying into the stock in the neighborhood of 37 (which we could have done any time within a five-week interval!).

Figure VI-5 shows the following action just as the ten-week average bottoms out. Extrapolation of the averages results in intersection with the stock price at 43 3/4. The stock has moved to this price from 35 1/8, or 8 5/8 points. We anticipate a further move of this amount to 43 3/4 + 8 5/8 = 52 3/8. As usual, we put a tolerance of ±10% of the total move about this price to get a zone of 50 5/8 to 54 1/8 with the target price of 52 3/8. As Figure VI-6 shows, the price of the stock rocketed into this zone the following week, remaining there for three weeks (plenty of time to get out using graphical methods and daily charts). The actual top-out price was 52 7/8!

This sell signal is, of course, also a sell-short signal. Suppose we had sold here and sold short at 51 to 52. Figure VI-7 shows the next reversal of the ten-week moving average. On this transaction, prices have oscillated wildly between 44 and 51 for nine weeks. We are somewhat concerned about our transaction, and wish to know whether or not we should cut and run! Extrapolation of averages provides intersection at 46 3/4. This is 6 1/8 points below the preceding peak. Prices should go down to 40 5/8, ±1 1/4, or into a zone from 39 3/8 to 41 7/8. The stock entered this zone two weeks later and bottomed out at 41!

This simple computational technique is one of the most powerful timing tools in your arsenal. It will not always provide as much information as in this example, but it should be the first computational technique you use as a backup to other methods. As usual, the whole armory of defensive techniques (trailing loss levels, etc.) should be employed to guard against the unexpected – which *does* occur occasionally. But, properly used, it can add materially to your confidence in making buy and sell decisions. Best of all, it is not an empirically derived method, but is solidly based on the existence and nature of the price-motion model!

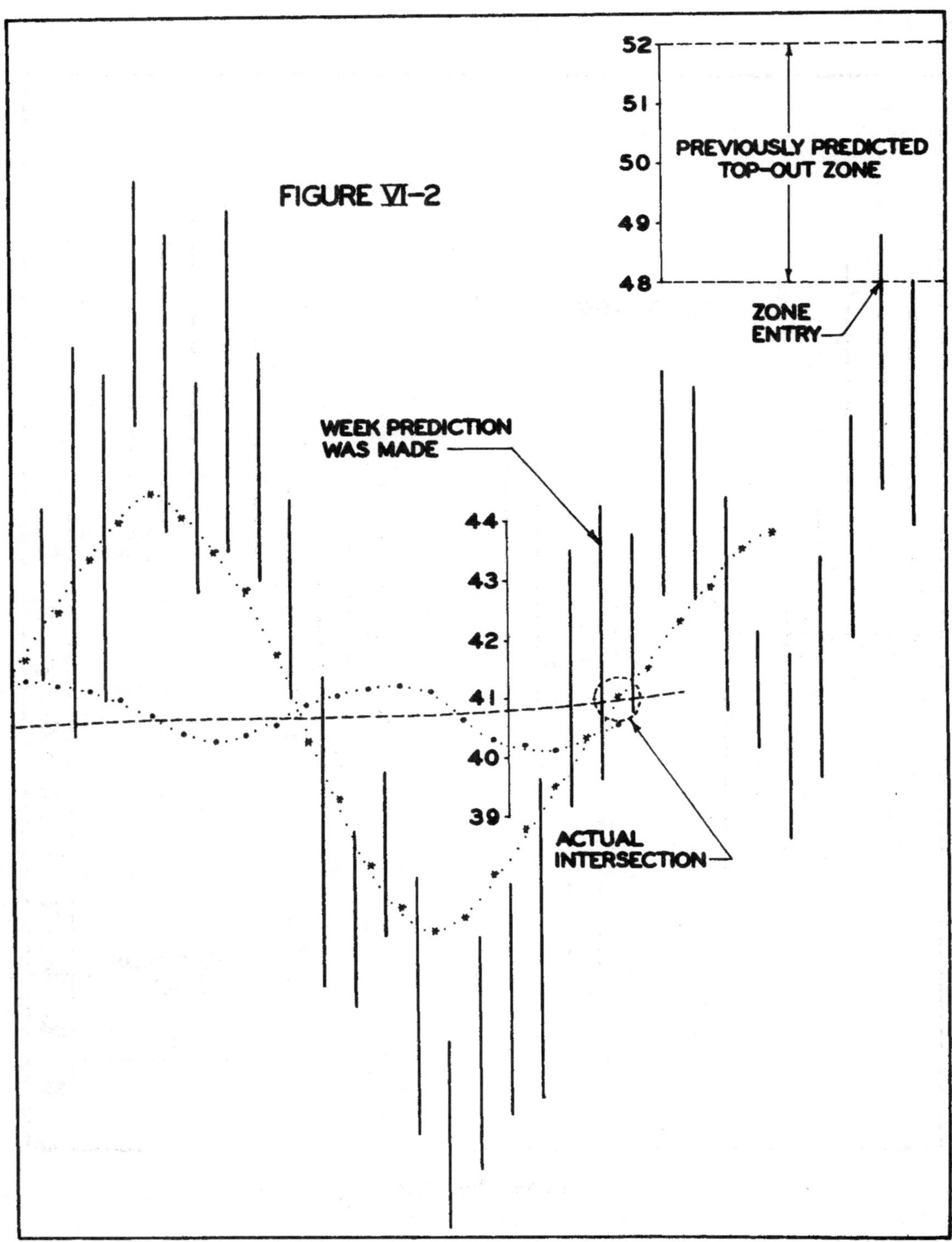


A Half-Span Average "Sell" And "Sell Short" Signal

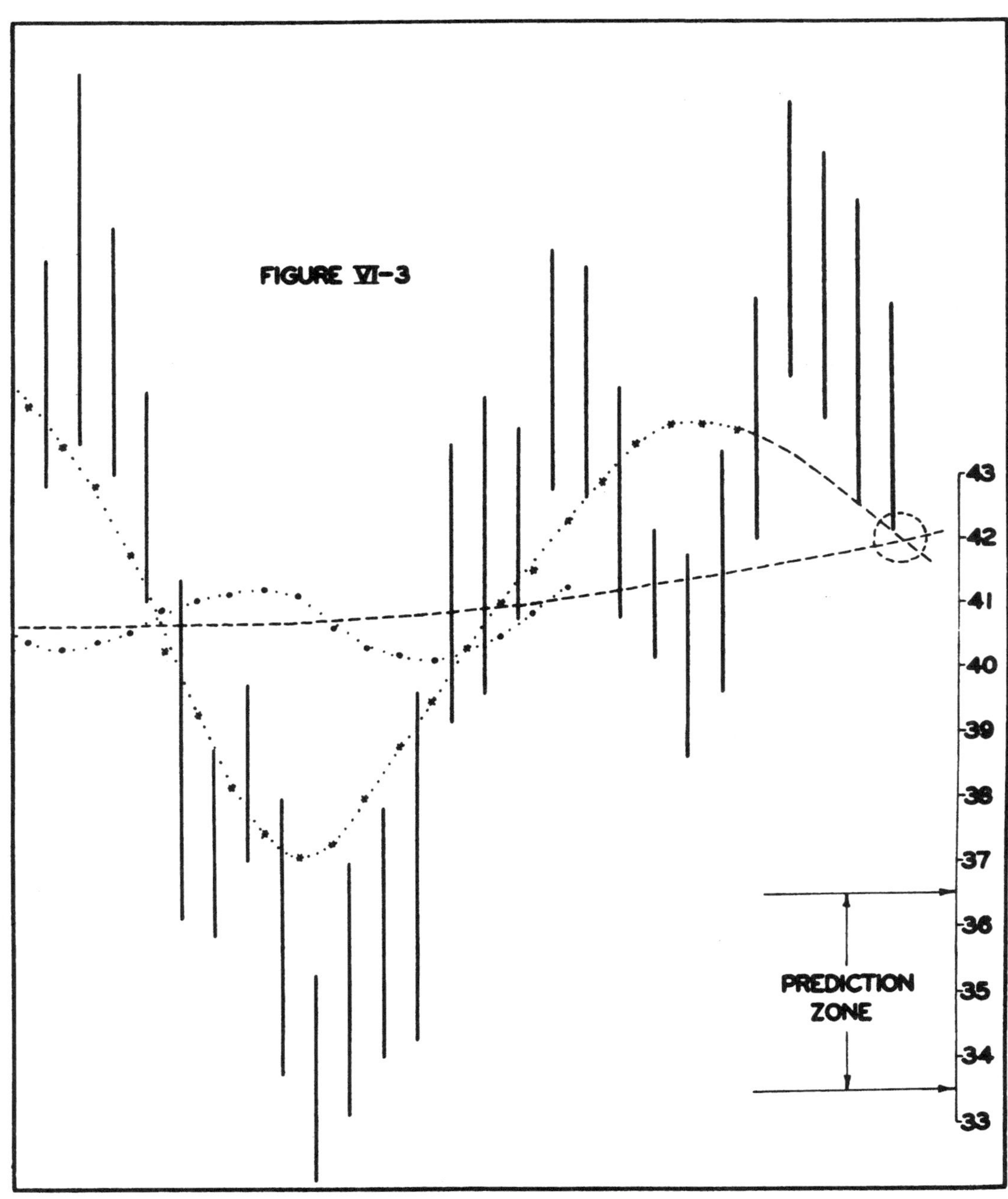


**The Next Prediction**

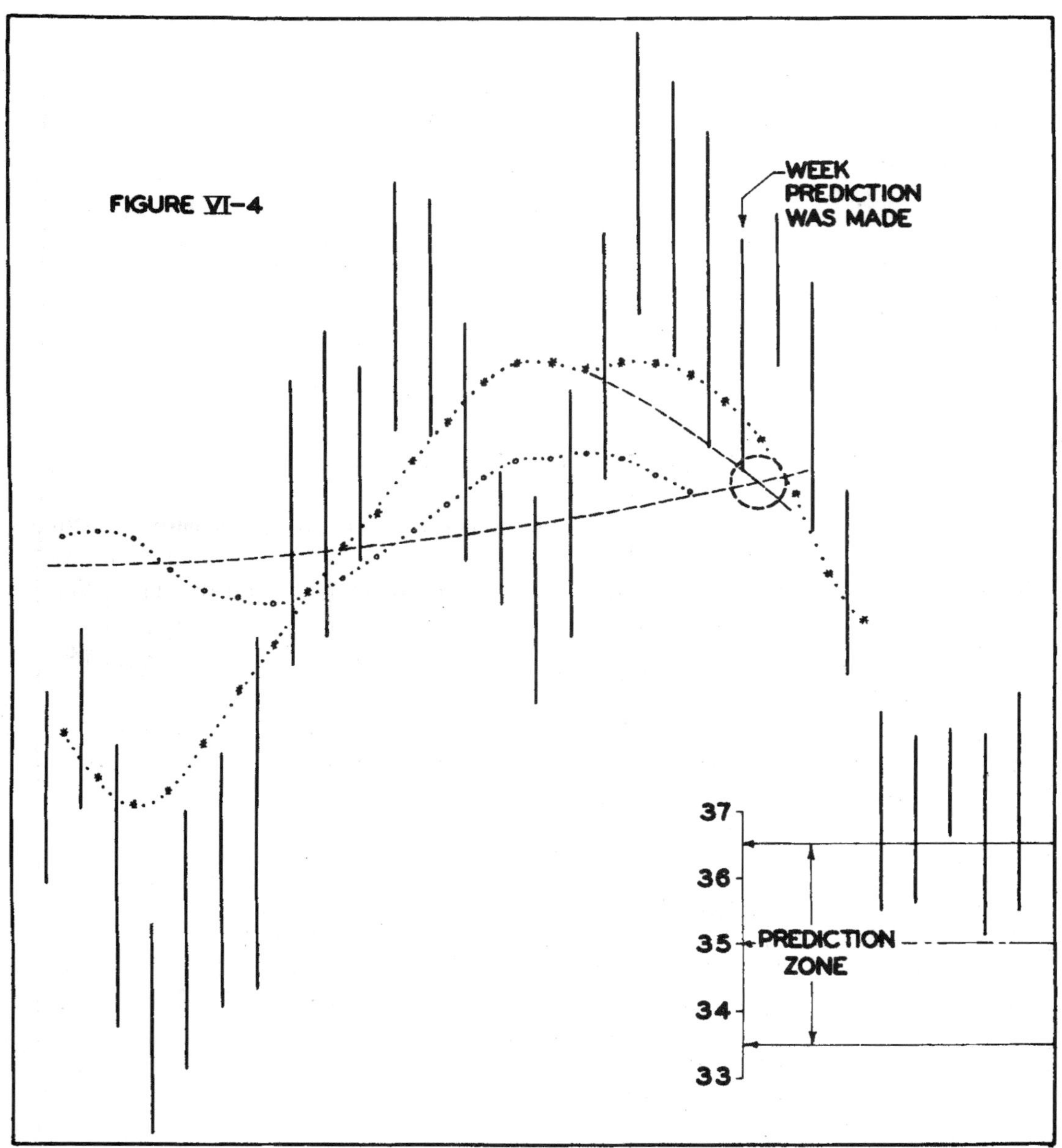


A Half-Span Average "Cover Short" And "Buy" Signal

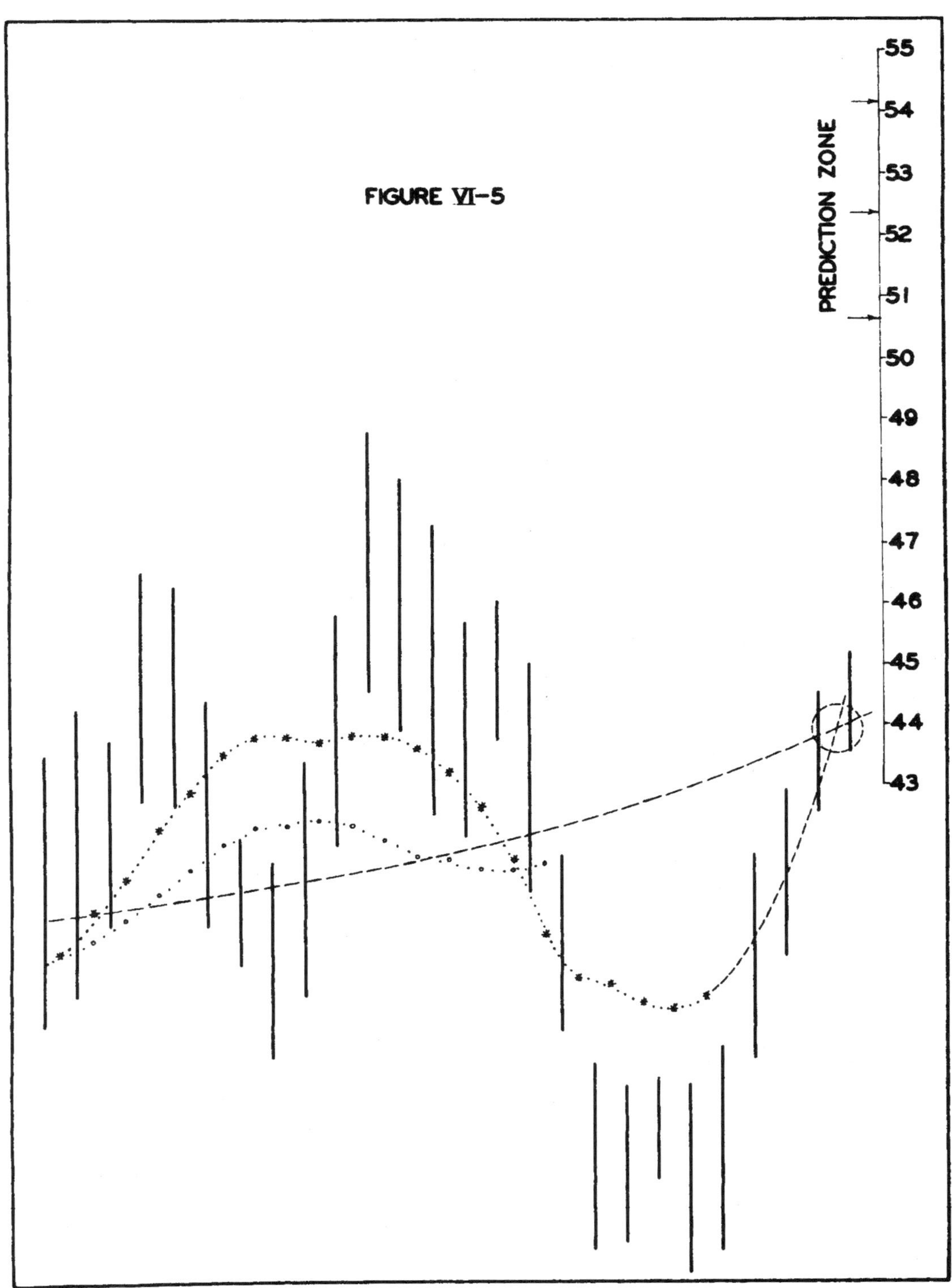


**A Half-Span Average "Hold Long" Signal**

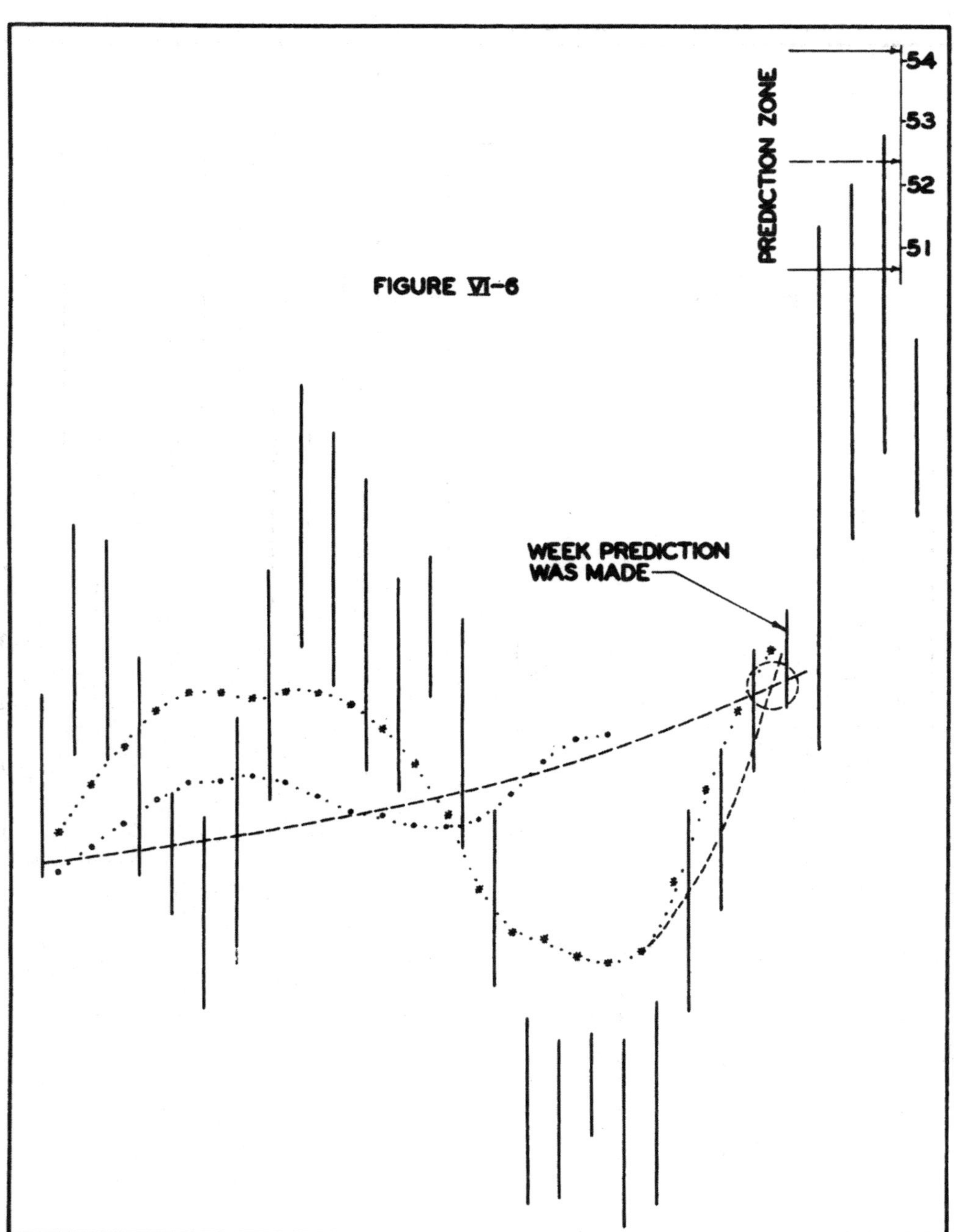


The Resulting "Sell" And "Sell Short" Signal

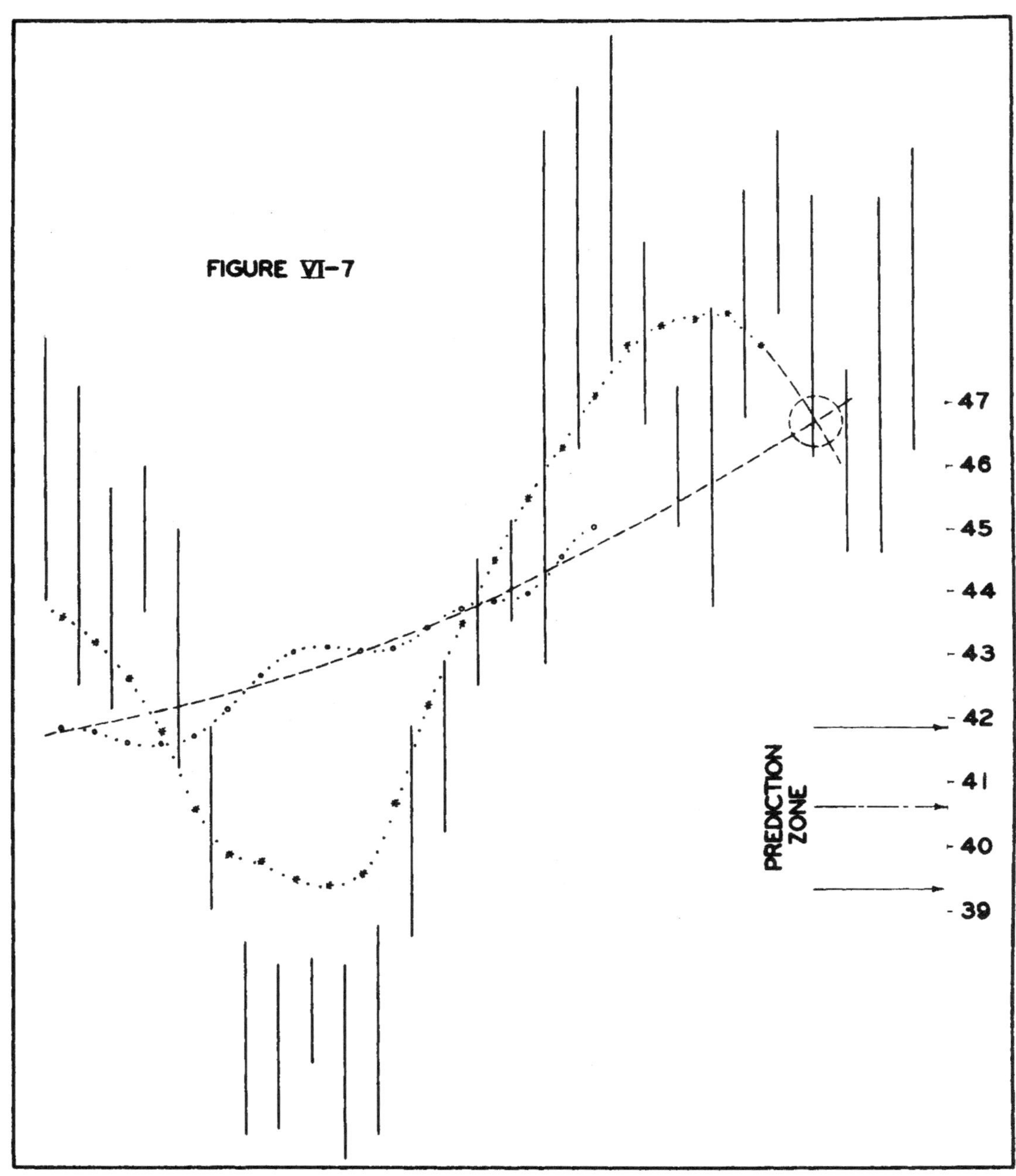


**A Half-Span Average "Hold Short" Signal**

## OTHER USES FOR HALF- AND FULL-SPAN AVERAGES

Graphical cyclic analysis should, of course, accompany the use of *all* techniques. In this case the two can interact very favorably. For example, looking back at Figure VI-6 we see that there is absolutely no doubt whatsoever about how the 20-week channel should be drawn. The 20-week moving average very nicely slices through the center of solidly visible peaks and valleys which provide points on the desired envelope.

You will find some issues in which the situation is not this clear. In such cases, "eyeball" the stock chart to get a rough feel for the dominant component. Construct a half- and full-span average based upon your best estimate of the duration of this cycle. You will find that plotting these averages makes identification of channel bounds very much easier. After your channel is constructed, you will be able to refine your estimate of trading cycle duration. If this is significantly different from the original, you will then want to reconstruct the half- and full-span averages based upon your revised durations.

Quite often a properly constructed set of averages will signal an envelope turn before either real or non-real time envelopes could possibly provide this information. Alloys Unlimited provides a typical example of this.

In Figure VI-5, it is impossible to know whether or not the 20-week channel is pivoting upward (about the 32 1/8 low) without the aid of the moving averages. In fact, the cycle high at 48 3/4 is lower than the preceding one at 49 3/4, leading to a suspicion that the channel direction is still down.

Inspection of the 20-week moving average tells us exactly what is happening. The trend here is definitely up—telling us that the sum of all components of duration greater than 20 weeks is moving up. Since this is the center line of the 20-week channel, this channel has to have bottomed with the 32 1/8 low and must now be curving upward. The approximate amount of curvature is obtained from one-half channel width measurements from the graphically smoothed 20-week moving average. The envelope bounds so defined give envelope analysis estimates of 20-week cycle moves that are in good agreement with those obtained by observation of ten-week moving average turns. *Note that this advance information was completely unobtainable from envelope analysis alone until a subsequent cyclic top was formed and confirmed at 52 7/8, a full three weeks later!*

From this example it is seen that the graphical and computational techniques can be used to aid and complement one another.

The same logic that leads to the use of half- and full-span moving averages to predict amounts of moves can be used to generate back-up time information as well.

As shown in previous paragraphs, a half-span average reversal signals the half-way point in a cyclic move in terms of magnitude. Now, when the half-span average reaches mid-channel, the price of the stock has preceded it down to the theoretical low for the move. But in predicting magnitude variation, we found it necessary to extrapolate the half- and full-span averages to intersection, which by definition is a best estimate of the point where the half-span average is at mid-channel. The theoretical low (in the predicted price zone) should take place one-half the span of the half-span average later.

Let's use a ten- and 20-week (half- and full-span respectively) case as an example.

The ten-week average has just topped out. We extrapolate both half- and full-span averages to intersection with the stock price. Note the calendar date on the chart at which this occurs. One-half the half-span average span is one-half of ten, or five. We expect the predicted low to occur five time units from the estimated intersection point date.

Return now to Figure VI-1 and VI-2. In Figure VI-1, note the time of estimated intersection. You now predict zone entrance and high five weeks later. From Figure VI-2 it is seen that zone entry and bottom-out took place nine weeks later. This is an example of about the poorest estimate correlation to be expected. In this case reliance would have had to be placed on other techniques to assure results.

From Figures VI-3 and VI-4 we note intersection at 42 and expect bottom-out five weeks later. Actual zone entry took place three weeks later, with a low achieved six weeks from intersection (an example of excellent correlation).

In Figures VI-5 and VI-6 intersection occurred at 43 3/4. Top-out was anticipated five weeks later. Zone entry occurred three weeks later with top-out at five weeks.

The reason for a larger percentage spread in timing is the existence of shorter duration components which tend to swell or depress prices as they peak or low out. Nevertheless, the method is of some use when allied with all of the other techniques available.

Generally speaking, graphical envelope analysis and valid trend lines can be depended upon for the most accurate and detailed information regarding move termination timing.

## NOW TURN YOUR MOVING AVERAGES INSIDE OUT

You're familiar now with the principal characteristics of a moving average, and how the price-motion model generates criteria for getting the most from them. In this section, you will find they have still more uses.

Let's ask ourselves the question: Is there useful information in what a moving average throws away?

We recall that a moving average "smooths" data. It does this by reducing the magnitude of short duration fluctuations, while permitting the longer ones to remain. In short, it throws away the short fluctuations.

### What a Moving Average Throws Away Can Be Recovered By Subtracting The Average From The Price-Motion Data

An example will clarify how this works. Suppose you form an 11-week moving average of the weekly mean prices of a stock. This means that in the moving average the magnitude of any cyclic component of duration exactly equal to 11 weeks is reduced to zero. Thus, the average contains only cyclic components present in the price motion which have durations longer than 11 weeks. Subtracting the average from the price motion removes all these longer duration fluctuations, leaving only those shorter than 11 weeks that did not appear in the average (or were "thrown away").

The only critical item to remember (as always) is to match the moving average and price data points properly before subtracting—taking into account the half-span time lag previously described.

## USE THE INVERSE HALF-SPAN AVERAGE TO IMPROVE YOUR TIMING

There are many ways in which you can make use of the inverse moving average. One of the most important of these is in connection with the half-span average concept. Let's see how it can work for you.

Direct your attention to Figure VI-8. Here is a weekly plot of Alloys Unlimited

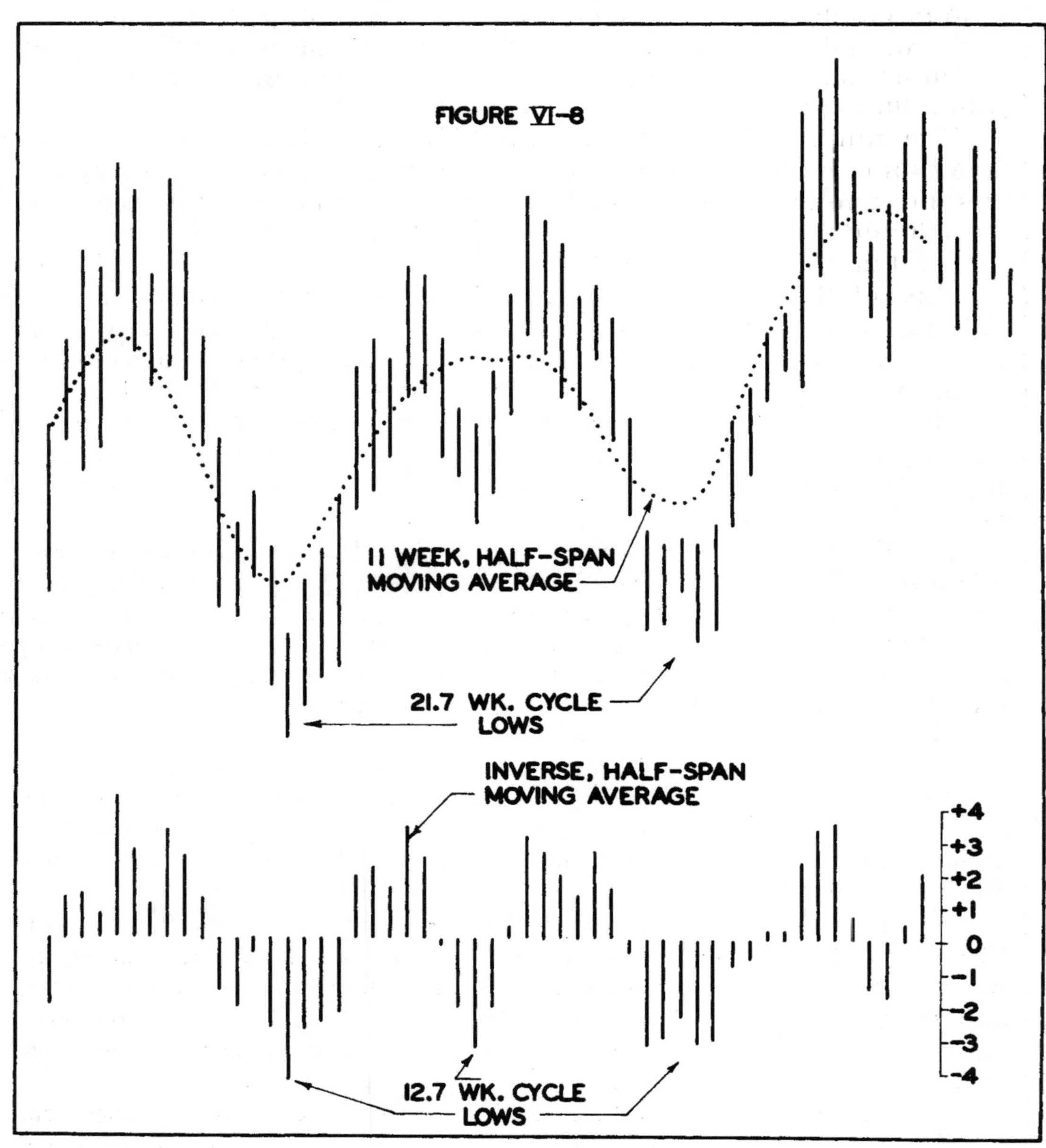


The Inverse Half-Span Average

over the entire time period covered by illustrations VI-1 through VI-7. This time, instead of using a ten-week average, an 11-week one is shown. With the number of elements of the average being "odd," each average datum directly corresponds (in time) to a weekly price datum instead of falling in midweek (as for the ten-week one). In this way subtraction can be accomplished directly without need for interpolation. As formed, each moving average is subtracted from the corresponding mean weekly price of the stock.

The results could be plotted as points about a "zero" base line, either by themselves or connected by straight lines. However, the process of erecting vertical lines from zero to the value of the difference (as in Figure VI-8) seems to provide the eye with more information.

What can we make of this plot?

First of all, the dominant cyclic component just shorter in duration than the trading cycle is now clearly evident. Counting weeks (low-to-low and high-to-high) and averaging gives a nominal duration of 12.7 weeks, with a "spread" from ten to 16. The correlation with an expected component of the price-motion model is obvious.

Secondly, it is seen that the magnitude of this cycle averages seven points peak-to-peak (±3 1/2 points). It is seen that the inverse average provides cycle magnitude directly, without necessity for, and without the error inherent in, the construction of envelopes!

Thirdly, we note that a simple process of subtraction converts a half-span average (which is vitally useful on its own) into that specific inverse average which is most capable of identifying the component of duration just less than that of the trading cycle. As seen in previous chapters, identification of this component is an essential part of the process of setting up trailing loss levels and sell signals in general. And, you will normally have already computed the half-span average anyway!

Now. How does all this aid transaction timing?

Return to Figure VI-6 and VI-7. In the discussions regarding these figures it is noted that the half-span average had put us in the stock short at 51 to 52. But, prices seemed to refuse to go down—oscillating instead from 44 to 51 for nine weeks. The half-span analysis assured us the stock was headed for 40 5/8. Does the inverse half-span confirm this conclusion?

In Figure VI-8, the inverse half-span average is two weeks away from a low of the 12.7-week cycle. The stock price is an additional five weeks along (due to the lag of the average). So, we're now seven weeks along on a component (next shorter in duration than the trading cycle) which averages 12.7 weeks, and varies from ten to 16 weeks. We expect the next significant low of this cycle in a time zone three to nine weeks from now.

In addition, the 21.7-week (average) duration trading cycle (which varies from 20 to 23 weeks in length) is now 19 weeks along from a low. We expect the next significant low of this cycle in a time zone one to four weeks from now. With both of these important cycles due to low out in the same general time period, we know the stock still has more to go on the downside. In fact, taking 6/13 of 7 points, we expect about 3.7 points more on the downside from the 12.7-week cycle alone. An additional

3/22 of 14 or 1.9 points remains in the 21.7-week cycle. The present price is 45 which, less 4.6, leaves 40 1/2 as a low-out estimate.

We conclude that the stock will reach approximately 40 1/2 within one to nine weeks. *This estimate compares almost identically with that obtained using the half-span average alone (40 5/8 in three weeks)—yet was obtained using information the half-span average "threw away"!*

With this additional reassurance, we do not hesitate to remain in our short position—and the stock proceeded to bottom out at 41 the next week, nicely within our tolerance zone!

## TRY THE INVERSE AVERAGE IN OTHER WAYS

An inverse moving average can be formed from an average of any span. Any time you wish to inspect a given component more accurately, simply form an average of span equal to the component duration. The associated inverse average *must* show the desired fluctuation at exactly the correct magnitude, since it is present in price to this extent but is precisely zero in the moving average. Taking the difference between the two displays this particular fluctuation on a zero baseline in all its glory!

This usage is particularly important as you are approaching buy and sell points. Extract the higher frequency components in this way, and you will never have to guess about trend line validity and channel turn-around.

Another excellent application: extract your trading cycle in this manner *before* you act on buy signals. The state of the magnitude-duration fluctuation situation is clearly discernible once the large, long components are removed. You may save yourself from acting on a perfectly valid buy signal only to find your trading cycle has shrunk to near zero in size!

Try the inverse average at triangle resolution points. Once again, the mechanics of formation of these patterns via magnitude-duration fluctuation of short duration components will be made very clear. In addition, the short duration component information derived will aid greatly in pinpointing pattern resolution times.

## TO SUMMARIZE

- Half- and full-span moving averages can be used to predict the extent of price fluctuations.
- Envelope analysis is used to identify and establish the average duration of a trading cycle.
- Two moving averages are then constructed. One has a span equal to the average duration of the trading cycle. The other has a span equal to one-half the duration of the trading cycle.
- These are plotted on the same chart as the stock, with due consideration for the time lag of each.
- When the half-span average reverses direction, important move prediction information is made available.

- Upon reversal, both half- and full-span averages are extrapolated to intersection with the stock price on the chart.
- The price move from the previous trading cycle peak (or low) to the intersection price represents half the total price move anticipated.
- The predicted price is generated by adding (or subtracting as the case may be) the peak-to-intersection price move to the intersection price.
- The total move is noted, and ±10% of this is used as a tolerance about the target price to create a prediction zone.
- A rough estimate of when zone entry or move peak-out will occur is gained by adding half the span of the half-span average to the date of intersection. The time zone tolerance about this date must be made quite broad.
- The half- and full-span average concept can be used to help establish correct envelope bounds.
- Use of the full-span average can detect trading channel trend changes before real and non-real time envelopes can do so.
- The technique is powerful, but should always be used in conjunction with all other methods of prediction available.
- The inverse half-span average identifies the all important component just shorter in duration than the trading cycle.
- Inverse averages display specific component magnitudes directly.
- Inverse averages used to extract a selected trading cycle can help establish the condition of magnitude-duration fluctuations of that cycle.

*chapter*

*seven*

# How to Select and Track Trading Issues

- **Alternative Ways of Selecting Investment Vehicles**
- **The Total Scanning Concept**
- **Making Use of Screening Criteria**
- **Selecting Candidates For Volatility**
- **Applying Stability Factors**
- **When You Should Use Alternative Scanning Methods**
- **Take Advantage of the "Stable" Concept**
- **How to Track Your Stable**
- **Summing Up Selection and Tracking**

Going back to Chapter One we recall that the four basic elements of a profit-optimizing trading system are as follows:

1. A profit-optimizing investment philosophy.
2. A fast and simple issue selection method.
3. Fast and simple transaction-timing analysis techniques.
4. Accurate and timely stock price tracking.

You now have in hand Items 1 and 3: This chapter suggests specific methodology for the accomplishment of Items 2 and 4.

## ALTERNATIVE WAYS OF SELECTING INVESTMENT VEHICLES

By this point you have realized that the existence of the "X" motivated cyclic phenomenon and methods of utilizing it in transaction timing negate the importance of many traditional ways of selecting issues on which to trade. Nevertheless, in keeping with the profit-maximization philosophy, much can be done at the level of selection to limit trading risk and provide increased profit potential per trade.

You can proceed here in one of a number of ways. You can, for example, depend wholly on issues brought to your attention via news items, brokerage recommendations, and the various stock advisory services. Once your attention is thus directed to specific issues, you can proceed to assemble the required data and perform the necessary cyclic analysis to determine when your commitments should take place.

Another route to go depends upon the daily newspaper, the *Wall Street Journal,* or Barron's weekly tabulations of stock data. Regular inspection of any of these sources is capable of quickly revealing stocks and groups of stocks toward which large-scale investor interest is directed. The most active list is a fertile source, or you can simply run your eye down the listings looking for extreme volume numbers or large percentage moves. The principal difficulty with this approach is the fact that by the time a stock comes to your attention in this way, it usually is well along on a major trading cycle, and you may have to analyze and track the stock for a long period before it provides you with the low-risk action signal you want.

As in the case of trailing-loss-level signals, it is far better to use a selection system soundly based on the price-motion model to begin with. Accordingly the rest of this chapter will be devoted to such a method, one which is truly in the spirit of the profit-optimization principle.

## THE TOTAL SCANNING CONCEPT

There are more than 2,000 issues listed on the New York and American Stock Exchanges. Since this number is far greater than needed to provide all the opportunities ever required for trading using the price-motion model, it is a good idea to limit your attention to these issues. The most important reason for this is the ready availability of data on stocks listed on these two exchanges.

We're concerned here with selecting those issues as trading candidates which:

1. Provide the highest probability of the greatest gain per trade, and:
2. Provide a high likelihood of generating a valid action signal in the very near future.

The object is always to have a "stable" of such issues at the ready, in order to reduce the inactive time between trades to an absolute minimum. Properly handled, the following techniques will assure a minimum of four or five action signals per day from a stable of 12 to 20 issues. If you do not need this many, you may always reduce the screening, analytical and tracking work required by limiting the size of your stable.

To implement the total scanning concept you require access to a comprehensive charting service. Among many, two such services provide you with freshly updated charts once each week on every stock and warrant on both major exchanges.

The Mansfield Stock Chart Service provides this coverage in the form of weekly high-low-close charts. This service can be obtained from:

R. W. Mansfield Co.
26 Journal Square
Jersey City, New Jersey (07306)

The Geiergraph Stock Chart Service provides the same coverage in the form of daily high-low-close charts. This service is available from:

Geiergraph
The Linden Building
1955 Merrick Road
Merrick, New York (11566)

Both may be requested air mail and special delivery, which puts them in your hands early on the weekend no matter where you live in the continental United States, leaving plenty of time for issue selection by Monday morning.

If these services are utilized, you will find that the task of selecting the highest probability performers for the following week from every issue on both exchanges will require little more than half a day. The rewards for this nominal amount of effort make it extremely worthwhile.

Let us assume that it is Saturday evening and you have the latest copy of one or both of these two services at your desk. The initial step in the selection process we will call the "scan." With a little practice you will be able to accomplish the scan almost as fast as you can turn pages.

You are looking for two things:

1. Issues that display dramatic visual evidence of dominant cyclicality.
2. Issues in which the general trend over the entire chart has just rounded a bottom (if you are interested in the market on the long side), or have just bent over a top (for your "short" candidates).

If a stock does not meet these two simple tests, ignore it and pass on. If it does pass the test, stop and examine the chart more closely.

Note the average volume traded. If it is less than 10,000 shares per week (or about 2,000 shares per day), better candidates are available.

Observe the approximate status of a dominant cycle on which you would like to trade. If either an edge- or mid-band signal seems imminent, write down the name of the stock and continue.

You will normally find that your list contains 80 to 140 issues by the time you finish the scan. If not, or if you desire more, relax your standards or re-scan using alternative scanning criteria discussed in later sections of this chapter.

## MAKING USE OF SCREENING CRITERIA

Typically the scanning process will provide you with an over-abundance of issues from which to choose. All are reasonable candidates, but what you want are the elite of the flock!

The following screening factors are based on information contained in the Mansfield and/or Geiergraph services so that they are available at your fingertips. You may use all or any part of these, with or without additions from your own background. Just remember this: whether or not you make money on a trade in one of these issues is considerably more dependent on your skill and diligence in applying the price-motion model than in the process you use for selection. Selection is of importance only insofar as it serves to *improve* the already high probabilities of turning a profit because of the existence (and your knowledge) of cyclicality.

## SELECTING CANDIDATES FOR VOLATILITY

There are three volatility factors of interest:

1. Capitalization: the number just under the stock name in Mansfield (in thousands of shares).
2. Percentage motion: the extreme left hand scale of Mansfield. Measure with a ruler the space between several scale marks and divide into the intervening percentage amount to get "percent per inch."
3. Short interest: the latest number in the top row of figures at the bottom of the Geiergraph chart.

Volatility is a very important concept in the optimization of profit. A stock may have an A+ rating, sell at a very low price with respect to earnings, have a high yield, show all kinds of earnings growth, attract considerable investor interest, and still move slowly in terms of percent per unit time. The principal factor involved is capitalization.

Capitalization is the number of shares of the company outstanding. Anything below 1,000,000 outstanding shares indicates the capacity for high volatility, meaning that small amounts of buying can create enough demand to cause a large and rapid increase in price. One to three million shares is considered to be light capitalization from the standpoint of volatility. Three to six million represents medium capitalization. Over six million shares usually requires tremendous volume to cause reasonable percentage moves. The lower the capitalization the better, as a measure of volatility.

Capitalization, however, is not the only key to volatility. An issue with three million shares outstanding may have two million of those shares held from circulation by corporate officers or other companies for the purpose of control, etc. Such an issue is the equivalent of one with only a million shares outstanding that are all available to supply demand. Average volume also affects the volatility potential of capitalization.

But a Mansfield chart has only so much space on which to plot two years of price action. If the plotting scales chosen are such that the price action runs off the chart, the entire chart must be replotted to a new scale. For this reason a rough measure of overall volatility is provided by the number of inches (or fraction of one inch) required to plot a one-percent change. This then is the meaning of the percent per inch measurement you have taken on the percentage scale. The larger the percent per inch number, the more volatile the stock.

Short interest is a measure of the number of shares that have been sold short (by borrowing shares to sell at current prices in the hope of replacing them at a later date with shares purchased in the market at a lower price). If an issue shows a high and increasing short interest, upward price motion, once started, may tend to be extremely volatile. As prices go up, the shorts rush to buy, causing extreme demand per unit time and per unit volume. A high and increasing short interest indicates high potential volatility.

## APPLYING STABILITY FACTORS

Four stability factors are available from Mansfield:

1. Rating: in the extreme lower right-hand corner of the chart. This is given in the form of: A, A–, B+, B, B–, etc. If none is present, use the Standard & Poor Stock Guide Rating (available from your stock broker).
2. Price earnings ratio: the number on the left in the box in the upper left-hand corner of the chart.
3. Yield: the number on the right in the same box as the price earnings ratio.
4. Earnings growth: a series of rows of numbers just below the volume base line. The one you want is marked "c" (on the left). This is the accumulated quarterly earnings for the past four quarters. Note the sequence of these from left to right to determine the earnings growth trend.

In the process of winnowing down the number of issues you are interested in analyzing, if all else is equal you might as well have a few of these so-called fundamental factors on your side.

The rating is a composite measure of the quality of an issue. It represents the considered judgment of fundamentals analysts as to the stability of the earnings and dividend potential of the issue. The higher the rating, the more desirable from a stability standpoint.

The price/earnings ratio is the current per share price of the stock divided by the yearly per share profits earned by the company. While not a stability factor in the same sense as rating, a low price earnings ratio makes the stock more desirable in the eyes of many investors. In assessing how low this ratio is for a given stock, the historical values of the ratio should be considered for the particular stock in question. Mansfield shows these ratios for most price turning points on the chart.

Yield is the current per share yearly dividends expressed as a percent of present per share price of the stock. A high yield signifies large dividends, low prices, or a combination of both, and adds to the desirability of the issue for the purpose of our stability screen.

The final stability factor is earnings growth. Investors tend to discount in advance the earnings potential of a company. That is, if the issue shows steadily increasing earnings, investors tend to buy with the intent of selling when the earnings are higher still, thus causing the issue to command higher prices than those paid. (This effect is to be found as part of the relatively smooth 75% of price motion caused by fundamental factors.) The more rapid the earnings growth indicated by the cumulative four-quarter earnings numbers shown in Mansfield, the higher the stability of the issue (for our purpose).

Summarizing the above characteristics, you desire:

| | |
|---|---|
| Rating | High |
| Price/earnings ratio | Low |
| Yield | High |
| Earnings growth | Large |
| *Capitalization | Small |
| *Motion | Large |
| Short interest | Large |
| Volume interest | Large |

This is what you look for if you are interested in *buying* the stock. If you are looking for short-sale candidates, all criteria should be reversed except those marked (*).

## A WORD OF CAUTION AND EMPHASIS

Of the above criteria, volatility is by far the most important. If you have avoided volatile issues in the past, remember that your situation and your capabilities have changed completely now that you are aware of cyclicality. Volatile issues go both up and down rapidly. This may have set an unacceptable risk level for you in the past. But as risk is decreased through improved timing capability, volatility becomes a major ingredient in the formula for profit optimization!

Do not make too much of an issue for yourself of the remaining screening factors. They should be used for one purpose only: to get your scan list cut down to useful size by the use of at least reasonably logical comparison criteria. Remember that *stocks fluctuate*—cyclically. If you make a "meal out of a sandwich" in your screening process, they will fluctuate on without you before you can get your analysis completed!

## WHEN YOU SHOULD USE ALTERNATIVE SCANNING METHODS

There are many variations of scan criteria. Cyclic readability, volatility, and imminence of action signals should always be considered before all else. However, if you cannot establish the number of issues you need on which to trade by these, or if you remain dissatisfied with the quality of the resultant choices, re-scan using alternative methods.

For example, scan looking for triangles in the process of formation (on either the daily or weekly charts). You have already witnessed the potency of using the price-motion model to resolve these chart patterns. At any given time you are unlikely to find more than a few, but these few are excellent candidates for your stable.

There is another technique which is soundly based on the model. While scanning Mansfield, focus your attention only on the nine-year, yearly-high-low sub-chart inset in the lower left-hand corner. What you are looking for is a steady and large decline for several years (the more and the longer the better!), followed by *no more than one year* of rising prices. Current price should still be low by comparison with the highs of several years ago.

If the stock does not meet this test, ignore it and pass on. If it does pass the test, turn your attention to the main body of the chart. Now you are looking for a cyclic pattern which is contained within a definite range over a period of nine to 24 months. This range will be contained within a more or less horizontal envelope. Note the upper bound of this envelope and whether or not the last week of trading has broken out of the band on the topside. If so, add the stock to your list of candidates to be screened as before.

What you are accomplishing, of course, is selection which assures you that the large smooth sweep of fundamental motivation has recently turned up. Quite obviously investor interest in the stock is now stirring again and you wish to take advantage of the resulting fundamental upward push—augmented by the cyclic action which rides the fundamental like frosting on a cake! The analog of this procedure which applies to short-sale candidates is obvious.

Many variations of the scan are possible, and each will produce trading choices of merit—*as long as:*

- The stocks are cyclically readable and volatile.
- The scan criteria you use are soundly based on price-motion model concepts.

## TAKE ADVANTAGE OF THE "STABLE" CONCEPT

Now that you've got a half-dozen or so prime trading vehicles in hand—what do you *do* with them?

Here's where the concept of a "stable" of stocks enters the picture. The purpose of the stable is threefold:

1. To center your full interest and attention on a specific group of stocks on which you will trade until the next periodic scan replaces issues with demonstrably better ones—or action signals are given and passed by because you are fully invested in other issues.
2. To force you to maintain current and up-to-date charts and analyses on your chosen issues!
3. To assure the maintenance *at all times* of sufficient "ready-to-go" issues, so that the idle time between trades is minimized.

For general awareness, you can clip out and use the Mansfield and Geiergraph charts directly. One simple way of handling these is to insert the daily Geiergraph and weekly Mansfield charts side-by-side into plastic 5½- by 8½-inch folders available at any stationery store. These already have a sheet of black "art" paper in them, against which the charts show up vividly. They are punched, and can be inserted in alphabetical order in a three-ring binder for the sake of compactness, or hung on hooks on a pegboard if you like. With care, these can be updated in pencil daily if you have chosen a short duration trading cycle. For long duration cycles, simply replace the charts periodically.

However, these charts are far too miniature for graphical analysis accuracy. For this purpose you must plot your own charts. The problem is data. Pulling daily highs and lows from a newspaper, or even weekly ones from *Barron's*, is very time-consuming (besides requiring maintenance of a tremendous back file of newsprint). One way around this is offered by the Investment Statistics Laboratory, a division of Standard & Poor's, in a publication called *ISL Daily Stock Price Index*. It comes to you quarterly, and contains tabulations of daily and weekly high, low, close, and volume data on all issues traded on the New York and American Exchanges. The books are hardback and durable, and back issues are available as far in the past as 1961. With this service it is a simple matter to extract and plot your own charts for analysis purposes. The maximum amount of newsprint you need ever keep on hand is for 90 days—and this may be discarded as soon as a new issue of ISL arrives.

With your stable charts in hand, complete your cyclic analysis on each. *Do not fail* to update these analyses as time passes and the price motion of the stock permits new or additional conclusions to be drawn. In addition, you may utilize the excellent daily and weekly charts in Mansfield of the DJ 30 Industrial Average for analysis purposes. This will keep you abreast of the market as a whole, and determine for you whether the climate is one in which you should be taking long or short positions.

## HOW TO TRACK YOUR STABLE

If your time is limited or if you are investing very large amounts, you will be forced to trade on longer duration cycles. In such a case, daily or even weekly updating of your charts may satisfy your tracking needs.

However, if you are pushing towards real profit-maximization through the use of short duration trading cycles, you will require more accurate methods of knowing what your stable is doing. This is especially true if you are capitalizing on the profit-compounding potential of mid-band action signals.

One way of accomplishing *fine* tracking is through the use of special buy and sell orders. In this case you are depending on the exchange floor specialist to track your stock for you. Unfortunately, there are severe drawbacks to this approach for our purposes.

A better way is to station yourself or an aid at a brokerage during the periods of time in which you are awaiting action signals. Use of the tape display and/or the electronic quotation devices there can provide you very fine tracking indeed.

The ultimate tracking tool is a combination dry-tape printer and analog computer available from Trans-Lux Corporation. Called the "Personal Ticker," this unit can be installed in your home or office. By a simple process of exchanging slip-in tabs, this unit is programmable for up to 40 particular stocks. Special arrangement with the exchanges permits input by wire of each trade of all stocks—exactly as at your brokerage. The unit then ignores all trades on stocks it is *not* programmed for—but the moment one of the stocks it *is* programmed for trades, the symbol, volume, and price are immediately displayed on tape. The unit acts as your personal watchdog. Remember, the techniques you have learned tell you *in advance* what to do the moment the stock price behaves a certain way. The personal ticker tells you instantly when this happens.

## SUMMING UP SELECTION AND TRACKING

- Any issue can be analyzed and traded upon using the price-motion model as long as data on past performance is available. This means that specific issue selection can take place in any of the traditional ways.
- However, for profit optimization, percent time invested must be maximized. This can be best achieved by maintaining a stable of issues on which analysis is complete, and in which action signals are constantly offered.
- Such a stable can be maintained through simple, but regular, scans of the charts of many stocks. Modern charting services suitable for this purpose are available.
- Cyclic readability, volatility, and imminence of action signals are the most important criteria to be used in scanning. However, any criteria that are logically based on the price-motion model may be used for this purpose.
- The chart services themselves provide general tracking capability. However, graphical cyclic analysis usually requires hand-drawn charts.
- Services are available which permit rapid extraction of data for the purpose of constructing charts to be used for analysis.
- Brokerage displays provide a means of fine tracking for mid-band action signals, or when trading on short duration cycles.
- The Trans-Lux Personal Ticker is the ideal instrument for fine tracking.

*chapter*

*eight*

# Trading by Logic Instead of by Guess

- The Tools at Your Command
- The Anatomy of a Trade
- Determining the "State of the Market"
- Selecting the Issue
- The Next Step Is Analysis
- Forming the Valid Downtrend Line
- Computing Potential and Risk
- A Model Transaction
- A Trading Experiment
- Prediction of the Averages
- The Results of Industry Group Predictions
- Specific Issues Involved
- Conclusions

The preceding chapters have provided the elements of a probabilistic system of profit maximization, based on a logical price-motion model. It is time now to pull these elements together and see how well such a system can be expected to work in actual practice.

## THE TOOLS AT YOUR COMMAND

What is available to you is a set of *general* and a set of *specific* tools. The nature of the price-motion model is such that these can be tailored to a wide range of investment objectives. Such objectives are, in turn, based on the amount of capital to be managed, market conditions, and the time and effort available for selection, analysis, and price-tracking.

The *general* tools at your disposal include the following:

- Understanding of the existence and nature of cyclicality in stock prices—and the implications for improved transaction timing.
- Understanding of the impact of improved timing on profit maximization. The essence of improved timing is reduction of trading risk, permitting shortened trades and profit-compounding. The yield on invested capital is ultra sensitive to these factors.
- Shortened trading intervals and the need for maximization of time invested demand rapid and efficient issue selection and analysis. The "scan" and "stable" concepts of Chapter Five meet the issue selection requirements—while the graphical and computational methods of Chapters Four, Five, and Six satisfy the analysis needs.

The *specific* tools available are all techniques for converting the concepts of the price-motion model into objective action signals. These include:

- Sufficient understanding of the cyclic model to permit envelope analysis.
- Sufficient understanding of the mechanics of formation of chart patterns to permit their resolution by means of cyclic analysis.
- The identification and resolution of triangles.
- The identification and resolution of valid trend lines.
- The meaning and use of the concepts of edge- and mid-band timing.
- The concepts of cyclic-channel-based "cut-loss" or "profit-preservation" trailing sell levels.
- Understanding and use of non-real time envelopes.
- The function, significance, and use of half- and full-span moving averages.
- Understanding of the interplay between moving average characteristics and the elements of the cyclic model, so that such averages can be used to interpret cyclic phenomena.
- The nature and use of inverse moving averages.

## THE ANATOMY OF A TRADE

The date is 1 November 1968. We're ready to put our new-found knowledge to work. How do we go about it?

The first question to be answered is: "Should we be looking for opportunities to buy or to sell short?" To answer, we must form a judgment of the cyclic status of the market as a whole. *The very first thing to do is to apply cyclic analysis to the averages!*

## DETERMINING THE "STATE OF THE MARKET"

Returning to Figure II-7, we find we're 24 months along on the nominal 4.5-year component of the cyclic model. We also see from Figure II-8 that in recent years this cycle has averaged 52 months in duration. We're almost half-way along—and top-out is approaching. This means we cannot expect buoyancy from this very large amplitude cycle for a long time to come. On the other hand, we do not expect a low-out on this component for another 28 months, which will place it in the vicinity of the first quarter of 1971. The push from this cyclic model element will be *slightly* up—to sideways—over the near term.

Now glance at Figure II-2. The low of 817.61 on this chart occurred during the week ending March 22, 1968. In the text accompanying Figure II-4, this low was shown to be due to the nominal 18-month cyclic component of our model—and is the last such low before the present date of November 1, 1968. Thus, we know we are 32 weeks along on this component, which (as shown in Chapter Two) has been averaging 71±4 weeks in the near past. A top-out is expected in this cycle at approximately 35 to 36 weeks, leaving only three to four weeks on the upside at most.

Comparing Figures II-2 and II-3, we see that the latest low of the 26-week component of our model occurred at the point marked "J" in Figure II-3. The Average reached a low of 863.33 at this time, the week ending 9 August 1968. We are now 12 weeks along on this cycle, which was shown in Chapter Two to have averaged 21.4±3.5 weeks in the near past. Thus we expect this component to have topped out one to two weeks ago—and to be gently on the downside by now.

Without going further we can state several conclusions regarding our trading operations in the near future starting 1 November 1968:

- The 4.5-year cycle is only several months from a top.
- The 18-month cycle is three to four weeks from a top.
- The 26-week cycle has already topped out one to two weeks ago.
- The combination of *slight* upward momentum from the 4.5-year and 18-month components should temporarily overweigh the 26-week component—but only for the next three to four weeks, after which both the 18-month and 26-week cycles will be downside, with only a flattening 4.5-year cycle to buck out.
- We expect a last near-term push to the market, followed by considerable downside activity!
- We should trade long for about a month—then switch to the short side of the market as our action signals develop!
- For the immediate future, we're looking for buying opportunities, *but*—we're going to be very cautious, keep the trades short, and be ready to reverse our stance quickly. We will not expect large yields per trade, since we are in the vicinity of a market top-out.

Here is an excellent example of the aid a minimal computational effort can provide. Since our cyclic analysis tells us we are approaching the market at a non-ideal time (conflicting action of several major cyclic components), we would like an independent evaluation of our conclusion regarding a short-term upside movement. We will apply the technique of half-span averages to give us this confirmation.

Figure VIII-1 is an expanded weekly plot about the 21.4-week cycle low of 9 August 1968. Using a ten-week moving average (as a close approximation to a half-span for 21.4 weeks), we see that the low of August 9 is indeed a low of the 21.4-week cycle. One-half of the half-span average span of ten weeks is five weeks. Five weeks from August 9 puts the DJIA in the neighborhood of 930. The action of the DJIA and

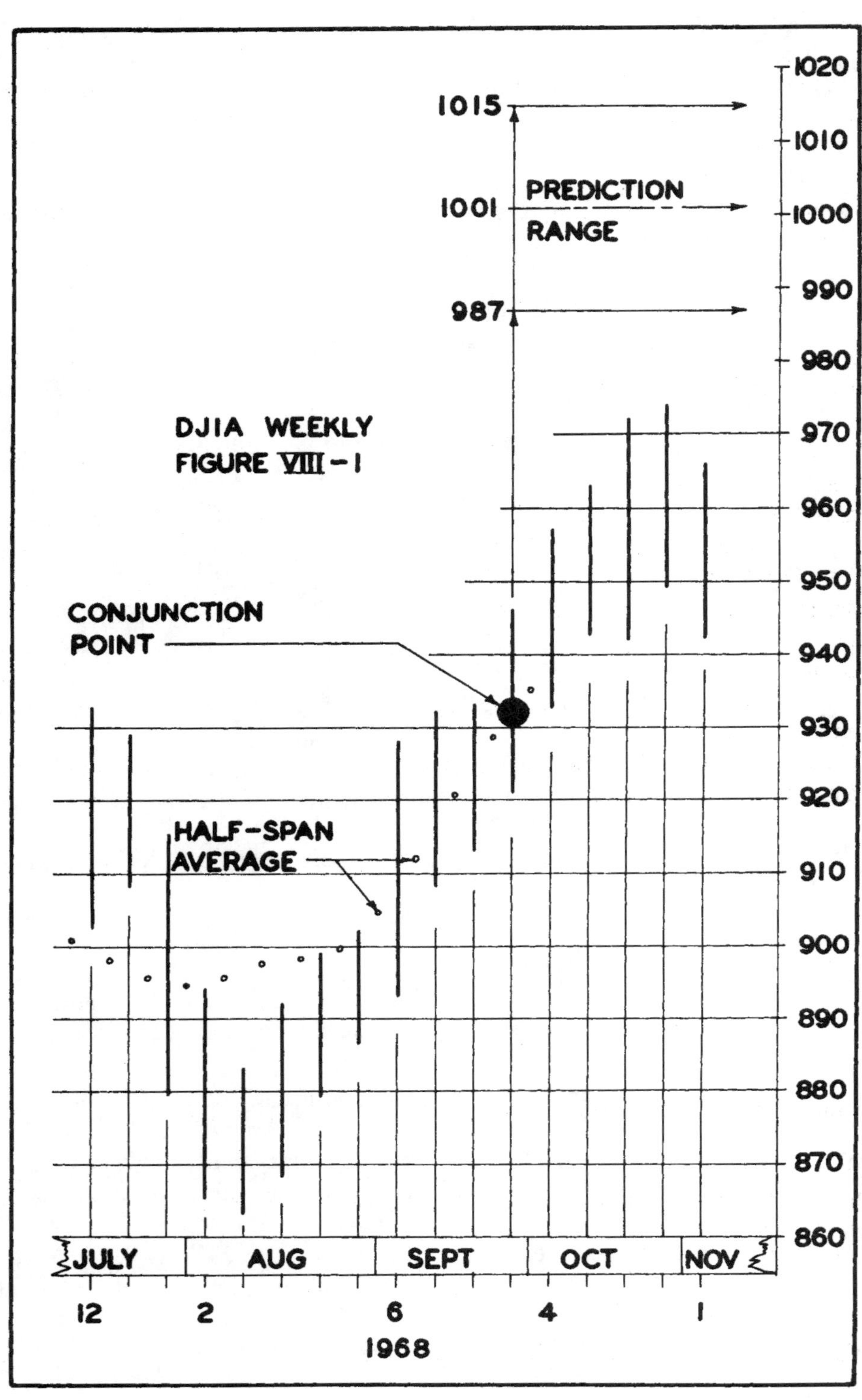


Analyzing The Dow

the ten-week moving average since that time confirms a conjunction point, the week ending 27 September 1968, at 932. We expect the move from the low of 863 to 932 to be one-half of the total move, which should continue to total 138±14. This would take the DJIA to 1001±14, or 987 to 1015 with a target of 1001. The closing value on Friday, 1 November 1968, was 948.4, so we are anticipating a *minimum* move of 39 points to market top-out.

This analysis neatly confirms the conclusions derived from cyclic status—and we can feel free to continue as planned.

## SELECTING THE ISSUE

Scanning the Mansfield charts of 1 November 1968, the techniques of Chapter Seven bring Screw and Bolt Corporation (New York Exchange) to our attention, among others.

This stock, after trading between 8 and 14 for 15 months, broke out to 18 in late September. As of November 1, the price has pulled back steadily for five weeks—and is now trading between 14 and 15. Pronounced cyclicality is evident in past price motion, suggesting simplified analysis requirements. The average volume is 30,000 shares per week—well over the minimum required to assure investor interest. A quick check with a bit of scratch paper confirms imminence of an edge-band buy signal.

Digging deeper, we find that volatility is assured by the above-average %/inch figure for the scale on the left side of the Mansfield chart. Capitalization is a small 1,663,000 shares, which along with the high average volume both explains and assures continued rapid price motion.

The quality rating of B and a cost-earnings ratio of 20 denote acceptable stability. Of still greater interest in this regard is the earnings growth trend:

CUMULATIVE 4-QUARTER EARNINGS

| | |
|---|---|
| 2nd quarter, 1967 | 0.83 |
| 3rd quarter, 1967 | 0.66 |
| 4th quarter, 1967 | 0.41 |
| 1st quarter, 1968 | 0.43 |
| 2nd quarter, 1968 | 0.51 |
| 3rd quarter, 1968 | 0.72 |

Earnings are seen to have reversed a downtrend and established a brisk rate of growth.

This issue (along with about 20 others of similar interest) is selected by the scan for further analysis from all issues on both the New York and American Exchanges for this particular Friday—November 1, 1968.

## THE NEXT STEP IS ANALYSIS

Let's follow Screw and Bolt through initial and detailed transaction timing analysis.

The weekly high-low data is taken from ISL (see Chapter Seven), *Barrons,* the *Wall Street Journal,* or other available sources. Carefully plotted, the results appear in Figure VIII-2. As usual at this point, little can be said as to whether the stock is a "buy," or has more to go on the downside, or when.

**"Setting Up" Screw And Bolt**

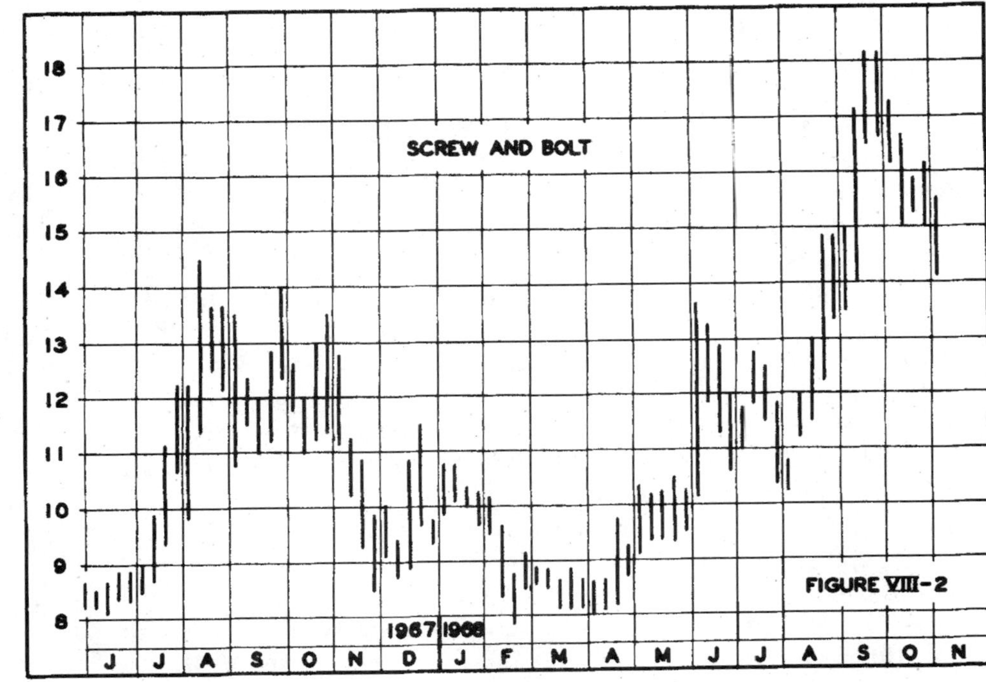


Tracing from this master chart we conduct a cyclic state analysis as shown in Figure VIII-3.

A single, constant-width envelope is drawn, and immediately generates pertinent information.

- The price motion up to the last 14 weeks demonstrates magnitude diminuation of a major cyclic component per the principle of variation.
- Two samples of the dominant component are present in the plot – of 20- and 16-week durations respectively. The average for these two samples is 18 weeks. We recognize this duration as consistent with the price-motion model.
- Each such component is seen to be sharply divided into two segments – of seven to 12 weeks in duration (average 9.2 weeks). While somewhat short to compare with the 13.0-week component of the model, we accept the results of our observation subject to verification.
- Each of these is further divided into two segments of four to seven weeks in duration (average 5.2 weeks). This is seen to compare to the 6.5-week cycle of the principle of nominality, with the tolerances of the principle of variation.
- The center line of the channel is *hard up* – telling us that the sum of all components *longer* in duration than the 18-week cycle is providing *up* impetus to price-motion.

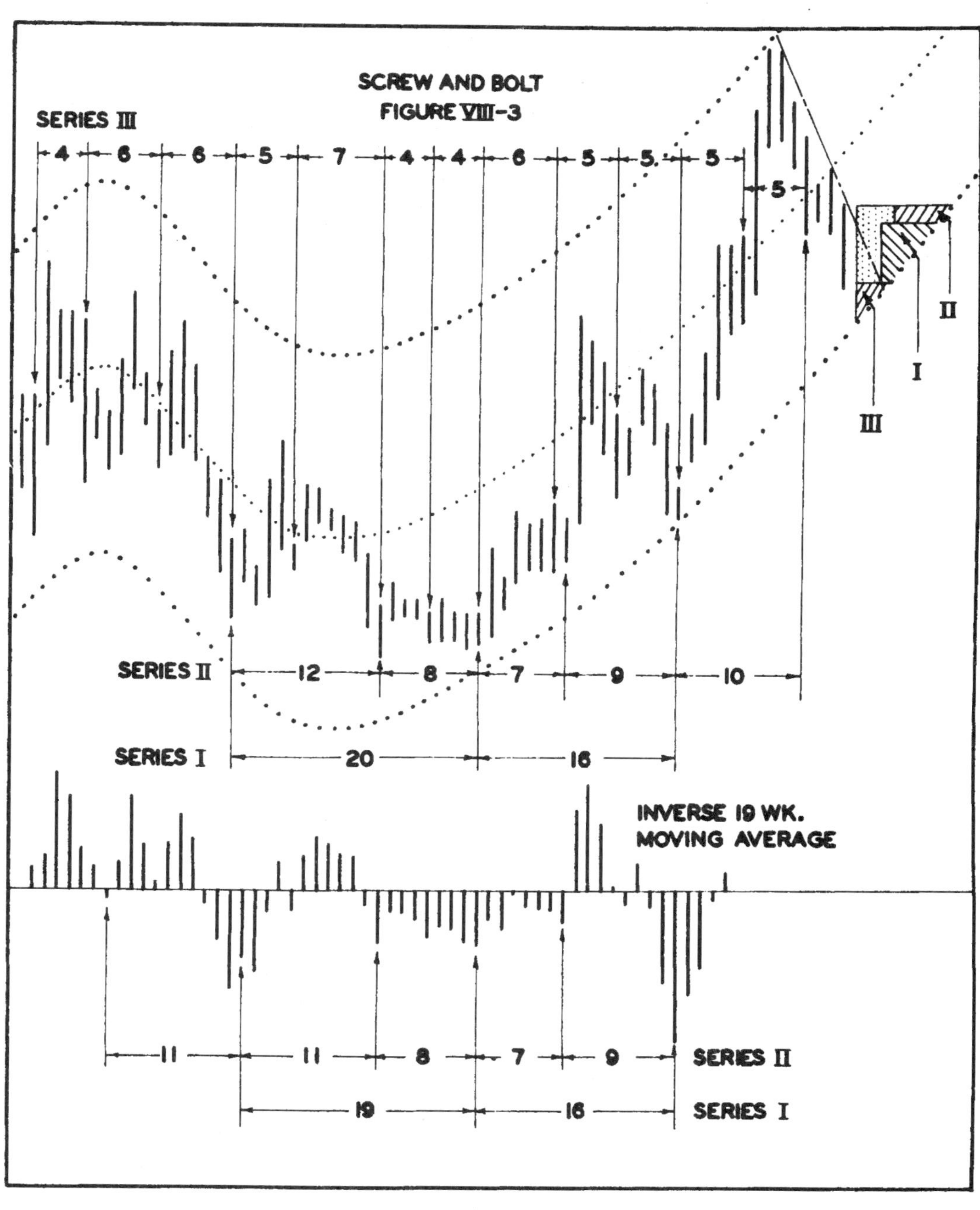


The Weekly Prediction Plot

Because of the rather large variation in observed duration from model nominal, we check our conclusions using an inverse moving average. A span of 19 weeks is chosen (18 would be ideal, but being an even number would require interpolation before subtraction from corresponding prices). The 19-week moving average of the weekly mean prices is formed and subtracted from the corresponding means. You will recall that the effect of this operation is to display about a horizontal base line the sum of all components shorter in duration than 19 weeks. The result is shown at the bottom of Figure VIII-3. With minor differences, the results of observation are found to be confirmed.

The next step is to extrapolate the average (and variation from average) durations of the three periodicities found, identified as Series I, II, and III in Figure VIII-3. To do this, we measure forward in time from the last identified low of each, and obtain the overlapping shaded areas marked I, II, and III. This is an expected nest of lows, and is seen to extend from present time to about three weeks into the future. We expect a significant buying opportunity in this stock—soon!

Having passed the initial analytical tests as an issue of interest, we now wish to construct our "working" chart. Gathering daily data from the last low of the 18-week cycle and plotting produces Figure VIII-4. The envelope and nest of lows are reproduced on this chart from the preceding figures.

As expected, going to daily data produces new information regarding still shorter duration components. The one that is most dominant is eight to 11 days long, or an average of 9.9 days. We are now ready to state the cyclic condition of the stock for the following week as follows:

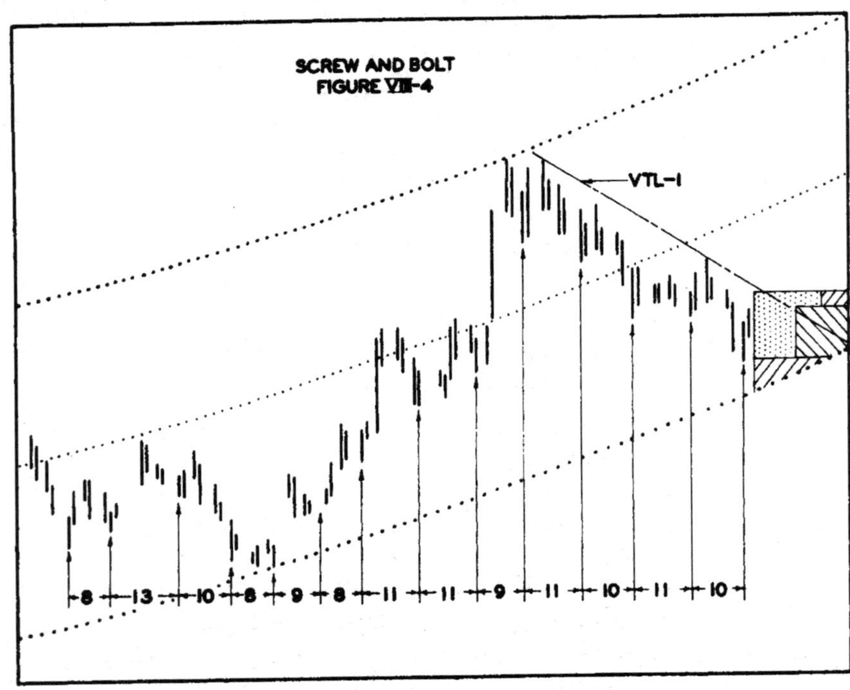


**The Daily Prediction Plot**

| | |
|---|---|
| • Sum of all long duration components | Hard up |
| • 18-week component | 14 weeks along.<br>Down, but due to bottom soon. |
| • 9.2-week component | 4 weeks along.<br>Up, but topping soon. |
| • 5.2-week component | 4 weeks along.<br>Down, but bottoming soon. |
| • 9.9-day component | 4 days along.<br>Up, but topping soon. |

The present score, three up and two down. Two of the ups are due to top out soon and two of the downs to bottom out soon—at the "nest." The cyclic status is one of near equilibrium at the moment, with nothing calling for further downside activity in the near future.

On the other hand, in a short time, around the nest area, the situation will be altered to the point where all five components will be simultaneously on the upside. We conclude that this stock is very near a buy signal.

## FORMING THE VALID DOWNTREND LINE

At this point we must identify the cyclic component on which we desire to trade. We know that the shorter the trading interval selected the greater the percent per unit time yield we can expect. We also know that we can increase our yield by passing by the up-coming edge-band buy signal, and waiting for a mid-band opportunity. The only considerations involved in making a decision are the amount of funds we wish to invest in this stock, and the amount of time we have available for analysis. Let us assume in this case that the funds involved are $100,000 or less (allowing us to get into and out of the stock relatively quickly), but that the amount of time available to us is somewhat limited. Accordingly, we make the decision to operate on the 18-week cycle, with the corresponding limitation on yield rate, in order to obviate the need to maintain a number of stocks analyzed and ready to provide numerous action signals.

With this decision made, we select the next shorter duration component as the basis for our valid downtrend line—or the 9.2-week one. We note from Figure VIII-4 that we're already over the top of the second 9.2-week cycle, and draw in the associated trendline, which terminates in the heart of the expected nest of lows as it should. We determine that if no other steeper valid trend lines form before, we will buy the stock as it crosses the trend line drawn.

## COMPUTING POTENTIAL AND RISK

At this point we can invoke a neat trick based upon half-span averages to estimate upside potential and downside risk.

We note that a ten-week moving average approximates a half-span for our trading cycle. If our analysis is correct, and the present downside trend is reversed within our nest of lows, a ten-week moving average must also halt and reverse a downtrend at this point in time.

However, this effect will not be seen for another five weeks (the lag period of the centered ten-week average). For the average to turn upwards now (as computed five weeks from now), the mean weekly price five weeks in the future must be greater than the one six weeks in the past. Referring to Figure VIII-2, we see that this critical price is 17 1/2.

This tells us that if our analysis is correct, prices will have moved from about 14 1/2 now to 17 1/2 in the next five weeks. But this will be only half of the total move expected (see the theory of half-span averages in Chapter Six). We would anticipate another 3 points, taking prices to 20 1/2 before the move is complete. Our estimated upside potential is thus 6 points, as compared to a downside risk of approximately 1/2 point plus commissions–since our first trailing loss level would be at 14. Such odds, plus the expected batting average of 80 to 90 percent correct decisions, confirm the desirability of the transaction.

We are now primed and waiting for an action signal.

## A MODEL TRANSACTION

Figure VIII-5 replays the subsequent events and the accompanying analysis.

The next day–Monday, the 4th of November– establishes the action of the preceding Friday as due to a top of a component of shorter duration than that upon which valid trend line #1 (VTL 1) was based. Accordingly VTL 2 is drawn, and it is determined that a single trade above this line will constitute a buy signal.

The market was closed Tuesday, November 5, but on Wednesday, the 6th, the stock opened above VTL 2, and the signal was complete for the placement of buy orders. We will assume that the order was executed at the mean of the high-low range for the day (15 1/2). Simultaneously, we draw in TLL-1 as our first trailing loss level, and we determine to sell instantly if prices trade below this value (14 1/8)–or alternatively, we enter a stop-loss order at this price.

The stock behaves as expected in the following several weeks until the move of November 26. This established the preceding pause in the vicinity of 15 1/2 as the stretched upward low of a short-term component which will be used later in establishing a valid uptrend line. Also, the duration of this element is noted, for the last several cycles, as being about 25 days. These durations are then used to establish the cross-hatched region, "A," as a potential next low for this component.

Meanwhile, we note that a ten-week moving average (constructed as a reasonably close half-span of the 18-week component) is just starting to turn down toward the expected low around the 1st of November. We know this average must bottom out in this time region, and turn up once again when prices have advanced approximately half as far as they will be pushed by the 18-week cycle. Since this has not occurred as yet, our prevailing signal is "hold," and we know that all is well with our trade, barring unforeseen fundamental factors that can override the cyclic expectations. This

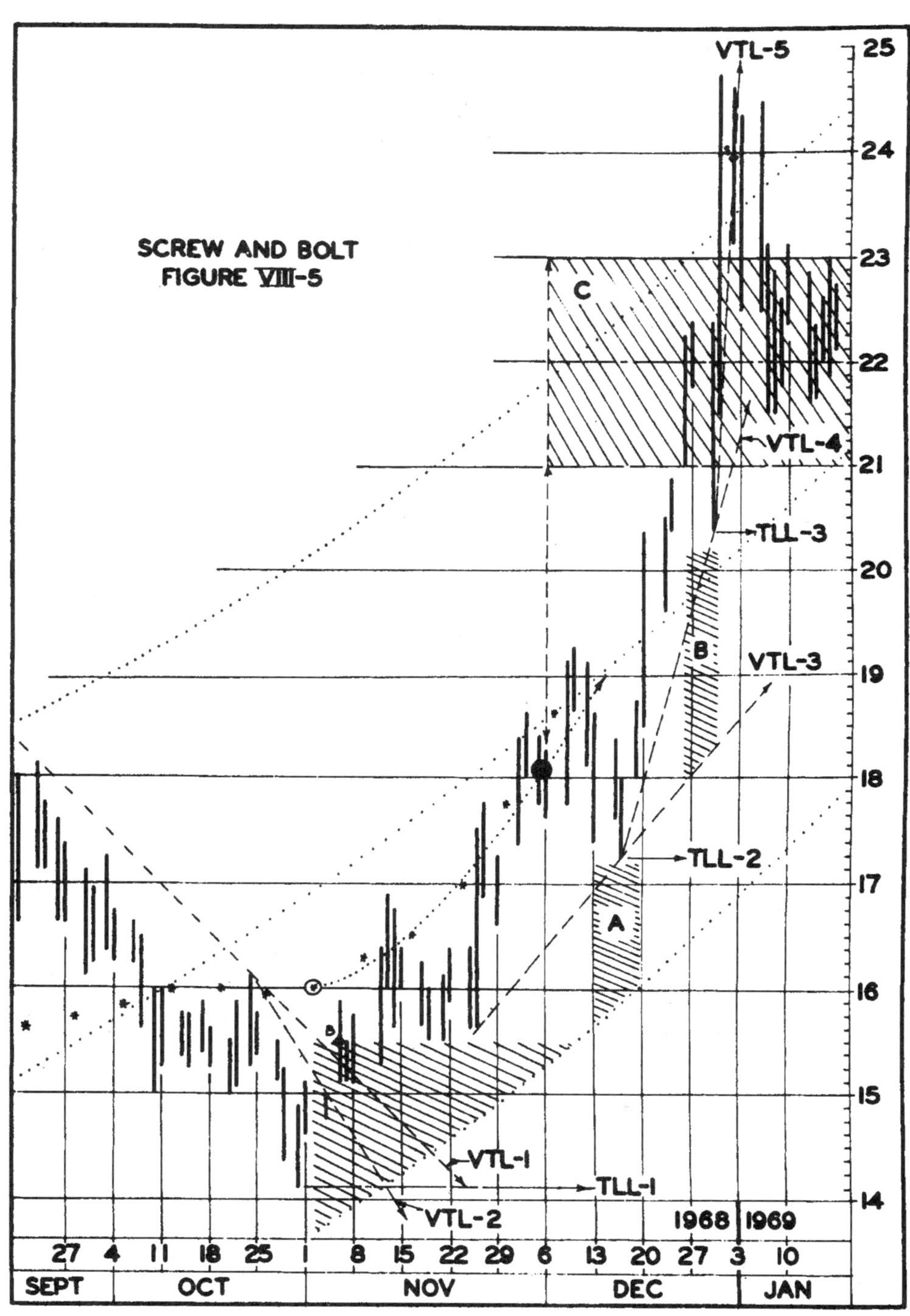


**49.7% Profit In 57 Days!**

possibility we have guarded against with our "profit preservation" or "trailing loss level" setup.

On Friday, the 6th of December, the expected upturn of the ten-week average occurs (as shown circled in Figure VIII-5). The extrapolation of the upturn is shown dotted, with an intersection with price motion at 18 1/8. (Remember to use the approximately equal time span between intersections of this average with the center line of the envelope which contains the component of which it is half-span as a guide to extrapolation. Alternatively, a 20-week average could be constructed and extrapolated to serve the same purpose.)

The move so far has been from 14 1/2 to 18 1/8. This is expected to be one-half of the total move, which now is targeted at 18 1/8 + 4 = 22 1/8. A tolerance of ±10% of the total move is applied, providing 22 1/8 ±.8. Rounding off and shifting down by 1/8 (for convenience and to be conservative), sets 21, 22, and 23 as the lower, target, and upper limits respectively of the anticipated move. This prediction area is shown cross-hatched in Figure VIII-5.

On December 19th, the action of the 17th is shown to be the low that was expected in region "A," and valid uptrend line VTL-3 is drawn. Four days later prices sweep into the prediction zone, and we have a choice to make. Either we can take profits now, or we can shift to the use of increasingly steep valid uptrend lines and ride out the remainder of the move, if any. If the latter course is chosen, we set up the cross-hatched area at "B" as the expected low time zone for the previously noted 9.9-day component, and this low is firmly established by the price action of December 31st. VTL-4 is established on this day. But prices have now swept well past our prediction zone to a high of 24 3/4. We are now nine weeks along on the 18-week cycle, and time is running out. The same price action that set up VTL-4 allows us to draw VTL-5 (from low-to-low of the last two days' motion). We determine that if prices continue to rise and remain above VTL-5 we will remain in the stock, but a puncture of this trend line on the downside will be interpreted as a sell signal. The following day this signal was flashed at a price of 23 7/8, 1 7/8 above our predicted target level. The use of increasingly steep valid trend lines based on very short duration components has extracted a tidy increment of profit for us.

The use of trend lines formed by daily lows is not to be considered a standard practice. The elements of the situation that dictated this action here were:

- Price levels were already above our prediction zone.
- Price levels were rising above even our extrapolated envelope bounds.
- Cyclic time was running out on our trading cycle.

Such a "blowoff" is normally followed by an equally rapid price contraction, and the steepest possible trend lines should be used to provide the take profit signal.

We bought at 15 1/2 on November 6, 1968, and sold in the vicinity of 23 7/8 on January 2, 1969. We made 49.7% profit on invested funds after costs in a total of 57 calendar days. The equivalent annual yield rate is 318% per year. Impressive as this seems, it must be kept in mind that still higher yields are possible if a selection is made of shorter cyclic components on which to trade. For example, this same issue was traded in the experiment described in the next section in which the objective of very short trading intervals was set. The result was a purchase at 16 1/2 and a sale at 17 1/2, in an elapsed time of one day. The gross percentage gain was only 6%, and the net (after costs) was further reduced to 3.2%. However, on an annual basis this amounts to 1168% per year. The price paid for this kind of performance was the necessity of having many other fully analyzed stocks in reserve so that the funds could be put back to work elsewhere immediately. By way of contrast, the previous example required time and effort to be spent on one stock only, over a period of nearly two months.

One further comment is in order before leaving this example. The amount of analysis described was that which was *just* sufficient to resolve the decision problems established by price action. If time is available, *all* the techniques described in previous chapters should be applied and the results updated regularly. In some cases some of the methods will produce no new information, but the occasional situation where extra analytical effort avoids an incorrect decision makes the additional time spent well worth while.

## A TRADING EXPERIMENT

The above issue was one of 35 that were analyzed and used in the first real-time trading experiment designed to apply the principles of the preceding chapters. This experiment was conducted from 28 October to 10 December 1968. The circumstances were as follows:

- Objectives were set at 10% return on invested capital in an average transaction interval of 30 days. Such a return, if continued without interruption, would compound $10,000 into $1,000,000 in approximately 44 months.
- It was decided that buy and profit-preservation signals would be used per the methods described, but that profits would be taken at the arbitrary level of 11.1%. In this manner it was planned to hold the transaction interval down and to establish as large a sample of trades as possible in the shortest possible interval of time.
- Operations were to take place from an office equipped to display the issues analyzed and tracked. A team of five was used to scan weekly charts, select issues for analysis, conduct analysis, and track prices for action signals.
- One member of the team used brokerage displays to track trades in the selected issues for action signals.

The results of this operation are summarized as follows:

- Three short term "market" turns were successfully predicted as shown in Figure VIII-6.
- Two Industry Group turns were predicted with the results shown in Figures VIII-7 and VIII-8.
- A total of 42 transactions was completed in 35 issues. Thirty-eight of these were successful, and four were failures, resulting in a success rate of 90.5%.
- The yield objectives were surpassed. Attained results were 8.9% net profit each 9.7 days. The equivalent annual yield rate achieved was 2474% per year as contrasted with the objective rate of 313.8%. The achieved rate of return, if continued without interruption, would compound $10,000 into $1,000,000 in approximately 15 months!

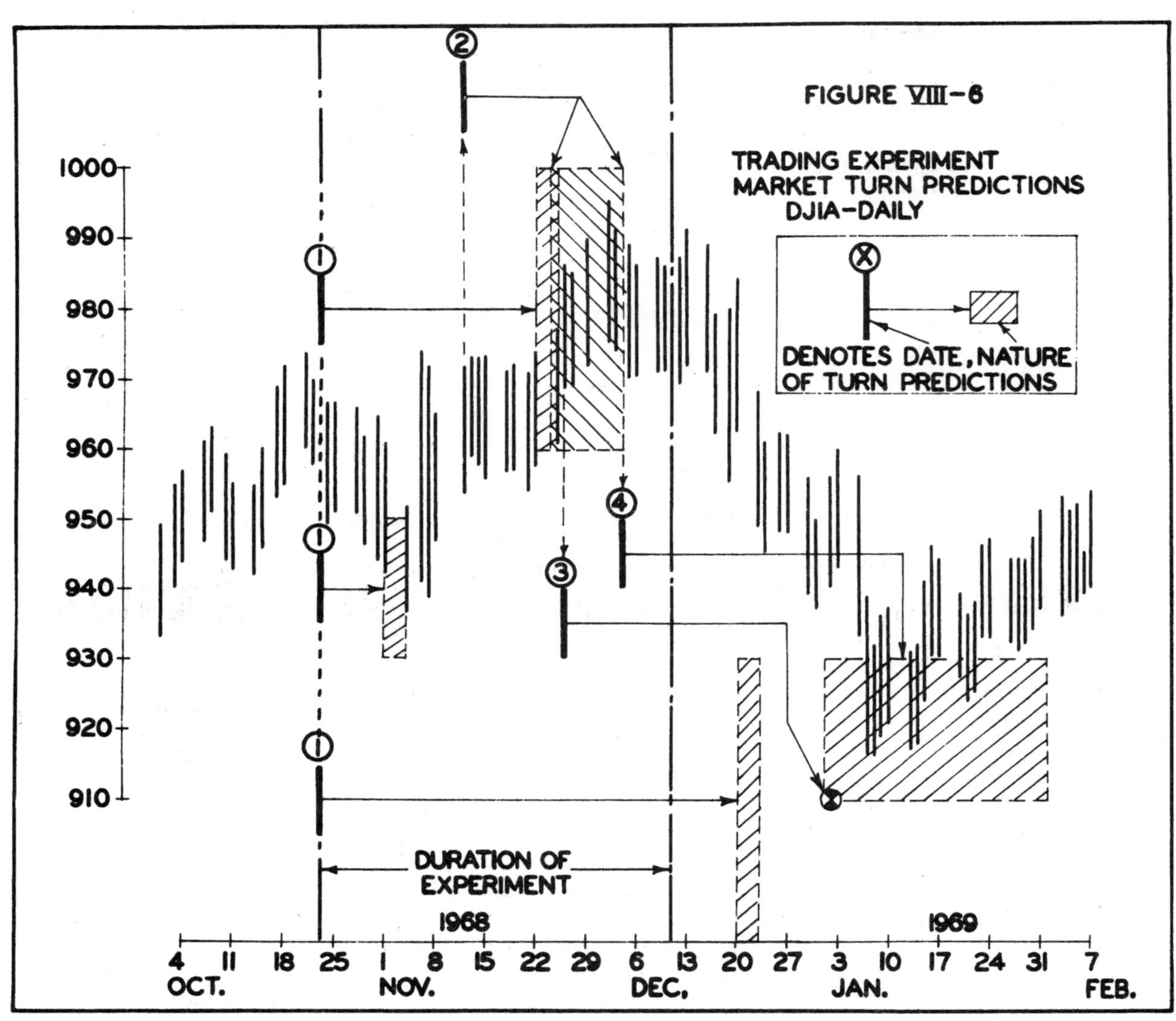


Predicting Short-Term Moves In The Dow

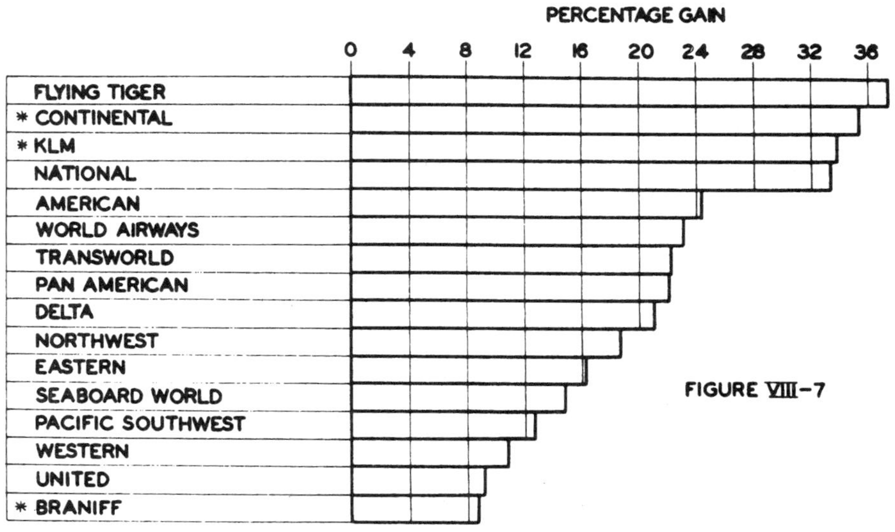


The Techniques At Work On Group Averages

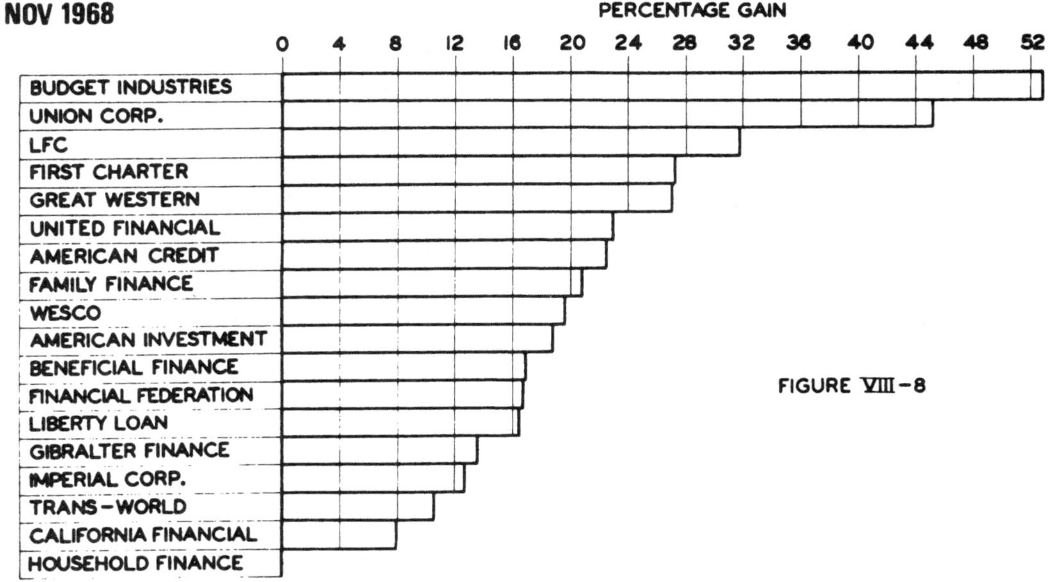


Another Group-Move Prediction

## PREDICTION OF THE AVERAGES

The operation began on 23 October 1968 with the analysis of the DJIA described at the start of this chapter. The analysis was extended by envelope and half-span average methods to produce the first three predictions shown in Figure VIII-6.

In this figure, the solid vertical bars show the times of predictions made, and the arrowed leaders indicate the time-price regions predicted. Prior to 23 October, the market was on the upside. The analysis called for an immediate drop to the 930-950 area, followed by a rise to between 960 and 1000. This was to be followed by a steep drop to between 890 and 930.

As time progressed, the initial short-term low was achieved, and on the 12th of November, the time region for the expected major high was refined and expanded as shown.

On the 25th of November, the time of the target low at 910 was revised from late December to early January 1969. *Note that this prediction was being refined even before the expected top in the vicinity of 1000 was reached!*

The final prediction of the series was made on the 4th of December. At this time the market had reached the target zone for a top-out, but had not as yet started the subsequent decline. Although the experiment was terminated shortly thereafter, the following market action shows how precise the prediction of the low to follow turned out to be.

## THE RESULTS OF INDUSTRY GROUP PREDICTIONS

Figure VIII-7 shows the results of the first Industry Group turn prediction of the experiment, and the subsequent price moves of all issues in the group during the experiment. The minimum move was 8.2%, the maximum was 37%, and the average move was 21.5%. Recalling that the experiment objectives were 11.1% gross, the predicted move provided an average safety factor of more than 2.0.

The Savings and Loan Group move was called on the 8th of November with nearly identical results, as indicated in Figure VIII-8.

## SPECIFIC ISSUES INVOLVED

The tabulation of Figure VIII-9 shows the specific issues analyzed and tracked through buy and sell signals during the experiment. All action signals for these stocks (as well as for the Dow and Industry Group Averages) were noted as they occurred and reported by daily memorandum to impartial observers. The asterisks of the figure indicate issues on which actual portfolios were managed. The remaining action signals were not acted upon, but were used as insurance to assure 100% time investment of funds (which was achieved throughout the experiment). The buy and sell prices are the actual values recorded by memorandum on the dates indicated, or the actual buy and sell prices for those cases where funds were invested.

**Trading Experiment Results**
**Analysis of Buy-Sell Recommendations**
**(10/23/68 Through 12/10/68)**

| | *Issue* | *Buy Date* | *Sell Date* | *Buy Level* | *Sell Level* | *%* | *Days Invested* |
|---|---|---|---|---|---|---|---|
| * 1. | CHD | 11/12/68 | 11/29/68 | 38-1/4 | 42-1/2 | +11.1 | 17 |
| 2. | CRI | 11/13/68 | 11/18/68 | 61-1/2 | 68-1/4 | +11.0 | 05 |
| * 3. | KLM | 11/7/68 | 11/12/68 | 59-1/2 | 69 | +15.9 | 05 |
| 4. | NWA | 11/8/68 | 11/29/68 | 85-3/4 | 95-1/4 | +11.1 | 21 |
| * 5. | GLP | 11/6/68 | 12/10/68 | 17-3/4 | 18-3/4 | +05.6 | 34 |
| 6. | FTR | 11/6/68 | 12/2/68 | 35 | 38-5/8 | +10.3 | 26 |
| * 7. | DMC | 11/7/68 | 11/15/68 | 39-1/4 | 46 | +17.2 | 08 |
| 8. | AJT | 11/12/68 | 11/22/68 | 30 | 34-1/2 | +15.0 | 10 |
| * 9. | ADB | 12/3/68 | 12/10/68 | 23-1/2 | 25-5/8 | +09.0 | 07 |
| *10. | PKE | 11/12/68 | 11/15/68 | 13-1/4 | 14-3/4 | +11.3 | 03 |
| 11. | AEX | 11/7/68 | 11/14/68 | 50 | 53-7/8 | +07.7 | 07 |
| 12. | BOU | 11/29/68 | 12/10/68 | 27-1/2 | 31 | +12.7 | 11 |
| 13. | CHI | 11/14/68 | 12/10/68 | 34 | 37-1/8 | +09.2 | 26 |
| *14. | PKN | 11/12/68 | 11/18/68 | 48 | 54-1/2 | +13.5 | 06 |
| *15. | AU | 11/7/68 | 11/18/68 | 45-1/2 | 50-1/4 | +10.4 | 11 |
| *16. | VIK | 11/7/68 | 11/12/68 | 30-1/2 | 34 | +11.5 | 05 |
| 17. | ARD | 11/12/68 | 11/22/68 | 157 | 174-1/4 | +11.0 | 10 |
| *18. | WYL | 11/8/68 | 11/15/68 | 38 | 42 | +10.5 | 07 |
| 19. | FAM | 11/8/68 | 11/12/68 | 27-1/2 | 29-3/4 | +08.2 | 04 |
| *20. | CAL | 11/8/68 | 11/18/68 | 20-7/8 | 23-1/2 | +12.5 | 10 |
| 21. | SCW | 11/8/68 | 11/27/68 | 15-1/2 | 17-1/2 | +12.9 | 19 |
| 22. | CRT | 11/8/68 | 11/15/68 | 35-1/8 | 39 | +11.0 | 07 |
| 23. | BNF | 11/12/68 | 11/22/68 | 20 | 22-3/4 | +13.5 | 10 |
| *24. | GWF | 11/12/68 | 11/29/68 | 25-1/4 | 30-1/4 | +19.8 | 17 |
| 25. | WBL | 11/13/68 | 11/22/68 | 9-3/4 | 10-7/8 | +11.5 | 09 |
| 26. | BCE | 11/26/68 | 11/27/68 | 14 | 15-5/8 | +11.8 | 01 |
| 27. | WOR | 11/12/68 | 11/15/68 | 9-3/4 | 10-7/8 | +11.5 | 03 |
| *28. | FCF | 11/13/68 | 11/13/68 | 35-1/4 | 39-1/8 | +10.7 | 01 |
| 29. | LPT | 11/25/68 | 12/2/68 | 21-1/2 | 23-3/4 | +10.4 | 07 |
| *30. | FTR | 11/25/68 | 12/2/68 | 35-1/2 | 38-7/8 | +09.5 | 07 |
| 31. | CRI | 11/26/68 | 12/10/68 | 65-1/2 | 71-3/8 | +09.0 | 14 |
| 32. | NWA | 11/26/68 | 11/29/68 | 90 | 90-1/4 | +00.3 | 03 |
| 33. | SCW | 11/26/68 | 11/27/68 | 16-1/2 | 17-1/2 | +06.0 | 01 |
| 34. | OX | 12/3/68 | 12/5/68 | 14-1/4 | 15-7/8 | +11.4 | 02 |
| **35. | CLI | 12/5/68 | 12/10/68 | 32-1/2 | 35-7/8 | +10.4 | 05 |

*Represents transactions in which actual funds were invested.

Ave. % = +11.1%
Ave. Days = 9.7 D
Ave. %/Day = 1.14%/D
Ave. % Costs = 2.2%

**Note: Multiple predictions per issue brought the total number of completed transactions to 42.

**FIGURE VIII–9**

## CONCLUSIONS

This trading experiment was conducted at a tempo which precluded exhaustive analysis. Only the absolute minimum of graphical work could be accomplished on the 40 to 60 issues of each weekly "stable" of stocks. It is undoubtedly true that such a paucity of analytical effort would not have been sufficient to handle a wide variety of market conditions. Nevertheless, the results were significant in several respects:

- It was demonstrated that transaction intervals of the order of ten days could be achieved with enough action signals generated to assure 100% time investment of funds.
- It was shown that the theoretical maximum of about 2400% per year yield on invested funds *could* be produced.
- It was found that the expectation of 90% decision accuracy could be achieved.
- It was learned that the average individual will do best by concentrating on a *thorough* analysis of a *few* issues. The analysis time requirements to handle a large number of issues is prohibitive unless a staff of personnel is utilized.
- The high expectation of decision accuracy eliminates the need for wide diversification. It is probably best to limit commitments to a maximum of two to four issues at any given time.
- It was shown that the theory is valid, and the methods work. All *you* need to do is to master the techniques—and avoid the psychological barriers inherent in extracting the magic from stock transaction timing!

# chapter nine

# Why Stock Prices Change

- How Decision-Making Enters the Picture
- Understanding Irrational Decision Processes
- What You Should Know About Fundamental Factors
- How Company-Related Fundamentals Affect Prices
- The Influence of Broad Environmental Factors
- Should You Sell in Event of War?
- What About Currency Devaluations?
- How National Crises Should Affect Your Decisions
- How the GNP Affects the Market
- Now Compare Cyclicality vs. History!
- The Impact of the Fall of France
- Here is How Long-Range Cyclicality Affects the Market
- Summarizing Price Change Causes

Up to this point the objective has been to put into your hands as rapidly as possible the essentials of a price-motion model, some methods of putting it to practical use in transaction timing, and an integrated approach to investing based upon it.

It is time now to fill in some gaps; to provide you with increased confidence in and understanding of *why* the techniques work. Such understanding is not needed when all goes smoothly, but can stand you in good stead if your emotions get out of hand or things don't occur quite as expected.

## HOW DECISION-MAKING ENTERS THE PICTURE

You must now force yourself to abandon many traditional investment concepts, replacing them with new ones. This is not easy to do, and a reasonable rationale for doing so is an aid.

For example, you must revise your concepts of *risk.*

Traditional investment procedures based upon research of fundamentals result in long-term trades with little possibility of capitalizing on the huge yield rates possible through short-term transactions and profit compounding. Price oscillations in this approach are evils to be survived, and the only way in which risk can be reduced to an acceptable level is to select good stocks, be thorough in your fundamentals research, have faith in business, and train yourself to be *very* patient. Short-term trading catches you up in the oscillatory action and presents inordinate risk in this type of investing.

However, you have now been exposed to a radical thought: namely, that these oscillations have a personality of their own, with characteristics which permit a certain degree of prediction—and hence *the risk of short-interval transactions is drastically reduced!* Many deeply ingrained investment traditions are thereby rendered not only invalid, but are put in the new position of *themselves* representing untenable risk.

To make the necessary attitude transition deep down, you must be able to accept the credibility of the phenomena described by the model. To aid you in this reorientation we need to go back to the basic tenets of the price-motion model and establish a creditability base.

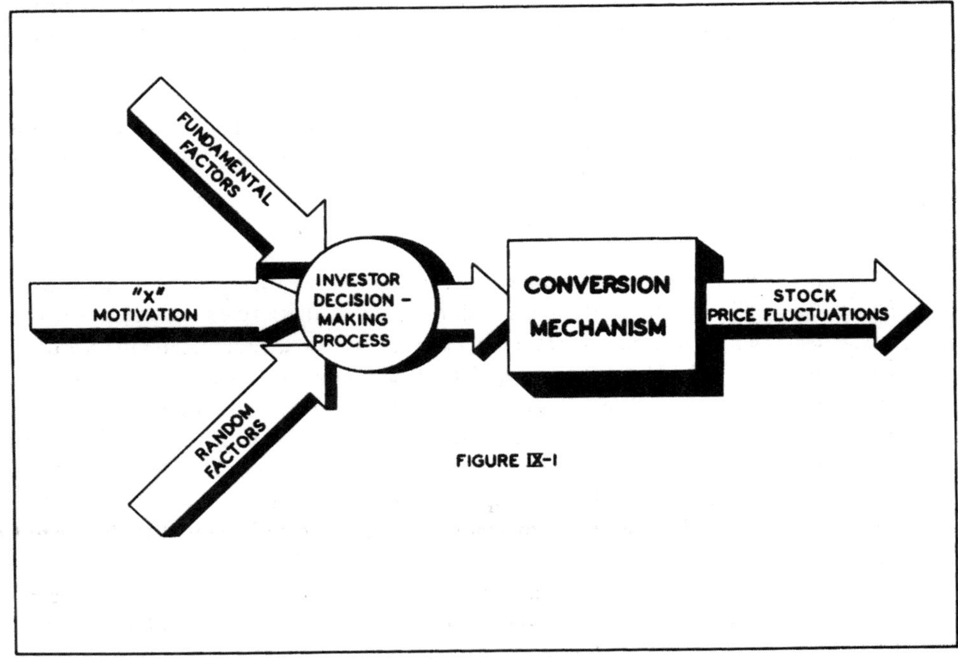


**How Prices Fluctuate**

Figure IX-1 is a block diagram of the anatomy of price change. Into the box labeled "Conversion Mechanism" we will put all processes between an investor decision to buy or to sell and the consummation of the resulting trade. Stock price changes are considered as an "output" of this box, such change being associated with each transaction. The processes within the box we will now proceed to ignore, since they are the direct but not the elemental cause of price fluctuations. *It is the decision to act that starts the whole process off.*

But what causes a human being to come to a decision? Logic? Emotion? The press of circumstances?

All of these and much, much more. It should be clearly understood at this point that the actual processes by which decisions are made are *not* understood—but the more that is learned on this subject, the more complex the process appears. Our particular need is to simplify the process in our own thinking to such an extent that we can logically *accept* the strange new facts on which we now intend to operate, even if we cannot fully understand what causes them to exist.

In Figure IX-1 such simplification is effected by lumping all possible contributors to the investment decision process under three headings:

1. Fundamental Factors
   We know for a fact that people *do* buy and sell on the basis of research and knowledge of these quantities. Therefore we must assume that such factors do influence investment decisions (hence price change) to some extent.
2. Random Factors
   We also know that investors sometimes buy and sell stocks for no better reason than to place excess funds or to raise cash. Such independent and non-price-level-correlated activity is most likely to create some level of random "noise" in price action.
3. "X" Motivation
   Now we simplify still more. For here we lump all other possible contributions, known or unknown, to the investment decision process—of any kind whatsoever.

Now we have an interesting handle on the situation. Consider:

1. You have seen examples in previous chapters of regular periodicity in price motion.
2. The nature and existence of such regularities can be described in detail. Techniques can be set up which can only work if such regularities exist—and can be shown to work.
3. The nature and existence of such regularities can be proven conclusively by analysis through some of the methods and results of Chapter Eleven and the Appendix.
4. But—and this is important—by definition, random price action (hence decision factors) *cannot* contribute to such regularity. Furthermore, to accept fundamental factors as the cause would force acceptance of the occurrence of fundamental events on a regular schedule, like a freight train, and we can readily show that this is not the case.
5. The conclusion is unavoidable that the cyclic regularities noted must be due to the lumped sum of all other possible contributors to human decision processes—or to what we have called "X" motivation!

And this is the concept that is difficult to accept. To do so, we must admit the possibility that something causes millions of investors operating from widely differing locations, making countless buy and sell decisions, at varying points in time, to behave more or less alike—and to do so consistently and persistently! How can this be?

The answer to this question is not known, although reasonable theories can be formulated. The best that can be done here is to show that many things do influence decisions—often without conscious awareness of the fact—and that the unknowns in the decision process can conceivably account for the startling behaviour of price fluctuations.

## UNDERSTANDING IRRATIONAL DECISION PROCESSES

First of all let's consider a hypothetical situation which has probably been experienced by every investor in one form or another.

Assume you have bought a stock on a fundamental tip. You are showing a paper profit and trying to make a decision as to whether you should sell or not. Let's say the fundamental factor is still in effect and the principal reason you are considering selling is the profit you would show if you did. What other factors might enter into your thinking at this time?

Perhaps you have been unsuccessful in your last several transactions and need the "ego boost" of a success. Your wife may be getting impatient, and you could fear a curtailment of your investment activities in favor of, say, redecorating the house if you don't show black in your ledger soon. You've seen paper profits dwindle to real dollar and cents loss before and you don't want it to happen again. Perhaps the automobile just broke down and you need the money anyway.

In making your decision, how can you possibly weigh and evaluate all of these considerations so as to arrive at a logical and rational decision? Obviously you cannot. So the resulting decision *must* be irrational in a sense!

Now let's add a purely emotional factor. Assume you've been giving the problem consideration, but have not made up your mind. One morning you awaken with a headache, the hot water is off, and you've got a flat tire. By the time you get to the office you're in a testy frame of mind. About mid-morning you suddenly pick up the phone and tell your broker to sell. What finalized your decision for you? It could be that with everything going awry that day you simply wanted at least one situation to be resolved favorably—in this case by a profit on your transaction. Suddenly your whole day seems brighter and you congratulate yourself on a good decision.

But supposing the next day the stock skyrockets in a short squeeze. You find you could have doubled your profits by waiting an additional two days. *Now* how do you feel regarding the validity of your decision?

This is a surprisingly good example of the way in which many decisions are made in the absence of sufficient facts on which to base a logical conclusion. Remove the facetiousness, rearrange the factors and circumstances a bit, and you could easily be describing many management decisions made by corporate executives. In fact, the ability to make good decisions in the absence of sufficient information is what distinguishes the successful executive (or investor) from the unsuccessful one!

So decisions are often based on other than a straightforward line of reasoning. Let's complicate the matter still more.

Recent experimental evidence tends to show that such intangibles as fatigue and frame of mind are influenced by the presence or absence of physical force fields. For example, Dr. Cristjo Cristofv (father of the "Cristofv Effect" used to detect nuclear explosions) reports that pilots of U-2's and truck drivers show increased alertness and job efficiency when the Earth's magnetic field, modified by the metal of the vehicle, is artificially restored. Now all of us exist in an environment that is simply riddled with force fields–gravitational, electrostatic, etc. If such fields can influence *some* physical and mental functions, might they not influence *others*–perhaps causing masses of humans to feel simultaneously bullish or bearish in the market, for example? Conjecture, but a possibility.

It is not being suggested here that the cyclic sub-model is based on this type of thing. It is enough to show that the possibility exists of external and unknown influence on investment decisions. Seeing how it *might* come about helps us to accept the evidence of our eyes and analyses, even when the results seem irrational by past experience.

## WHAT YOU SHOULD KNOW ABOUT FUNDAMENTAL FACTORS

The discussions of the previous sections should help you to accept and apply the non-traditional concepts presented in earlier chapters with increased confidence.

In like vein, let's go back to several statements in Chapter Two which are a part of the price-motion model, but were presented without substantiation. One of these was: national and world historical events contribute in an utterly negligible way to the performance of the market as a whole, and that of individual issues in particular.

That this is a foreign and alien concept is amply illustrated by every financial column and commentary you read and hear. The market is constantly being cited as weak or strong depending on the progress of Vietnam peace talks or ten dozen other such factors.

Fortunately, it's not too hard to check on just how much such things influence the market. We've plenty of recorded market price history on which to draw, and the Almanac supplies corresponding dates of such events. Let's look into this one, because if you think such things *do* influence the market you cannot help letting it influence your decisions. And if they do *not,* you are quite likely to make wrong decisions with attendant loss.

It was also stated without amplification that company-oriented fundamental factors contribute heavily to the broad, smooth sweep of price motion. Let us investigate all of these areas simultaneously.

There are certainly at least three broad classifications involved.

1. Factors related solely or primarily to a given company and its operations. New products, new management policies, and key personnel changes serve as examples.

2. Factors not intimately related to any individual company, but which are a decisive element of the specialized environment in which the company must operate. The effect of tight-money situations on a savings and loan company would be an example here.
3. Factors not necessarily related to a specific company, nor even to its specialized environment. A general monetary crisis or the eruption of armed conflict somewhere in the world would exemplify this type of environmental factor.

The question is whether or not any of these contribute to cyclicality.

It is difficult enough to conceive of the complex interaction of these three types of factors as being capable of inducing a cyclic response in the decision-making process with regard to any single stock, but when we consider what we learned in Chapter Two about the synchronization in time of the cyclicality of many issues, it becomes simply impossible. Certainly the factors which most closely affect one issue, but should not affect another in the same way if at all, *cannot* be held responsible for the fact that both issues demonstrate time-coordinated cyclicality!

But there is another part to the question. We have already admitted that random events do occur and must have some influence on stock prices. We have seen that the impact of this type of event must be approximately 2.0% of the total stock price. We have also seen another possible source of additional random effects in the irregularity of the variations in fluctuation magnitude with time.

Likewise we admit to the existence of fundamental factors, and feel instinctively that there must be some impact of these on the decision-making process, and hence on stock prices. Can we gain some sort of feeling for the magnitude and nature of this impact?

## HOW COMPANY-RELATED FUNDAMENTALS AFFECT PRICES

Of the three types of fundamental factors discussed, the first two may be considered together for our purposes. The effects are likely to be quite similar except that a factor relating to only one company will exert most of its influence on the price of that company's stock whereas events influencing a group (steels, oils, etc.) will show effects more or less across the group.

This situation requires very little consideration and no specific examples. We have all observed a stock in which selling suddenly soars. If trading becomes sufficiently panicky, trading in the stock may be suspended for a time. The stock may re-open (hours, days, or even weeks later) at half the price at the time trading was halted. In the interim, the news regarding the specific fundamental factor involved has probably become common knowledge. The stock price changed *not* because of the fundamental factor itself, but because of the effect of that factor on the thinking and decision processes of investors. Nevertheless, the correlation of stock price change, through the decision process, to the fundamental factor is obvious and undeniable. The same type of thing takes place on the upside, notably in recent years upon the advent of a conglomerate takeover type of tender offer. These are certainly examples of the more obvious impact of fundamental factors. It is highly likely that many less obvious effects are incurred as well. In fact, given the knowledge that random effects are small and that cyclicality is synchronized, all other observed differences between individual stock price motions must be considered as being caused by fundamental factors!—or at least by what investors *think* the effects of these factors should be. That the result in terms of magnitude of influence is quite large is at once evident when we study the price patterns of stocks in any of the wide-coverage stock chart services now available.

But is this all we can learn of the influence of fundamental factors? It would certainly seem that the above reasoning, while straightforward and valid, is difficult if not impossible to quantify. So let's try another approach!

## THE INFLUENCE OF BROAD ENVIRONMENTAL FACTORS

Every day we are told in innumerable ways about this or that world or national situation which, it is implied, is the principal cause of the current behavior of the market. True, any analyst worth his salt will admit to the simultaneous existence of *many* such factors—some purported to have bullish influence while others presumably favor the bears. It is, supposedly, the on-balance sum of all these push-pull forces which shapes the course of market action. In order to better examine the influence of such factors, Figure IX-2 was prepared. Let's see if we can detect the influence in the market of the major historical events shown!

## SHOULD YOU SELL IN THE EVENT OF WAR?

First of all, note the shaded areas emphasizing the behavior of the market throughout periods of armed conflict. Can we honestly say that if these shaded areas and the dates at the bottom of the chart were removed, we could detect *any* abnormal behavior of the market that would permit us to identify the war periods? Not really. During the Korean War a 52-month cycle topped out and ended, just as similar cycles have been behaving since 1897. It was complete down to the three (nominally) 18-month cycles we have come to expect. The same action has occurred since the start of the Vietnam War. A 52-month cycle was about half-way along at this time, and it just continued and terminated as expected in 52 months' time, whereupon another promptly started! And yet, if the news were suddenly flashed on the broad-tape tomorrow that the U.S. was involved in still another war, wouldn't *you* be concerned about the impact on the price of the stocks *you* hold? But, *should* you be concerned?

## WHAT ABOUT CURRENCY DEVALUATIONS?

Remember the panic about the foreign currency devaluations of 1949? Did this situation change the course of the market? Both an 18-month and a 52-month cycle were four months along at this time, and each continued to completion in blissful ignorance of the currency troubles! But, you say, when the British pound was devalued in late 1967 the market took a tumble. So it did. But you notice that it was falling *before* the devaluation took place. Furthermore, the drop was predictable—as much as

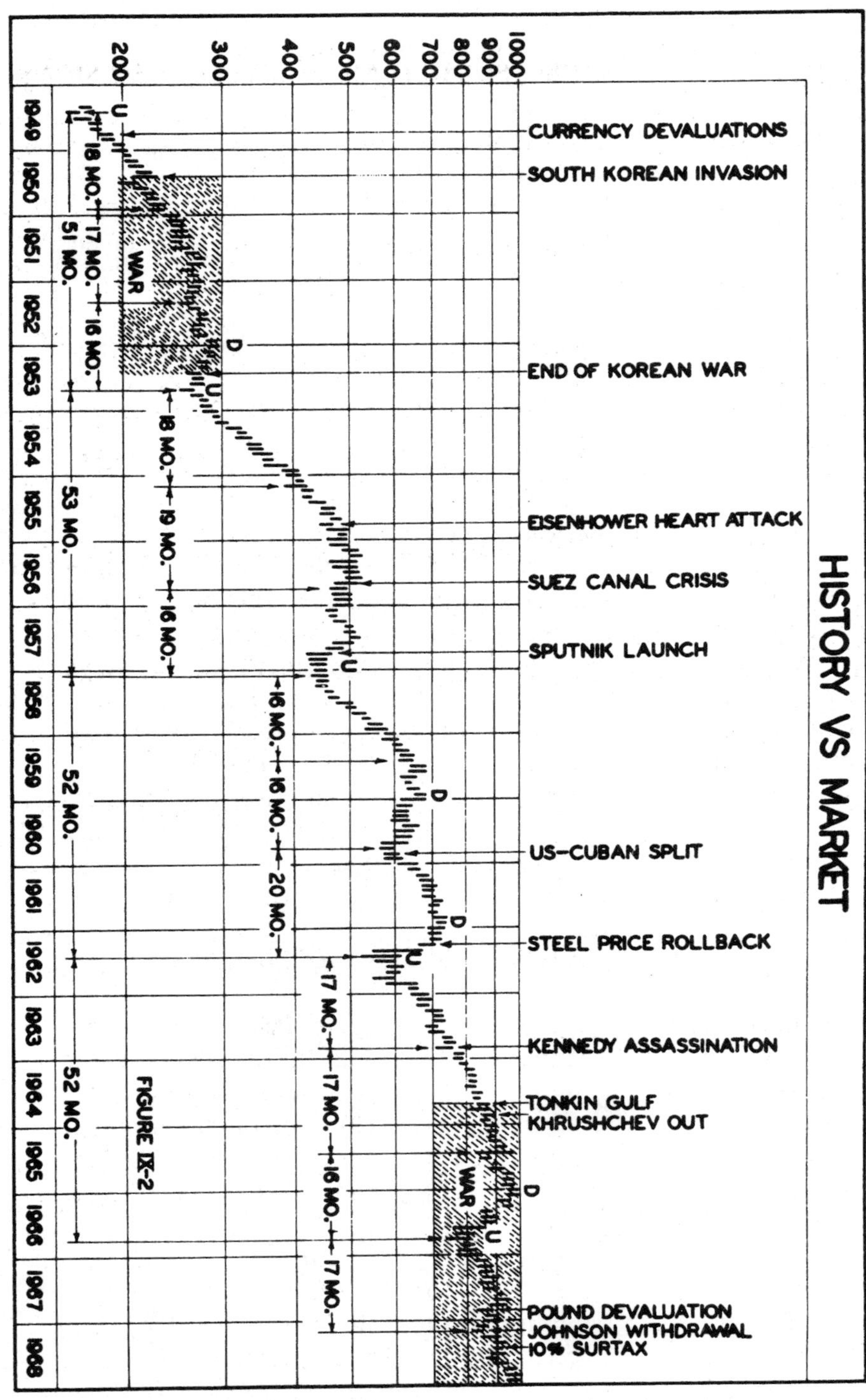

FIGURE IX-2

How History Does Not Influence The Market!

one and a half years in advance! The pound devaluation simply took place during the termination phase of a (nominally) 18-month cycle that has been going up and down with the regularity of clockwork for nearly a century.

## HOW NATIONAL CRISIS SHOULD AFFECT YOUR DECISIONS

How about when President Eisenhower was stricken by a heart attack while in office? Could you spot this occurrence in the history of the market if all markings were removed from Figure IX-2? The market dropped, yes. But if you expand this period of time, you will find that the drop perfectly coincided with the end of the first of three 18- to 20-week cycles in the second of three 18-month cycles of the 52-month cycle that began in late 1963!

The U.S. and Cuba had a big falling out in late 1960. What did the market do about it? It was time to start an 18-month (in this case 20-month) cycle, so it did. In fact, the market disdained even to show the courtesy of a mild reaction to this momentous turn of events!

Can anyone ever forget the 15 minutes of panic selling that hit the market on the news of President Kennedy's assassination? There is certainly no doubt whatsoever as to the relationship of that frenzied few moments of price action to the tragic news that inspired it. The powers that be even closed down the exchange. Yet, in retrospect, it cannot be denied that the slight drop in the market at this time signaled the *expected* end of the first 18-month (17-month in this case) cycle of the 52-month cycle which started in 1962. Here was a case where a popular president was cut down violently and unexpectedly in office and the presidency of the U.S. was assumed by a new administrative head, yet the market barreled uninterruptedly upward until the pullback in 1965 which terminated the second 18-month cycle of the 52!

Try to relate the significance of the Suez Canal crisis, the Sputnik launching, the attack on U.S. destroyers in Tonkin Gulf, the political demise of Premier Khrushchev, etc., to market activity. The unavoidable conclusion that *must* be reached is major world and national historical events have negligible impact on stock prices!

## HOW THE GNP AFFECTS THE MARKET

Yet, we notice one thing more from this figure. Prices moved from about 160 in 1949 to over 1000 in 1966, but the sum total of all the cyclicality of the price-motion model accounts only for price motion within the envelope surrounding the 52-month highs and lows (as demonstrated in Figure II-10). Our observed cyclicality *does not* account for the price motion represented by a center line drawn between the bounds of this envelope. If random events, cyclicality, and major world affairs do not account for this panoramic price change—*what does?*

Take a look at Figure IX-3. Overlaid upon our now familiar plot of the DJ 30 Industrials from 1949 through 1968 is a plot of the Gross National Product of the U.S. in billions of dollars. Now it is an interesting coincidence that the scales of the DJ 30 and the GNP in billions of dollars match almost perfectly. The scale on the left therefore represents both the value of the average and the value of the GNP expressed

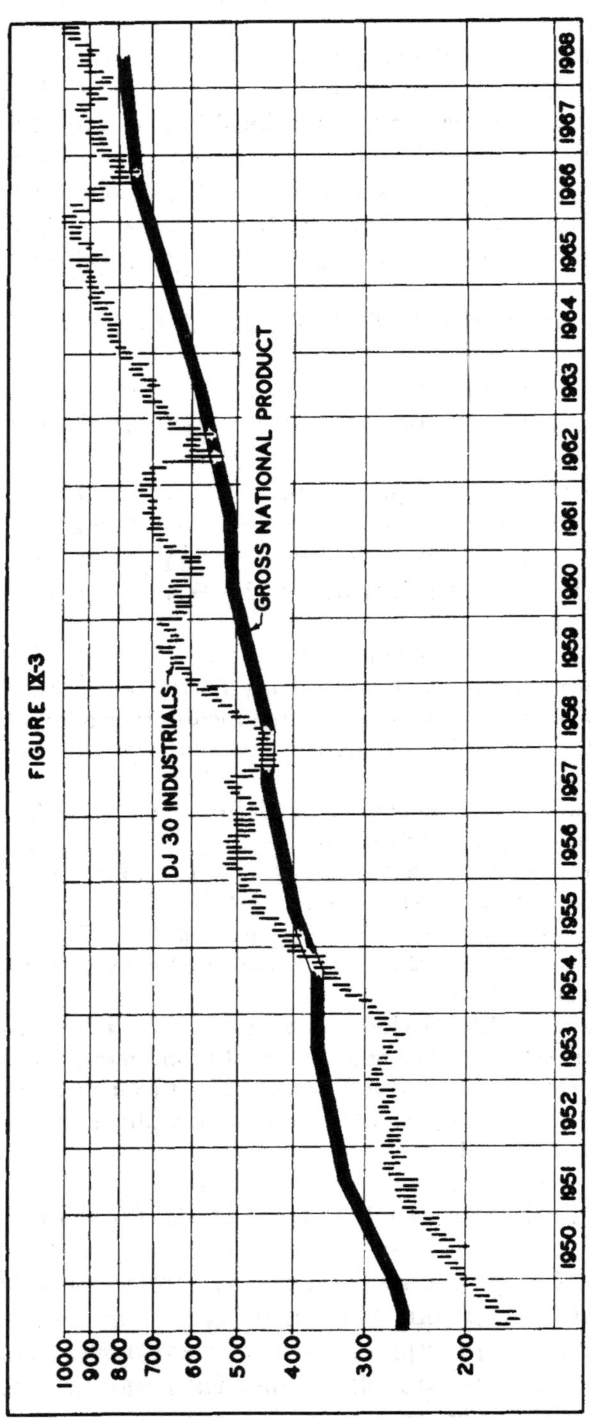


Which Came First: The Dow "Chicken" Or The GNP "Egg"?

in billions of dollars. The correlation is striking. There is even an indication in the GNP of the ups and downs of the 52-month cycle! We must be cautious to the extent of remembering that the observed correlation does not necessarily imply a cause and effect relationship. In fact, it may well be saying that both the DJ 30 and the GNP simply react to the same causes. Or the relationship may even be purely coincidental. However, here is a "fundamental" factor which undeniably *does* correlate to market action over the time period shown, and at the same time seems to account for the part of price motion not accounted for by cyclicality. It certainly stretches the imagination less to impute a relationship here than in the case of historical events!

## NOW COMPARE CYCLICALITY VS. HISTORY

Consider Figure IX-4. This may well be one of the most informative charts in this book. It's certainly a well belabored one, requiring more than three million separate computations to produce.

The weekly closing prices of the DJ 30 Industrials are used this time–from 1935 through 1951. Again, the major world and national events that we're told make market history are accurately overlaid. Now, without peeking at the dateline or captions, can you pick out the period of time in which World War II was in progress from market action alone?

Taking events one at a time again:

1. No events of major significance could be found for 1935, '36, and '37. Yet the market roared mightily during this period and subsided with a thump in 1937 and early 1938. What caused all this price motion–far more extensive than any that took place during all of WW II?
2. WW II started in 1939 and no immediate effects are seen at all. For nearly a year the market drifted sidewise to slightly down.
3. The Pearl Harbor hammer blow hit in 1941 and the market plunged some. But it had been going down for months before–at the same rate!
4. The German and Japanese surrenders show no impact at all. The market had been rising sharply for three years, and neither accelerated nor decelerated its pace because of these monumental events.
5. The fall of France in 1940 is closely associated in time with a fierce and very rapid plunge in the market. Could *this* be an impact of a fundamental event? It is noted that the market plunge took place *before* the event, but perhaps the market was simply "discounting" the possibility in advance (a favorite phrase of the fundamentalist). Well, let's take a closer look.

## THE IMPACT OF THE FALL OF FRANCE

Figure IX-4 also displays a series of six wavy, dotted lines. These are cyclicalities that have been identified for this time period and were removed using the same analytical techniques that were employed with Warner Co. in Figure II-11.

Now let's see if any of these look familiar. The periodicity marked "6" shows 92 samples over 884 weeks for an average of 9.6 weeks per cycle. When this form of analysis is carried through to more recent years, it is found that this oscillation slowly

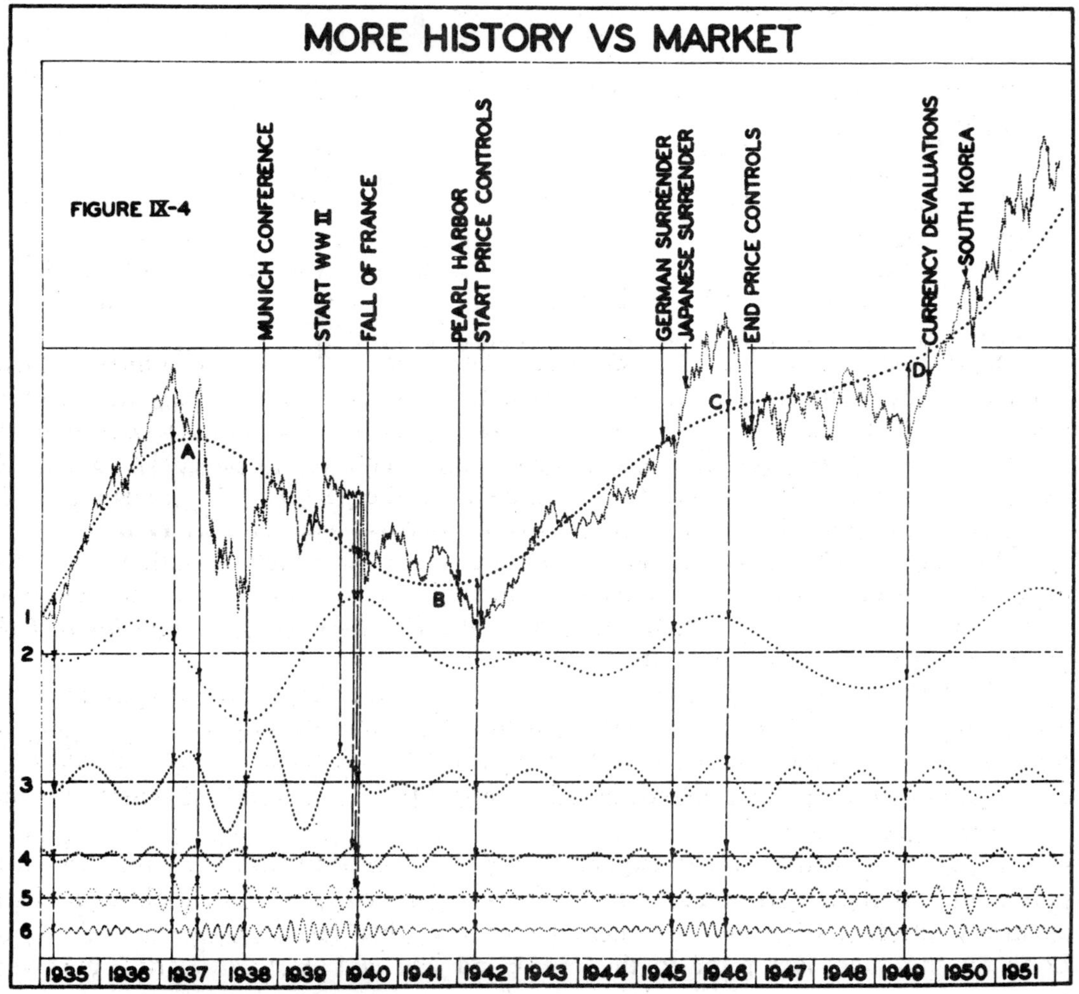


**History, The Market, And Cyclicality**

reduces its duration to between six and seven weeks. This is the 1936-1951 counterpart of the 6.5-week cycle of the model!

What about Number 5? There are 44½ samples present in 884 weeks. The average duration is 19.85 weeks. Sound familiar?

Number 4. An average of 34.6 weeks is obtained from the 25½ samples present. This is the 1935-1951 equivalent of the (nominal) nine-month component of the model.

Number 3. The average duration of the 13 samples in 204 months is 15.7 months or 67.98 weeks. Familiarity again!

Number 2. Here sample durations are as follows:

- Sample 1 — 38 months
- Sample 2 — 43 months
- Sample 3 — 28 months
- Sample 4 — 54 months
- Sample 5 — 58 months (the total duration estimate for this one is based on the one-half cycle present)

Now we note the same effect we've seen before, only this time in connection with our 54-month cycle: short durations associated with low magnitudes—and magnitude fluctuation with time! In fact, the shortest sample (28 months) is associated with the 1942, '43, '44 time period in which oscillation magnitude almost went to zero. So there seems to be little doubt that Number 2 is the 1935-1951 equivalent of the 4.5-year component of the model.

Number 1. This one represents the sum of all possible oscillations longer in duration than those we've been calling (nominally) 54 months. Notice the high points in this curve at A and C, and the lows at B and D. *These are highs and lows of the nine-year periodic oscillation of our model!*

Once more a comment on randomness: It is perfectly evident that none of the smooth curves one through six are random in nature, yet *the sum of these six non-random curves adds up to the curve representing the DJ closing prices within ±1%!*

If non-random motion makes up all except ±1% of the total price motion, what then is left to be random?

Now we've been unable to explain the price action of the average during this time period by looking to historical events. Let's see if we can do better looking at things cyclically, starting with the one question mark we had left over—the fall of France. Look on the chart just prior to this event and you will see three vertical lines with arrows on the ends. These lines relate a specific part of the DJ price action to the cyclic constituent status at the time in question. The earliest of these three lines shows the following:

1. Component 1 — is moving rapidly downward.
2. Component 2 — is going over a top and contributing nothing.
3. Component 3 — is hard down.

4. Component 4 is going over a top and contributing nothing.
5. Component 5 is hard up.
6. Component 6 is hard up.

So what's happening to the average as a result? Two components are going up, two are going down, and two are sidewise—and (you guessed it!) the average is going sidewise (with a *tiny* uptick due to component 6).

Now try tne next line to the right:

1. Component 1 is still down.
2. Component 2 is still sideways.
3. Component 3 is still down.
4. Component 4 is just starting down.
5. Component 5 is now going over the top and contributing nothing.
6. Component 6 is still hard up.

Two going down, one just starting down, and one going up. What's the average doing? It's just starting down—gently.

Now look at the third line:

1. Component No. 1 is still down.
2. Component No. 2 is still sideways.
3. Component No. 3 is still down.
4. Component No. 4 is now hard down.
5. Component No. 5 is now hard down.
6. Component No. 6 is just going over the top and becomes hard down right through the precipitous drop preceding the fall of France!

Five down and one sideways—and the bottom dropped out! Now remember this: each of these components had existed and had been oscillating regularly up and down for years before the events leading to the fall of France even had their embryonic beginnings! Was it then anticipation of the fall of France that caused the market to drop?

## HERE IS HOW LONG-RANGE CYCLICALITY AFFECTS THE MARKET

If we cannot find historical events which relate to market activity, let's go back to the average and pick significant turning points and see if they relate to cyclicality, and how. We'll take eight cases in this 17-year time span.

**Case I: The Major Market Rise Starting In Early 1935.**

Component 1 hard up
Component 2 bottoming and heading up
Component 3 bottoming and heading up
Component 4 bottoming and heading up
Component 5 bottomed and heading up
Component 6 bottomed and heading up

No wonder the market went up!

### Case II: The Minor Market Drop Of Early 1937

| | |
|---|---|
| Component 1 | flattening across the top |
| Component 2 | hard down |
| Component 3 | hard up |
| Component 4 | bottoming and heading up |
| Component 5 | topping out to head down |
| Component 6 | topping out to head down |

One hard up, one bottoming to head up, one flattening across the top, two topping to head down and one hard down. So, the market went down. But it didn't go down very far, and then bounced right back up again. Why? Because by that time Components 4, 5, and 6 were due to bottom out. They did so and the market responded by bottoming also.

### Case III: The Big Drop of 1937 And 1938

| | |
|---|---|
| Component 1 | flat across the top |
| Component 2 | hard down |
| Component 3 | hard down |
| Component 4 | topping and heading down |
| Component 5 | topping and heading down |
| Component 6 | topping and heading down |

There was simply nothing here cyclically to cause up action, and plenty to cause down action—and the bottom *really* dropped out from under!

### Case IV: The Up Market Of 1938

| | |
|---|---|
| Component 1 | hard down |
| Component 2 | bottoming and heading up |
| Component 3 | hard up |
| Component 4 | hard down |
| Component 5 | hard up |
| Component 6 | hard down |

Three down and three up. The ups won, because of the magnitude and longevity of Components 2 and 3, but the rebound was not nearly as furious as for Case I where everything was up.

### Case V: The Market Rise Of 1942

| | |
|---|---|
| Component 1 | up |
| Component 2 | up |
| Component 3 | down |
| Component 4 | up |
| Component 5 | up |
| Component 6 | topping and down |

Four ups and two downs, so the market went up. And it continued to go up because down Component 3 soon bottomed and lent up impetus, while down

Component 6 was short-lived and small in amplitude and really only caused small wiggles anyway.

**Case VI: The Spurt Of 1945**

| | |
|---|---|
| Component 1 | hard up |
| Component 2 | hard up |
| Component 3 | bottoming and heading up |
| Component 4 | hard up |
| Component 5 | bottoming and ready to head up |
| Component 6 | down, but due to bottom soon |

With all this working for it, the surge was understandably huge. It was relatively short-lived however, since up Component 2 was not too far from a top-out at the time.

**Case VII: The Hard Down Market Of 1946**

| | |
|---|---|
| Component 1 | up |
| Component 2 | down |
| Component 3 | down |
| Component 4 | topping out to go down |
| Component 5 | up |
| Component 6 | down |

With a preponderance of downs, the plunge was precipitous. Again short-lived however, because Components 3 and 4 contributed heavily to the fall and were of short enough duration that they soon turned, arresting the downside activity.

**Case VIII: The Big Up Market Of 1949**

| | |
|---|---|
| Component 1 | up |
| Component 2 | up |
| Component 3 | up |
| Component 4 | bottoming to go up |
| Component 5 | up |
| Component 6 | bottoming to go up |

Here we have nearly an identical situation to that of Case I, and the market behavior is identical: i.e., the longest and steepest upward move since the one starting in 1935!

So. Just as world events cannot explain market oscillations, it appears that cyclicality can and does. And the importance of this remarkable fact is especially apparent when we keep in mind the following:

1. Although our derived results apply strictly to the DJ 30 Industrial Stock Average, data in the Appendix shows that many, if not all, individual issues behave similarly.
2. All these periodicities persist in time. They have been regularly bottoming out, going up, topping out, and going down again for years on end—completely independent of all the things that we normally think make stock prices change.
3. Sufficient periodicity spells semi-predictability, which in turn spells transaction timing aid!

Figure IX-4 is one of the most useful charts in the book, and is worthy of intense study. Here is seen the regularity, persistence, deviation from regularity, and manner of combination of most of the periodic oscillations that comprise stock price actions.

## SUMMARIZING PRICE CHANGE CAUSES

- You don't need to understand the causes of price change in detail in order to profit by the price-motion model—but it helps when the unexpected occurs.
- The traditional concepts of risk versus trading interval are out-dated by the existence of the price-motion model.
- The determining element of price change is the human decision-making process.
- Decision-making is complex and little understood. Emotions and unrelated influences often play a large part. The unknowns in the process probably mask the true cause of price motion cyclicality.
- Although the cause of cyclicality is unknown, the nature of the effect is certain.
- The implications of cyclicality include possible external influence of the decision processes of masses of investors more or less simultaneously. If this is fact, you must guard yourself carefully against the same influences.
- Cyclicality is probably not related to rational decision factors.
- The lack of relationship between cyclicality and historical events is clear-cut.
- More specific fundamental events cause wide differences in individual stock price action, and must always be taken into account.
- There may be a link between gross national product and non-cyclic price action in the market.
- True panics due to wars, currency devaluations, etc., represent buying opportunities if the cyclic picture is also ripe.
- The extent of non-random cyclicality precludes any major contribution to price action by random events.
- All price fluctuations about smooth long-term trends in the market (as represented by the DJIA) are due to manifestations of cyclicality.

*chapter*

*ten*

# Pitfalls and How to Avoid Them

- **Why the Unexpected Occurs**
- **Recognizing Psychological Barriers**
- **Counteracting the "Outside Influence"**
- **Overcoming Greed**
- **Beat the "Persimmon Effect"**
- **The Bugaboo of "Time Distortion"—and What to Do About It**
- **Dealing With "Scale Effect"**
- **Combating Emotional Cyclicality**
- **In a Nutshell**

Understanding provides control and control permits attainment. This is true in all areas of human endeavor, and no less true as regards the market.

Before the Dow theory of price motion was formulated, little or no true control was possible in investing. A few gifted individuals did indeed make fortunes in the market, but it is to be suspected that they did so by intuitively acting on information inherent in price motion.

In more recent years chartists and other "technicians" have advanced the measure of knowledge of price fluctuations still more, and an improved degree of control has become possible as a result. It is the author's conviction that recognition of cyclicality in price motion advances the cause a step further.

This is certainly not the end of the line. Other bits and pieces of knowledge will fall into place as time goes on. This means that the predictive processes described here are not perfect. This further means that operation with these concepts will not always produce the desired results.

It is the purpose of this chapter to outline a few of the resulting pitfalls in the hope that you may then more easily avoid them.

## WHY THE UNEXPECTED OCCURS

There are three principal causes of cyclic analysis going awry. The one which must be most guarded against is the totally unpredictable fundamental factor which hits a specific stock without warning. This differs completely from the long-term, smooth, underlying fundamental push characterizing 75% of price motion. This is the factor that either throws investors into a selling panic, or causes them to flood the issue with buy orders no matter how high the price is driven.

If this occurs in such a sense as to *aid* your transaction, you should shift immediately to the use of terminal sell signal criteria. If it occurs in such a sense as *not* to aid your transaction, let your trailing loss level signals be your guide.

These situations do not occur often. When they do, proceed as described and put your funds to work in another issue.

The second cause of difficulty is the unpredictability of magnitude-duration fluctuation of your trading cycle.

Go back now to Figure IX-4. A study of this variable in the cyclic components shows that you can usually avoid trouble here by using sufficient past data in your analysis. The variations are not sudden, and an increased span of past data can help warn you when magnitude is due to dry up on a particular cycle.

A publication that is of considerable help in this regard is Standard and Poor's *Trendlines, Current Market Perspectives.* Although this service does not include all of the issues in which you will be interested, it does include nearly 1000—on both exchanges. These are weekly high-low charts covering about four years.

Never overlook the signs of occurrence. These are:

1. Failure to fill constant-width envelopes, and
2. The formation of triangles, coils, wedges, and diamonds, in the manner of the first one described for Figure III-9.

When this occurs due to components of shorter duration than your trading cycle, it can be a great aid. But when it occurs due to the trading cycle itself, trouble is at hand, and investment in the issue should be temporarily avoided.

Once again you will find it rather rare to be caught in these circumstances, but if you are, your trailing loss levels will protect you against major loss.

The third source of difficulty is caused by overlooking the status of longer term components. Sometimes these will be just emerging from a crossover point of magnitude-duration fluctuation, and hence are not readily observable in past data. At other times this occurs because of the use of an inadequate span of past price history in your analysis.

To guard against this, always keep clearly in mind *all* of the components of the price-motion model. When performing a cyclic analysis the status of as many of these as practical must be taken into account. If doubt exists, resort to the computational methods of Chapter Six, or select another issue on which to trade.

## RECOGNIZING PSYCHOLOGICAL BARRIERS

Your techniques can be mastered to perfection and you can still get into trouble with trading. The reasons are psychological in nature. There are several varieties of these barriers and the most important single thing you can do to overcome them is *simply recognize that they exist.*

## COUNTERACTING THE OUTSIDE INFLUENCE

This one is always present, but is of special significance if you have been operating in one way in the past and decide to convert to the methods described in this book.

Let's see how it works by example:

You've been trading in the market for some time with mediocre results. You haven't really had any logical basis on which to make your decisions–no consistent and unified trading method. You have relied heavily on advice from friends, your broker, etc.

Now you are suddenly exposed to the price-motion model and the resulting techniques of trading. You test it on past stock price-action data. It works in the tests, and you're excited; you are eager to put it to the *real* test!

You conduct your scans, pull together a stable, and complete your analysis. You are now waiting for an action signal, and have funds free for the transaction when the time comes.

Before this comes about, however, the phone rings. Your broker is on the line. He says XYZ company is the object of an acquisition move. The stock is now at 21 and the prospects are for 32 when the tender offer is made public. He strongly recommends a purchase.

You hesitate. You know your broker has your best interests at heart. His suggestion is tempting. He's been in the business for a long time and knows it inside and out. You, however, are only a neophyte. You've just latched onto a method you think will work, but it hasn't really made you any profits yet. And the last time he gave you a tip you made $1000 in three days. Your self-confidence drains and you eagerly put your waiting funds into XYZ.

Now it doesn't really matter whether you make or lose money on this particular transaction. The point is *you are still following your old method of trading on information, which has proven that it provides mediocre results in the long run!*

You have:

1. Made up your mind to try something else, because of the evidence that the old method doesn't work consistently.
2. Suddenly changed your mind, and reverted to the old method anyway, because of *outside influences.*

Now, no real harm has resulted in this case since we're only really talking about whether you inaugurate a new system right now or some time later. However, let the same thing occur *after* you have made the switch–and you're in trouble.

*You can only expect a system based on probabilities to develop the expected degree of success if it is followed with utter consistency!*

In fact, it requires remarkably *little* deviation from consistency to *radically* affect the odds.

Let's try another example.

You've set yourself mentally and financially to try the new method. (Maybe the XYZ transaction didn't turn out so well: merger news situations are sometimes tricky.) You steel yourself and say: "From now on I will be influenced *only* by my own analysis of the situation!"

Suddenly, ABC stock trades one day in such a manner that it is apparent a new two-week low has been established. But your extension lines on the non-real time envelope tell you that this low should have been two points lower, *if* the past downtrend was still intact. You compute and plot in the new low, use your channel envelope measure, and sketch in the reversal—complete with the next expected intra-channel high and low values. The downtrend is broken! The analysis is confirmed by all other aspects of your graphical constructs. The stock has signaled a 30% move over the next week and a half!

You call your broker to place an order to buy. But the market has been going up for the last two weeks. The DJ Industrials have risen 25 points in the last six days. Your broker, anxious to avert a costly mistake on your part, says, "The market is weakening. It's time it took a breather—after all it's been up 25 points in the last week. The tick has just started to deteriorate. I would strongly advise that you delay all purchases until the market reacts a little."

You think: "That's true. Is the method *really* that accurate? I can't be absolutely sure I just saw a cyclic low. Maybe that cycle was stretched a little. Maybe a short-term fundamental factor popped the stock up a bit. I sure don't want to sit in it at a loss for the next two weeks." Aloud you say "Maybe you're right. Forget the order: I'll wait a while."

However, your broker (and perhaps you) did not realize that ABC has been going *down* during the last six days the market has been *up*. You are aware of the close time synchronization between cyclic activities of individual issues and the overall market, and are also aware that for short periods of time the shorter duration periodicities *can* get out of step. Nevertheless, you worry a little about the latter. As a matter of fact, the last significant up-move in ABC started two weeks *before* the average turned, and ABC soared 20% under cover of a down market! In short, the cyclic components of ABC are just slightly out of time synchronization with the market as a whole at this particular time. You've heard the Wall Street expression: "This is a market of stocks, *not* a stock market." You know this is true by virtue of three facts:

1. Price changes between stocks vary because of fundamental differences.
2. Price changes between stocks vary because of magnitude-duration fluctuation differences.
3. Price changes between stocks vary because of small differences in cyclic time synchronization.

You have just seen an example of the latter, doubted your own analysis, and missed your 30% move in ABC! *You were defeated by the psychological impact of respected outside influences!*

The outside influence doesn't have to be your broker. It can be an earnings statement you see in the newspaper. It can be an article on the company in *Barron's.* It can be anything whatever that creates doubt in your mind, and prevents you from acting when the stock price behavior tells you what it is going to do next! All of this is not saying that you are always going to be right while the next fellow is always wrong—but if you are going to trade on fundamental information and tips, you must do so consistently. If you are going to trade on cyclic analysis, you must do this consistently also. Mix your methods, and the best features of each will not dominate your results!

Now that this powerful agent of difficulty has been identified, the question is what can you do to train yourself out of trouble?

It will help a great deal if you will keep just one fact very firmly in mind:

When you tested the methods on paper, they worked—and you didn't have any outside influences deflecting your purpose then. In fact, you did not even need the date nor the name of the stock in order to derive the needed conclusions from your analysis.

You will find also that there is no substitute for analytical practice. You simply cannot apply the methods in this book too often on paper. You must do this, checking out every statement made, over and over again. Keep meticulous track of what the results would have been had you been invested. Lean over backward not to cheat. In this manner you can build sufficient confidence in the efficacy of the methods and in yourself to assure a stiff spine when the barrier is approached.

It will help to consciously prepare your mind to give these methods the good old "college try." You must inform your friends that you are trying something new and you do not want to hear any news about investments. Then, you must pre-make your decision as to what way you will react, and what you will do if outside influences sneak in anyway, as they will. You will probably still not be able to refrain from succumbing at first. If you do so, follow the transaction both ways—and keep a record of the results! After you have a series of these results on record, go back and see how all would have worked out *if* you had been able to master outside influences!

## OVERCOMING GREED

It may sound trite to you, but you *must* be able to overcome greed. You now have available a logical and complete basis on which to trade in the market. After training yourself to overcome outside influences, the next most important psychological barrier you will meet is simple avarice.

Let's say you have followed all the steps in this book in detail. You have selected issues, pulled data, plotted, and analyzed. Right off the bat you notice several situations which seem to fit all criteria—almost. Not all factors are aligned in your favor, but most of them are. For example, everything is right except for some confusion on the status of the 13-week cycle. But everything else says *buy.* Besides, to locate better candidates would require another several days of work, and your opportunity may be past by then in the issue before you.

**Don't Trade on the Issue Where Confusion is Present!**

Remember this: you can work diligently without trading at all for three and a half weeks, discarding prospect after prospect before you find a situation that leaves no doubt in your mind. It is perfectly possible to trade on that one issue and capture a 10% gain in half a week. Recall the compounding example of Chapter One. Starting with $10,000, making just one 10% trade per month, your capital compounds to over $1,000,000 in something like four years! On the other hand, trade on all the "almosts" that come along and you're sure to strike some losers. Each time you lose you will diminish self-confidence.

The same thinking applies to sales. Ride your profits only as long as there is no doubt as to what the techniques are telling you to do. If doubt occurs—take your profit, and be content. You don't need much per trade for the principle of profit compounding to make you rich!

This barrier is particularly hard to contend with when you see situation after situation where "almosts" go right ahead and do what you expected them to. The temptation gets very great to jump on the next one, in spite of the fact that the daily effort required to identify the ideal situation is far less strenuous and exacting than your work-a-day job. The trait at fault is simply *greed*—and greed can defeat you just as effectively in the market as if you attempt to trade without system!

## BEAT THE "PERSIMMON EFFECT"

As you practice graphical analysis you will note a common situation over and over again: *The ideal time to buy a stock is exactly when it looks the least interesting!* Similarly: *The ideal time to sell a stock short is when it looks as though it will never stop going up!*

You will put a stock into your stable and patiently track it for a buy signal. The price continues to drop and the amount of daily or weekly variation dries up along with volume. Your cyclic analysis tells you to expect this, but it certainly looks as though all investor interest has completely vanished.

At such a time it is very difficult indeed to convince yourself that you should actually take action when that buy signal comes along.

Anyone who has experienced the varied taste treat of the persimmon can form the appropriate analogy. Even knowing the situation with regard to this fruit, it is still difficult to force yourself to select the nearly rotten looking ones which are sweet and tasty. But the penalty for biting into the smooth, firm, and desirable looking fruit is severe!

Quite often when the cyclic situation is ripe a full day's trading all at one price and on vanishing volume will signal in advance a buy signal the very next day!

You will have to consciously recognize and train yourself to avoid the persimmon effect!

## THE BUGABOO OF TIME DISTORTION–AND WHAT TO DO ABOUT IT

This element of the psychological problem is of particular importance in any technical approach to the market. In a technical approach, decisions are made on the basis of what a stock *does.* To remain aware of what it does requires charts. Charts accomplish the purpose because they provide at-a-glance perception of what a stock is doing over large periods of time. This very reason for the effectiveness of charts is the heart of the time-distortion problem!

To see this, consider:

The relationships between stock price motion and time are presented in a chart in vastly compressed time. Price motions that took months to occur are perceived in a chart in seconds. The mind is free from considering time when a chart is studied. But the mind is never free from time considerations when a stock is in motion, *and you're in it!* Time-price relationships which are easy to sense in looking at a chart refuse to make themselves even noticeable as *real* time crawls along.

The effect is closely analogous to a motion picture film. Viewed frame by frame all fluidity, grace, and even reality of motion cease to exist. Speeded up into an acceptably compressed time scale, exotic dancers can delight as though real.

In the case of stock charts, the situation is just reversed. The chart presents information over past time on a compressed time scale like that of a movie film running at normal speed. But real life stock price changes are viewed as additions to the chart at movie film frame-by-frame speed!

You will find that you can analyze a chart with perfect objectivity over all past time. But start adding real-time data at frame-by-frame speed, and objectivity vanishes just when you need it the most.

You can set up a powerful demonstration of this for yourself in this way:

Assemble a series of past Mansfield chart issues. Sort out all the white "Page Ones" in chronological order. Clip off all parts of the page except the weekly chart of the DJ Industrial Average. Staple the left-hand edges together.

Now bend the package in the middle and fan the sheets before your eyes as if you were shuffling a deck of cards. Concentrate your attention on the 18- to 20-week cycle. If you fan at a reasonably constant speed, you will find that you will know, in advance, what motion in the average is coming up. Your charts will come to life with cyclic motion! Then, when you come to the last chart, the motion will subside—but you will retain a strong impression of what comes next!

What this accomplishes, of course, is to force each added data point on the chart (insignificant in itself when presented in real time) to be perceived as part of the entire fabric of price-time action. In this way, price-time rates may be qualitatively sensed, as they cannot be with a static, add-on chart.

As always, the mere recognition of this problem gets you a long way toward a solution. The use of positive, advance-decisions possible when using the objective action signals is also a definite aid.

You can also take specific steps to train yourself. Practice selection of an issue from chart services of the past. Do the plotting and analysis work just as if you were going to trade in the stock. After all analysis is complete, add one new datum (daily or weekly high-low). Repeat analysis, paying particular heed to the impact of the addition. Continue in this way, always striving to attach special significance to each new bit of evidence. You will gradually gain a sense of relationship between *chart time and real time.*

It is even more effective if you do this as real time goes along. Carry a number of fully analyzed issues along day by day and week by week *before* you start to trade. It is truly difficult to over-emphasize the importance of this barrier to your success. All time spent in this manner will reap large rewards as you swing your new abilities into actual practice!

## DEALING WITH "SCALE EFFECT"

This is another highly significant factor when dealing with charts. The kernel of the problem is that no chart is unique. The time-price pairs that constitute the data on which the chart is based *are* unique. Once established, they appear in your *Wall Street Journal* just exactly as they appear in "Friend Jack's Journal," 2000 miles away.

However, when *you* construct a chart of this data and *Jack* charts the same data you will sometimes have difficulty believing that the two charts describe the same stock. In fact *the significance of time-price relationships in a stock can be suppressed and/or lost if care is not used in the selection of scale factors!*

Now, the time scale factor that you choose is simply the space that you allot on your chart to represent a particular unit of time (day, week, etc.). Similarly, the price scale factor is the space you allot on your chart to represent a specific unit of price (one-eighth, one-point, etc.). Thus, by choice of scale factor, a chart can minimize time effects while emphasizing price motion, or vice versa.

If you fix your time scale factor, you can accomplish the same results by varying the price scale factor. Or you may select both so that you must stand yards away in order to see relationships without receiving a surrealistic effect. Through compression of both scales, you can convey a sense of unimportance and insignificance for both time and price motions—hence of the stock itself!

The problem is thus seen as one in which you must first know what it is you're looking for on a chart. Then you must choose scale factors which optimize the ease of perceptivity of the desired information.

You will want to experiment on your own in this area, but a few guidelines can be drawn:

1. Use daily charts for components with periods of one to 13 weeks.
2. Use weekly charts for components of 13 weeks to nine months in duration.
3. Use monthly charts for components of nine months and longer.
4. In general, arrange the scale factors so that the price motion over the time period of interest forms a nearly square chart.
5. To suppress the effect of short components while emphasizing the longer ones, plot the price motion in *less* space while retaining the same scale factor for time.
6. To suppress the effect of long components while emphasizing the short ones, plot the price motion in *more* space while retaining the same scale factor for time.

7. If a pattern you're analyzing (a triangle, for example) seems insignificant to you, *enlarge* both price and time scale factors.
8. If your attention seems riveted on what you know are insignificant phenomena, *reduce* both price and time scale factors.

Chart services present a different version of the same problem. In such charts, the space available is fixed, as is the time span covered. This means that the time scale factor never varies from chart to chart and issue to issue.

At the same time, the price motion of *all* stocks charted by the service must be displayed in a fixed amount of chart space for the total time covered.

Thus, a highly volatile issue will have a *compressed* price scale (with all that this implies), and a sluggish issue will have an *expanded* price scale (with undue emphasis on short duration fluctuations). Use is made of this fact in Chapter Seven, where the scale factor of the Mansfield chart is actually measured as an indication of volatility.

All of this means that the same types of cyclic phenomena occurring in two different stocks charted in this manner require a shift in your thinking in order to effect the required same interpretation. Either this, or one or the other of the two charts must be replotted.

For the methods described in this book, replotting for analysis purposes is required anyway. This is the time to consider the impact of scale factor. However, in order to make effective use of chart services in scan and selection, you must practice negating the effect of scale factor change from chart to chart.

## COMBATING EMOTIONAL CYCLICALITY

This may or may not be a real psychological barrier. Nevertheless, assumption that it exists at least helps to overcome the persimmon effect, and hence does no harm. If it *does* exist, experience in overcoming it is essential.

Return in thought to the price-motion model. It has been emphasized that human decisions are what set in motion the chain of events that result in price change. But a decision is an effect which demands a *cause.* A human decision is caused *by* something. If the decision is a logical one, the decision is based on deductions which are reasoned from facts. If a decision is made in the partial or total absence of sufficient facts on which to base a logical conclusion, then we may say that emotion or feeling has been the determining factor.

Now couple the above line of reasoning with the fact that *something* causes masses of investors to make buy and sell decisions which result in a fair chunk of price motion being cyclic in nature. Furthermore, they do this pretty much in unison. Add to this the surety that individual investors *never* have *all* the facts needed on which to base logical buy and sell decisions–and often have very few. It becomes a fair assumption then, that many buy and sell decisions are characterized more by emotion than by logic. The obvious implication of all this is that the emotional attitudes or feelings of masses of investors vary in a cyclic manner, and that cyclicality in stock prices is nothing more than a reflection of this.

However, regardless of whether or not this is a valid explanation of *why*, it is certainly a fact that people in general do *not* get more and more in the mood to buy stocks as prices go down. Conversely, the mood to sell does not strike harder and harder as prices rise. Yet the exact opposite of this mood is absolutely mandatory if we are to "buy low and sell high," and this is precisely what we must do in order to profit in the market.

Therefore, if we condition ourselves to behave as though something is cyclically causing our emotional outlook to vary (which in turn causes us to be bearish or bullish at the wrong times), and if we consciously try to combat the assumed forces, we will find ourselves doing all the right things: i.e., being in a frame of mind to *sell into rising markets* and *buy into falling markets.* This alone cannot guarantee us profits, but combined with a workable timing theory it can work wonders.

In actual practice it is very hard to force yourself to adopt such contrary frames of mind. Invariably the temptation exists to buy stocks ebulliently just as soon as you sell one at a profit, even though (or perhaps because) the fact is clearly evident that prices have moved strongly upward for some period of time.

The price-motion model and resulting techniques provide excellent objective evidence of market (and individual stock) turning points, but it is indeed difficult to accept and act on the results unless you've trained your emotions to the reverse of the natural bent.

## IN A NUTSHELL

- Nothing is perfect—there are pitfalls.
- Cyclic analysis can be wrong due to transient fundamental factors, magnitude-duration fluctuation, and overlooked long-term components.
- Trailing loss levels will protect you in most cases.
- The most important antidote for psychological barriers is awareness of their existence and importance.
- Outside influences, however well meant, can upset the statistical balance of things for you.
- Greed is a problem. Use knowledge of the effectiveness of profit compounding to counteract it.
- A stock seldom appears interesting at the ideal time to buy. It usually looks too good to be true when it's time to sell.
- There is a psychological effect attributable to chart time vs. real time.
- When using charts, scale factors are important.
- You must train yourself emotionally to sell into rising markets and buy into falling ones.

*chapter*

*eleven*

# Spectral Analysis — How to Do It and What It Means

- Why Numerical Analysis
- The Meaning of a Frequency Spectrum
- How to Do Fourier Analysis
- Assembling Your Data
- Separating Your Data Into Two Sequences
- Determine the Frequencies in Your Analysis
- Now Compute the Corresponding Amplitudes
- How to Get Composite Amplitudes
- The Kind of Results You Can Expect
- How Numerical Filters Can Help You
- What You Must Know About Filter Operations
- The Part of "Weights" in Numerical Filters
- How to Design Your Own Numerical Filters
- Applying Your Numerical Filter to Stock Prices
- Take Advantage of Curve Fitting
- Fit Your Data With a Straight Line
- How to Use Other Kinds of Curve Fitting
- Summarizing Numerical Analysis

This chapter is provided for those individuals of curious mind who would like to investigate the fascinating intricacies of market cyclicality on their own, but who have little or no background in the required methods of numerical and spectral analysis.

It is intended as an introduction to the subject which, when augmented by study of the appropriate references in the bibliography, can launch you on your own sea of investigation.

## WHY NUMERICAL ANALYSIS

A stock history is a record of a phenomenon; namely, the price changes in a stock as a function of time. Other events of the world also establish such time histories: take the matter of the temperature at a specific location in downtown Los Angeles as an example. This temperature is a quantity which changes continuously as time passes. A pen and ink recorder associated with a suitable thermometer will record a continuous wavy line as temperature changes, minute or large, occur. Such a history is referred to as a continuous "function of time."

A stock price history is a little different. The nature of the events which cause price change is such that the result is not continuous. It is only when a specific transaction takes place that a price change is noted, with the result that stock histories consist of a sequence of price numbers instead of a continuously changing price. Even assuming that stock price changes are a mirror of some unknown continuous variable, such as investor emotional attitudes, does not change the fact that the price changes themselves are only available to us as samples in the form of separate and distinct numbers.

The techniques of numerical analysis were formulated to handle just such problems as ours. What we wish to do is to extract as much information as possible from a time series of discrete numbers. This is precisely what numerical analysis makes it possible to do.

## THE MEANING OF A FREQUENCY SPECTRUM

The quantities heretofore referred to as fluctuations, regularities, or periodicities are more precisely called *sine waves.* A frequency spectrum is a map of the existence and nature of such sine waves. The durations previously referred to are a characteristic of sine waves called the *period.* The magnitude (or size) of these is measured from positive peak to negative valley and is known as the *amplitude.*

In Figure III-6, two such sine waves are depicted, one of which is slightly displaced from the other in time. This characteristic is spoken of as the phase-relationship of two sine waves. The analogous time relationship of a specific sine wave to an arbitrary (but fixed) reference point in time is similarly noted as the *phase time* of that particular sine wave.

Thus a sine wave is completely and uniquely described mathematically (or numerically) in terms of the associated period, amplitude, and phase.

Another descriptive quantity can be derived from the period, and is somewhat more useful in numerical analysis. This is the *frequency* of the sine wave. It is simply computed, once the period is known, by taking the reciprocal of period. In symbols:

$$f = \frac{1}{T}$$

where $f$ = frequency in cycles per unit time;
and $T$ = period in the same units of time.

The relationship between these two quantities is most easily seen by means of an example.

Given: a sine wave with a period of six months or a half-year. The corresponding frequency is: $f = \frac{1}{1/2} = 2$ cycles per year—or, leaving time in units of months: $f = \frac{1}{6} = \frac{1}{6}$ cycle per month.

There is another form of the frequency quantity which is still more meaningful in some applications. This is called *angular frequency.* It comes about because the amplitude of a sine wave can be related to the angular measure of a circle, 360 degrees (or $2\pi$ radians) of a circle corresponding to one period of a sine wave. It is simply derived as follows:

$$\omega = 2\pi f = \frac{2\pi}{T}$$

where: $\omega$ = angular frequency in radians per unit time
$f$ = frequency in cycles per unit time
$T$ = period in units of time
$\pi$ = constant = 3.14159 . . .

Now, just how does all of this relate to the market?

It is a true fact that any given time history of any event (including the price history of a stock) can always be considered as reproducible to any desired degree of accuracy by the process of algebraically summing a particular series of sine waves. This is intuitively evident if you start with a number of sine waves of differing frequencies, amplitudes, and phases, and then sum them up to get a new and more complex wave form. In such a case you already know the nature of the sine wave content of the final result. As you recall, several very simple examples of this process were shown in Chapter Three, except that a sloping straight line was added in as well. But if the straight line had not been included, the frequency spectrum of the resultant would have been described by a plot similar to that of Figure A I-1, but with only one or two frequency "lines" present.

In the references to Fourier Analysis in the bibliography you can find proof of the fact that even the straight line of the last paragraph can be accurately represented by the sum of a series of properly chosen sine waves. If the spectral plot were expanded to include these components as well, we would say that we then have a complete spectral analysis of the wave forms generated as examples in Chapter Three.

In similar manner, the frequency, amplitude, and phase of a sine wave series which adds up to any given wave form, no matter how complex, can always be found to any desired degree of accuracy by using the techniques of Fourier Analysis (subject to certain mathematical and conceptual restrictions which do not apply to market data).

The results of such an analysis are called the frequency spectrum of the wave form, and the process is called spectral (sometimes harmonic) analysis.

It should be clearly understood that while nearly all wave forms have a frequency spectrum, this does not necessarily imply that the wave form was initially generated by a process which sums sine waves. In our case, the fact that stock price histories have frequency spectrums does not guarantee that they were generated by a process which starts out with sine waves and adds them up. However, methods are available whereby such processes can be detected. In the case of stocks, the random and fundamentally motivated parts of price motion are *not* generated in this manner, while the "X" motivated portion of price motion *is* generated in this way. This is a vital consideration since if this were not true, knowledge of spectral components would not necessarily imply predictability. In any case, the starting point in looking for such useful results as "X motivation" cyclicality is the process of spectral or harmonic analysis.

At this point we can state the following in support of the need for numerical analysis in any comprehensive study of the market.

1. Stock price histories consist of sequences of numbers.
2. We need to be able to accomplish spectral analysis of price motion using these numbers.
3. Spectral analysis may be accomplished in several ways but the one which permits direct application to stock price numbers is numerical analysis.

## HOW TO DO FOURIER ANALYSIS

As you look into the references on this subject in the bibliography, you will find that there are several varieties of the Fourier methods. The one chosen for presentation here is described by Lanczos, in a simple and straightforward manner, and will suffice as your introduction to the subject.

## ASSEMBLING YOUR DATA

Your stock price data must be equi-spaced in time–that is, daily, weekly, monthly, etc.

You must choose one value that you consider representative of the price over the chosen increment of time. In the case of daily data this can be the closing price, the mean between high and low for the day, or any other price you feel typifies the day. Once you have chosen it, however, you should use the same criterion for each day's data. The price most often used is the closing one (for the day or for the week, etc.).

Choose an odd number of such price datums, in the proper time sequence, for your analysis. The larger the number of such that you use the better your resulting frequency spectrum will be resolved.

Have your data tabulated before you in chronological order.

## SEPARATING YOUR DATA INTO TWO SEQUENCES

Note and mark in your tabulation the one data point in the exact center of the series. You are going to form two new data sequences now, and this central number is going to be the starting place.

To form the first new sequence, proceed as follows:

1. The first number in the sequence is just the middle number of your stock price series.
2. Now add together the two numbers on either side of the mid-point number of your original price series. This is the second number in the new sequence.
3. Next, add together the two numbers one removed from, and to either side of, the mid-point number of your original price series. This is the third number in the new sequence.
4. The fourth number is obtained by adding together the two numbers of the original series that are two removed from the central number.
5. Proceed in this manner until you get the last element of your new series by adding together the first and last prices in your original stock price series of numbers.
6. Now take the last number only in your new series, and change it by dividing by 2.0. This operation completes the first new sequence you must make.

To form the second sequence, proceed as follows:

1. Do just the same as for sequence No. 1, except for the following:
   - Enter zero as the first number of this sequence.
   - Instead of adding the appropriate numbers to get new ones, subtract. Always subtract the earliest number in your original series of stock prices from the later number.
   - Do not divide the final number by two as you did before. Instead, change the last number to zero.
2. Identify this whole new tabulation as sequence No. 2.

This completes your two new sequences of numbers. All further operations will be conducted on these number series rather than on the original stock prices.

## DETERMINING THE FREQUENCIES IN YOUR ANALYSIS

Remember what it is you are accomplishing in doing a Fourier analysis. You are trying to determine the angular frequency, amplitude, and phase of a predetermined number of "slices" through the frequency spectrum of the stock price history being analyzed. The thing that determines how finely your analysis will "slice," and therefore how well you are able to separate any frequency peaks or valleys that may exist, is the amount of data you assemble to analyze and the length of the time period involved. So the very next thing you must do is to determine the precise angular frequencies associated with your particular analysis.

Let us assume that you have selected "$m$" price data points for analysis. Form the quantity $\left(\frac{m-1}{2}\right)$. Then divide this into the constant, $\pi = 3.14159\ldots$ Call the resulting quantity:

$$Z = \frac{\pi}{(m-1)/2}$$

Now form a new page for data tabulation. Head the first column "$\omega$," representing the angular frequencies about which your analysis is going to provide you with information. Calculate these frequencies as follows:

- The first one is zero (zero frequency represents infinitely long periods, or in other words a value without oscillation).
- The second one is just the value of "$Z$" that you found earlier, divided by the digital data spacing you have chosen.
- The third one is two times "$Z$," divided by digital data spacing.
- The fourth one is three times "$Z$," divided by digital data spacing.
- Continue calculating frequencies and tabulating them in this manner until the number you are multiplying "$Z$" by is the number, $\frac{m-1}{2}$, that you computed earlier.

At this point you can see clearly just how many samples your analysis will provide of the frequency spectrum of the stock you are analyzing. You may convert any of these angular frequencies ("$\omega$") to the corresponding sinusoidal period by the relationship:

$$T = \frac{2\pi}{\omega}$$

A word here about units. If you have selected daily data to analyze, the angular frequencies calculated above will be in units of radians per day. If your selection was of weekly data, the frequency will be in units of radians per week, etc. It is a good idea always to convert your computed frequencies to some common unit of measure to avoid confusion. Radians per year is a good choice. Thus, frequency in radians per week must be multiplied by 52 to get radians per year, and so forth. Similarly, when you convert angular frequency in radians per year to period by using the relationship $T = \frac{2\pi}{\omega}$ the period "$T$" will come out in years. If you had used frequency in radians per week in this conversion, the period would have come out in weeks.

## NOW COMPUTE THE CORRESPONDING AMPLITUDES

The reason for separating your original price series into two new sequences was to allow computation of the amplitudes of not only a sine-wave series, but an associated cosine series as well. A cosine wave is shaped just like a sine wave but is 90 degrees out of phase (one-fourth cycle) with the reference sine wave. The sum of two such wave forms is simply another wave form with the same frequency, but with differing amplitude and phase. We will now calculate the amplitudes of the Fourier sine and cosine waves associated with each of the frequencies you've found that the analysis considers–for the particular stock price sequence you're using. Afterwards, you will be shown how to combine these into a single spectrum.

We will start with sequence No. 1, which provides the amplitudes of the cosinusoidal components.

First, find the amplitude of the cosinusoidal component associated with the first angular frequency ($\omega = 0$) in your tabulation. To do this, add up all the numbers in sequence No. 1, and divide by the number, $\frac{m-1}{2}$, that you found earlier. The result is the amplitude you seek.

The amplitude of the cosinusoidal component associated with the second angular frequency in your tabulation is found as follows:

1. Note the value of the first number in sequence No. 1.
2. Now find the cosine of the number "$Z$" from a set of trigonometric tables. Multiply this by the second number in sequence No. 1. Add the result to Item 1 above.
3. Now find the cosine of the number $2 \times Z$. Multiply this by the third number in sequence No. 1. Add the result to Item 2 above.
4. Find the cosine of the number $3 \times Z$. Multiply this by the fourth number in sequence No. 1, and add the result to Item 3 above.
5. Proceed in this manner until you run out of numbers in sequence No. 1.
6. Divide the final result (sum of results of all intervening steps) by the number, $\frac{m-1}{2}$.

   Enter this as the amplitude of the cosinusoidal component associated with the second angular frequency in your list.

The amplitude of the third cosinusoidal component is found as follows:

1. Proceed exactly as for component No. 2–except before looking up any of the required cosines in the trigonometric tables, multiply the quantity obtained before by two, then look up the cosine of the result.

For the fourth component, proceed as for the third, but multiply by three before finding the cosine in the tables.

Proceed in this manner until you have found a corresponding cosinusoidal amplitude for each angular frequency in your tabulation.

Now compute the amplitudes of the sinusoidal components associated with the same frequencies. The process is similar to the one you have just completed with three small differences:

1. You will use the numbers in sequence No. 2 now instead of No. 1.
2. Instead of looking up cosines in the tables, you will look up sines.
3. The amplitude of the first sinusoidal component is zero.

With these exceptions, proceed exactly as you did when finding the cosinusoidal amplitudes.

## HOW TO GET COMPOSITE AMPLITUDES

Now go back to your frequency tabulation. For each frequency you now have an associated amplitude for a cosinusoidal and a sinusoidal component. Form the square root of the sum of the squares of these amplitude pairs for each frequency. This is the composite amplitude of the oscillatory component of the frequency associated with it in your table, which exists in the original stock price data. Plot the pairs of amplitudes and frequencies as shown in Figure A I-1. You may either plot amplitude vs. angular frequency, or you can first convert angular frequency to period, plotting this against amplitude. With this step your Fourier analysis is complete!

## THE KIND OF RESULTS YOU CAN EXPECT

This kind of analysis has been completed using 2300 weekly close data points of the DJ 30 Industrial Average. The results are plotted in the Appendix, and the interpretation of them is given along with correlations to spectral analysis using other methods.

You must always remember that such a Fourier analysis does not necessarily imply that the resulting oscillatory components are in the original data because of having been generated separately and summed to the total. For example, you may draw a sloping line on a piece of paper, then tabulate the pairs of points making up this line. A Fourier analysis of the resulting data will produce a set of oscillating components which can be made to approximate the original line (when summed) as closely as you desire. The analysis has found the spectrum of the line for you, but this does not imply that the line was originally formed by adding up this series of components. As a matter of fact, you formed it by simply drawing a ruled line!

A Fourier analysis is always a good starting point when you suspect hidden periodicities, but other techniques must be used if you wish to learn more about whether the originating process put all or part of the periodic components into the spectrum to begin with. If they were not brought about in such a manner, the resulting spectral analysis may tell you many things, but it will not permit prediction by extrapolation of periodicities.

This is the really fascinating point about which this whole book revolves: the fact that about 23% of all price motion is not part of an artificial frequency spectrum, but instead represents a basic, intrinsic process whereby that part of price motion is formed. The case for this is further developed in the Appendix.

## HOW NUMERICAL FILTERS CAN HELP YOU

The most familiar example of a filter is a sieve. Such a device allows particles under a certain size to pass, while holding back those that are larger. A sieve thus separates granular material into two parts. One of these contains particles smaller than a certain size while the other contains particles larger than that size. The basic function of a filter is to separate something into parts according to some specified characteristic of that which is being separated.

A numerical frequency filter behaves the same way. It separates that part of digital data which contains frequencies below a certain value from that part of the data which contains frequencies above that same value.

When a filter just separates data into two parts, it is known as a "cutoff" filter. A moving average is a crude filter of this type as shown in the Appendix. The moving average process stops the passage of high frequencies (short periods), and permits the passage of low frequencies (long periods). Just as the size of the mesh in a sieve sets the separation point for granular material, so the span of a moving average sets the frequency separation point.

But a sieve divides particles into two parts, large and small. The moving average seems to throw away high frequencies, while saving the lows. Recall now the "inverted" moving average of Chapter Six. This is the numerical filter equivalent of the sieve process that allows retention of the small particles. The inverted average throws away the low frequencies and retains the highs. By using both the normal and the inverted moving average on data, the full function of the sieve is duplicated with regard to the frequency characteristics of data instead of the size characteristics of physical particles.

But filters can do even more than this. Suppose you used a sieve to separate sand into two piles. Then suppose you screened the pile with the largest particles, using a sieve with slightly larger holes. You would then have three piles of sand. One of them contains all grains smaller than a certain size. The next contains all grains between this certain size and another larger one. The third contains all particles larger than those in the second pile.

These processes can also be duplicated by frequency filters. The filtering process which produces results that lie between two fixed bounds is called a band-pass filter operation, and is particularly useful in the analysis of stock price data. Such filters were employed to produce the results of Figures II-13 and IX-4 and a good part of the results in the Appendix. Filters of this nature are an indispensable tool when you undertake research of the price motion of stocks.

The type of filter that passes low frequencies but not highs (à la a moving average) is called a low-pass filter. Similarly, a filter that passes high frequencies but not lows is called a high-pass filter. All three types, low-pass, band-pass, and high-pass, belong in your arsenal if you desire to research market data.

## WHAT YOU MUST KNOW ABOUT FILTER OPERATION

We have already noted in the case of the low-pass filter operation known as a moving average that there is a time lag to the output. This simply means that the latest data resulting from the filter operation never reflects up-to-date events. Put another way, it means that current time filter output results depend on events which have not yet occurred.

This is an example of a general characteristic of all numerical filters. To obtain precise knowledge, using a filter, of the nature of the frequency content of data, you must sacrifice knowledge of how that spectrum is affected by recent data. In fact, the more precisely you construct a frequency filter to perform the function of separating frequencies, the more time lag you must tolerate. A moving average is a rather poor instrument for frequency separation, and as a result it has a rather small time lag associated with it. Much more effective filters can be constructed and used, but only at the cost of increased lag.

Because of the minimal lag and reasonable frequency separation capability, the moving average is an acceptable compromise for use in the kind of real time, predictive analysis presented in previous chapters. In such work, the lag must be kept small, and a moving average does as good a job for its lag as any filter can do.

On the other hand, lag is not nearly as important as effective frequency separation when you are researching for helpful relationships in market data. Plenty of past information is available, and tests of applicability of results to the real-time situation can always come later.

To improve the frequency separation characteristics of a filter, you must increase the span of time it covers. With such an increase, the lag automatically increases, since it is, as for the moving average, half the span of the filter. Some of the filters described in the Appendix have time lags of many years!

When using filters you should become familiar with the term "frequency response." This is a characteristic which completely identifies and describes the effectiveness of a filter. Conceive of the numbers you derive via a filtering process as the output of the filter. Similarly, picture the stock price data on which the filter operates as the input to the filter. If you then divide the numbers of the output by the numbers of the input, the resulting quantity is called the "amplitude ratio." If a sine wave is present in the stock data of a given amplitude, and it is reproduced in the output at the same amplitude, the amplitude ratio is one (for sine waves of that particular frequency). In short, the filter has not changed the amplitude—or has "passed" it intact.

Similarly, if a sine wave of a given amplitude is present in the data but is completely non-existent (or of zero amplitude) in the filter output, the amplitude ratio of the filter for that frequency is zero. Clearly, for the filter to perform its function of frequency separation the amplitude ratio of the filter must vary from 0.0 to 1.0, dependent on the frequency of the sine waves put into it.

There is another characteristic of frequency response with which we will not be overly concerned in this introduction, but of which you should be aware. This is called "phase response." Phase response is a measure of how much if any a filter operation changes the phase-time of a sine wave on which it operates. Thus, it is seen that a filter can modify an input sine wave both as to its amplitude and with respect to sliding it backward or forward in time.

The two quantities, amplitude ratio and phase response, together make up the frequency response of a filter. These quantities vary as the frequency elements of the data input to the filter vary, and between them they completely describe the qualities and capabilities of a filter.

## THE PART OF "WEIGHTS" IN NUMERICAL FILTERS

You have already learned how to design normal and inverted moving average filters in previous chapters. There is a very large number of ways in which more effective numerical filters can be designed to make them do what you want. The bibliography contains a broad sample of references to some of these. As an introduction to the subject and to get you started, the design criteria of just one class of these will be presented here. You will undoubtedly wish to follow up the references to develop more capability in this highly interesting field.

All such filters have one aspect in common. They use what are called "weights" to achieve the desired results.

Weights are simply numbers which are derived as a result of filter design. In applying a numerical filter, you simply multiply each weight by the proper stock price datum and sum up these products to obtain the filter output. Determination of the number and precise value of these weights in order to achieve the needed filtering results is the object of filter design work.

This is true even in the case of a moving average, although the usual process of moving average application masks this fact. Recall that to cause a moving average to do what you want it to do, you set a cutoff frequency by selection of the span of the average. Suppose the resulting average utilizes "$N$" data points. The process of forming the latest possible moving average output consists of summing up the last "$N$" stock prices, then dividing by "$N$." This is precisely equivalent to the more arduous task of dividing each of the last "$N$" stock prices by "$N$," and summing up these fractions. This, in turn, is the same as multiplying each of the last "$N$" stock prices by $\frac{1}{N}$ and summing results. From this it is seen that a moving average simply uses constant weights. Each weight has a value of $\frac{1}{N}$.

If you plot these moving average weights in the chronological order of the stock prices to which they are applied, the result is a square wave. In essence, all price data prior to the $N$'th one before the last are multiplied by zero. All price data from the $N$'th one to the last one are multiplied by $\frac{1}{N}$. All future prices are likewise not involved in the average, or are effectively multiplied by zero. The resulting square wave you've plotted is the so-called "weighting function" of a moving average.

The four square corners of this weighting function cause many of the adverse characteristics of a moving average (which are discussed in the Appendix). To improve the characteristics, these must be rounded in a particular manner. The following design criteria accomplish this, resulting in one specific class of numerical filters suitable for research work.

## HOW TO DESIGN YOUR OWN NUMERICAL FILTERS

The design presented here is one of several developed and discussed by Joseph F. A. Ormsby in a paper dated March, 1960 (see bibliography for details).

The techniques of this paper have been combined to form band-pass design criteria in this example, since this will be of the most use to you. The reference will provide you directly with the corresponding low- and high-pass filter designs.

There are several decisions that you must make before you can start a design.

First of all you must decide the time spacing you are going to use for your stock price data. This will become a design parameter of your filter, and that particular filter must always be applied against stock data of the same time spacing.

Secondly, you must decide how many filter weights you are going to use. The number you select must be odd.

Finally, you must determine the steepness of skirt slope you desire your filter to have. This means how rapidly the amplitude ratio of the filter rises from 0.0 (at the lower-bound cutoff frequency) to a value of 1.0 (at the lower-bound rolloff frequency). This ratio will then remain more or less constant over the passband of the filter, until the upper-bound rolloff frequency is reached. It will then start to diminish, becoming zero again at the upper-bound cutoff frequency. The meaning of these terms will become clearer to you as you study the sample filter design of Figure XI-1.

All three of these quantities are involved in determining filter error. Error in filter design is unavoidable. This means that although we can approach ideal filter characteristics as closely as desired (at the expense of increased computational difficulty), we are never able to achieve the exact performance we want. Filter design is a matter of forming the required compromise in such a way as to accomplish our purposes to the best extent possible.

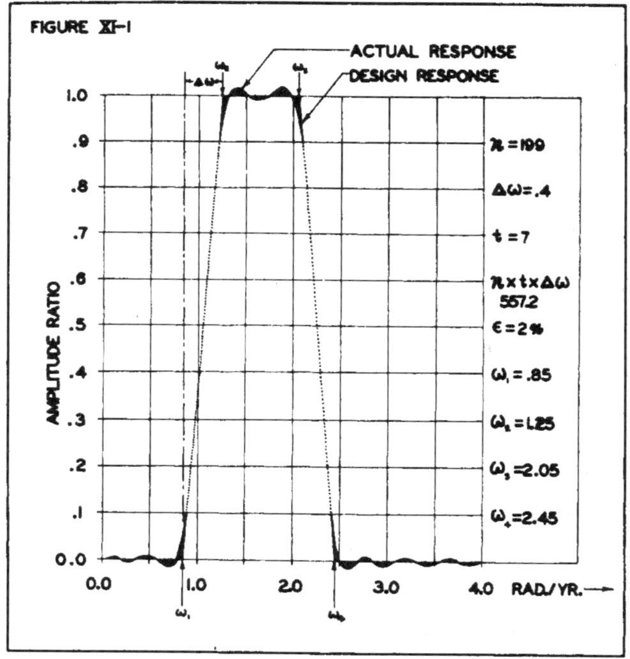


**A Typical, Digital-Filter Response Curve**

Precision filter error analysis is a very complex subject. To avoid getting into this and yet provide you with workable tools, Figure XI-2 has been prepared. This figure will bring you as close to being able to pre-determine your filter error as you will need to be.

Notice that error is a function of the product of three factors:

1. $\Delta\omega$ = frequency difference between cutoff and rolloff frequencies–or the measure of filter skirt slope, in radians per year.
2. $n$ = number of weights you use in your filter design.
3. $t$ = time spacing you choose to use between stock price data points in weeks.

**How To Control "Error" In A Digital Filter**

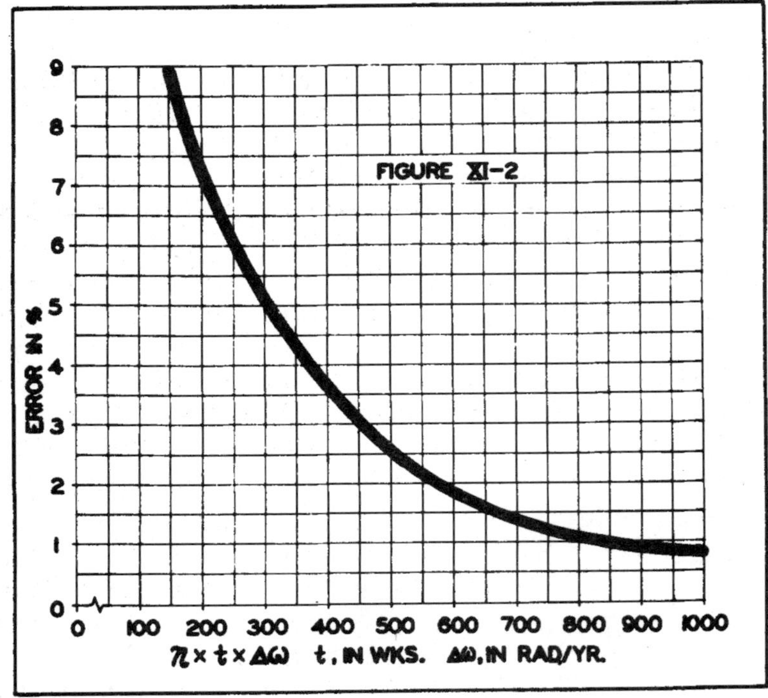


These are the same three quantities discussed in previous paragraphs, now related to filter error in percent.

For stock research work you should shoot for an ($n \times t \times \Delta\omega$) product of between 500 and 700. This will result in filter errors of about two and a half and one percent respectively.

Keep this in mind as you make your choices: You will want at least six or seven data points in the output of your filter for each cycle of the shortest duration frequency component that can be in your filter output. This will put a basic limit on how big you can make "$t$." Then, the larger you make $n$ the more work you will have to do both in designing and applying the filter, but the smaller you can make $\Delta\omega$ (which makes your filter more effective). Similarly, to reduce the amount of work, you may reduce $n$ but you will then have to make $\Delta\omega$ larger, reducing filter efficiency. In extreme cases you can even use filter errors of up to five or six percent–and you will still be surprised at how effectively you can extract cyclicalities.

At this stage of filter design you have made the following choices:

1. $\omega_1$ = the lowest frequency of the four: that frequency below which you wish amplitude ratio to be zero, and for which you wish higher frequencies to start being "passed" by the filter.
2. $\omega_2$ = the next higher frequency of the four: that frequency at which you wish amplitude ratio to first become equal to 1.
3. $\omega_3$ = the next higher frequency of the four: that frequency at which you wish amplitude ratio to still equal 1.0, but at which you desire higher frequencies to start to be attenuated.
4. $\omega_4$ = the highest of the four frequencies you must select: that frequency at which

you wish amplitude ratio to have again reached 0.0, and beyond which you want all higher frequencies to be attenuated to zero.

5. $t$ = time spacing in weeks between the data points you are going to use representing stock prices.
6. $n$ = number of weights in your filter.

These quantities are illustrated graphically in Figure XI-1. For this design the number of filter weights is 199. $\Delta\omega$ (the measure of skirt slope) is .4 radians per year. The data spacing to be used on stock prices, "$t$," is seven weeks. The product of these is 557.2, resulting in an error of about two %. The low-end rolloff frequency is $\omega_2$, while that for the high end is $\omega_3$. The low-end cutoff frequency is $\omega_1$, while that for the high end is $\omega_4$. The shaded areas show the error, or the amount by which actual filter performance is different from the response we were trying to achieve by the design.

These design choices provide 50% or more filter response across a pass-band of frequencies corresponding to sinusoidal components with periods of 2.8 to 6.0 years. Such a filter is suitable for investigation of oscillations of the order of four and a half years' duration–a dominant element of the price-motion model.

Note that $\Delta\omega$ is simply $(\omega_2\text{-}\omega_1)$ or $(\omega_4\text{-}\omega_3)$. At this stage of your experience you should make $\Delta\omega$ equal for both high and low rolloff.

The next step is the computation of several quantities that will be common to the calculation of all $n$ weights. Where necessary, these quantities will be assigned symbols so that you can keep them straight.

1. First set:
   - Calculate the quantity: $\frac{n-1}{2}$
   - Calculate the quantity: $\omega_n = \frac{104\pi}{t}$
2. Second set:
   - Calculate the quantity: $\lambda_1 = \frac{\omega_1}{\omega_n}$
   - Calculate the quantity: $\lambda_2 = \frac{\omega_2}{\omega_n}$
   - Calculate the quantity: $\lambda_3 = \frac{\omega_3}{\omega_n}$
   - Calculate the quantity: $\lambda_4 = \frac{\omega_4}{\omega_n}$
3. Third set:
   - Calculate the quantity: $\lambda_5 = \lambda_1 - \lambda_2$
   - Calculate the quantity: $\lambda_6 = \lambda_4 - \lambda_3$
4. Fourth set:
   - Calculate the quantity: $2\pi\lambda_1$
   - Calculate the quantity: $2\pi\lambda_2$
   - Calculate the quantity: $2\pi\lambda_3$
   - Calculate the quantity: $2\pi\lambda_4$
   - Calculate the quantity: $2\pi^2\lambda_5$
   - Calculate the quantity: $2\pi^2\lambda_6$

The final step is the calculation of the weights themselves. Only one-half of these and the unique central one must be computed, since the weighting function will be symmetrical about the middle weight.

Compute the first weight as follows:

- Look up the cosine of $2\pi\lambda_3$ in your trigonometric tables.
- Subtract from this the cosine of $2\pi\lambda_4$.
- Divide the difference by $2\pi^2\lambda_6$.
- Make a note of the resulting quantity, identifying it as "A."
- Now look up the cosine of $2\pi\lambda_2$.
- Subtract from this the cosine of $2\pi\lambda_1$.
- Divide this difference by $2\pi^2\lambda_5$.
- Make a note of the resulting quantity, identifying it as "B."
- Form the difference, A-B.
- Tabulate this as your first weight.

Compute the second weight exactly the same way as the first except for the following differences:

- Multiply $2\pi\lambda_3$, $2\pi\lambda_4$, $2\pi\lambda_2$, and $2\pi\lambda_1$ by two before you look up the cosines.
- Multiply $2\pi^2\lambda_6$ and $2\pi^2\lambda_5$ by $2^2$ or $2 \times 2$ before you use them as divisors.

Compute the third weight exactly the same way as the first except for the following differences:

- Multiply $2\pi\lambda_3$, $2\pi\lambda_4$, $2\pi\lambda_2$, and $2\pi\lambda_1$ by three before you look up the cosines.
- Multiply $2\pi^2\lambda_6$ and $2\pi^2\lambda_5$ by $3^2$ or $3 \times 3$ before you use them as divisors.

Continue in this manner until you are ready for the central weight. Compute it as follows:

- Form the sum, $\lambda_3 + \lambda_4$.
- Subtract from this the sum, $\lambda_1 + \lambda_2$.
- The result is the value of the unique central weight.

The next weight after the central weight is identical to the weight just before it.

The second weight after the central one is identical to the second weight before it.

Continue tabulating the remaining weights until you have all $n$ of them written down. Now sum all of the weights you've tabulated and divide the result by $n$. Subtract this quantity from each of the previously calculated weights to get new values for each.

The design of your filter is now complete.

## APPLYING YOUR NUMERICAL FILTER TO STOCK PRICES

There is no shortcut to applying this type of filter to stock price data as in the case of a moving average. Each output data point must be obtained in the same way, namely by summing the products of each weight with the associated stock prices.

Proceed as follows:

Tabulate your stock prices in chronological order on a continuous, long strip of paper. Be sure to use the data spacing for which you designed your filter.

Tabulate your filter weights (in the order in which they were derived) on another long thin strip of paper.

Starting at the beginning of your price data, lay the filter weight strip alongside so that the first filter weight is opposite the first price datum. Mark your filter strip at the center. This mark will coincide with the price datum to which the first filter output applies.

Now multiply each stock price by the associated (opposite) filter weight to get $n$ sums. Add these all together. The result is the filter output associated with the central price datum.

Now slide your filter strip one data space forward. The center of the strip picks out the next price datum to which the filter output applies. Repeat the multiplications and summing process to get the second filter output number.

Repeat the process until you run out of prices. You will note that you have no filter output corresponding to the last $\frac{n-1}{2}$ stock price data. This is normal, and represents the one-half span lag of the filter.

Now you may plot both the stock prices and the filter outputs on a single chart in order to see visually what the filter has done for you.

Figure IX-4 is an excellent example of what can be accomplished. In this case, Items 1 through 6 on the chart are the outputs of six different band-pass filters, so designed that their response curves overlapped. As noted in Chapter Nine, over three million computations were required to design and apply the filters which produced this chart. However, the insight gained by the effort into the nature of price motion fully vindicated the work involved. Who knows what you may accomplish as you start to design and use these interesting spectral analysis tools for yourself!

## TAKE ADVANTAGE OF CURVE FITTING

Once you obtain results from spectral analysis, you must be able to derive conclusions from them if they are to be useful. One of the most effective techniques to help you here is the process known as curve fitting. You will find in the index cross-references to the bibliography as well as to the text of this book that will enable you to pursue the subject as far as you like. As in the case of filters, just enough will be provided here to get you on your way.

Suppose you have designed and applied a numerical filter to stock price data. After plotting the results, you tabulate and plot the resulting periods of the sine-wave output. On your plot of this you notice that period (or frequency) as a function of time oscillates back and forth between narrow bounds, but generally trends either up or down. You would like to establish a straight-line "fit" of this frequency data in such a way that the equation of the resulting straight line is known. Further, you would like to use some logical criteria to do this based upon the data itself, rather than depend upon sketching such a line in by hand. The technique you want is called fitting to the data a least-square-error straight line.

## FIT YOUR DATA WITH A STRAIGHT LINE

The equation of any straight line is of the form:

$$P = A + B(t)$$

"$P$" is the variable you would plot vertically on a graph, and "$t$" is the variable you would plot horizontally.

"$A$" and "$B$" are constants for a given line. In fact, when known, these describe a particular straight line as uniquely as the quantities period, amplitude, and phase describe a particular sine wave.

Your present problem is to find values of "$A$" and "$B$" for a straight line which comes as close as possible to fitting all of the points on your frequency vs. time plot. For consistency we can rewrite the line equation using the symbols assigned to frequency and time earlier in the chapter:

$$\omega = A + B(t)$$

As rewritten, $\omega$ is the angular frequency you are measuring. (Remember that you can measure "period" from the filter output, then convert this to angular frequency.)

The quantity "t" now represents time from any arbitrary "time zero" (usually taken at the start of your data).

To start, arrange your data in two vertical columns, one for the measured frequencies, and the other for the times associated with them as measured from the chosen time zero. It is a good idea right here to make your time units compatible: i.e., if you use radians per year to describe frequency, use fractions of years to describe time, etc.

Now looking across the tabulation, the data appears in pairs–an angular frequency associated with a time in each case. Count the number of such pairs and label the result as "N."

You must now do the following things with this data and jot down the results:

1. Add up all the "ω's" and label the result "C."
2. Add up all the "t's" and label the result "D."
3. Square all the "t's" (multiply each one by itself), and add up these values. Label the sum "E."
4. Multiply each "ω" by the associated "t" and add up all the products. Label the result "F."
5. Square the sum of all the "t's" found in Step 2. Label the result "G."

You have now written down six numbers: N, the number of pairs of data points you have, and the numbers labeled C, D, E, F, and G.

The next step is to compute the numerical values of the equation constants desired, A and B. To do this, proceed as follows:

1. Multiply D by F and subtract the result from the product of C and E.
2. Multiply N and E together and subtract G from the product. Divide this result into the result of Step 1.
3. The number you get is the value of the constant "A" that you seek.
4. Now, multiply C by D and subtract the result from the product of N and F.
5. Divide the result of Step 4 by the number you used as a divisor in Step 2.
6. The number you get is the value of the constant "B" that you seek.

By replacing "A" and "B" in your basic equation with the corresponding values you have just derived, you establish the equation of the best-fitting straight line to your original data points.

Now you may select any two values of "t" that you wish, put them one at a time into your equation and solve for the corresponding "ω." This gives you two points to plot on the graph of the original data. Draw a straight line through them and see for yourself how well your best-fit line describes your data!

## HOW TO USE OTHER KINDS OF CURVE FITTING

You can find a way in the references to fit nearly any kind of curve you wish through data. However, two additional kinds of fits will handle 99% of all your market research work. Each of these requires somewhat more extensive arithmetic manipulation than that used for the straight-line fit, so the basic technique is located in the Appendix. Here we will discuss the need and use of these methods.

You recall that stock price data spacing became a design parameter for numerical filters. This means that you will probably find yourself faced from time to time with a situation like this:

- You have designed one filter using a given data spacing. The filter output then has this spacing also, say five weeks.
- You have designed another filter using a different data spacing. Let's say this one is three weeks.
- You desire to compare directly (or sum, or difference, or otherwise operate with) the outputs of the two filters. But the outputs will not compare directly because of the difference in the spacing of points where the values of each are known.

You can solve this problem by use of curve fitting techniques. What you must do is to fit a section of a curve such as a parabola through each possible consecutive set of three filter output data points. The resulting equations can then be solved to give you "in-between" values for both filter outputs which are associated with common times, and can therefore be directly compared. For the charts in this book, all filter results have been interpolated in this manner down to a common interval of one week. The technique for doing this you will find in the Appendix.

The third exceptionally useful data-fitting technique derives its utility from the nature of the results you get in analyzing stock price data. This is the Prony method of fitting curves to sine waves. The application is obvious in the analysis of filter results to determine objectively the frequency, amplitude, and phase of resulting sine waves. This technique is also described in the Appendix.

## SUMMARIZING NUMERICAL ANALYSIS

You now have at hand, or know where to go to get, the basic tools you need to research stock price data from the frequency spectrum standpoint. There are many other powerful aids available to you through numerical analysis, and as you pursue the references you will start to see their applicability to your own special problems. As you dig further into this field you should bear in mind the following:

- There are a number of ways in which you can analyze "spaced" or "sampled" data (such as stock prices) that can get you into trouble regarding conclusions. Always search the references for these stumbling blocks before applying a new method.
- Fourier analysis is a powerful tool for stock market research. However, the results achieved should always be verified and expanded by other spectral analysis methods before conclusive decisions are reached.
- Digital or numerical filters are a natural next step in the spectral analysis process.
- The disciplines of statistical analysis and the methods of curve fitting provide additional tools with which to work.
- The tools of numerical analysis are widely applied at universities and research institutes to help find solutions to a great variety of problems. They do not appear to have been used with equal vigor in the analysis of stock price motions. Why don't you try them for yourself–perhaps it will make the "competitive edge" difference you've been looking for in your stock market operations!

# *APPENDICES*

| | |
|---|---|
| appendix one | The Not-To-Be-Expected "Order" of Spectral Relationships in Stock Price Data |
| appendix two | Extension of "Average" Results to Individual Issues |
| appendix three | The Source and Nature of Transaction Interval Effects |
| appendix four | Frequency Response Characteristics of a Centered Moving Average |
| appendix five | Parabolic Interpolation |
| appendix six | Trigonometric Curve Fitting |

*appendix*

*one*

# The Not-to-Be-Expected "Order" of Spectral Relationships in Stock Price Data

- **The Implications of Fourier Analysis of Stock Prices**
- **Coarse Frequency Structure**
- **Fine Frequency Structure**
- **Amplitude-Frequency Relationship**
- **The Use of Comb Filters**
- **The Variables Involved**
- **Best Estimate of Spectral Line Spacing**
- **The Line Spectral Model**

In Chapter Two, a price-motion model was formulated that implied a surprising degree of order in the frequency spectra of stock prices. The basic tenets of the model were demonstrated primarily by observational methods, and were then shown to be sound by use of a number of price-predictive techniques which could work only if the theory behind them was reasonably correct.

Then, in Chapter Three, it was noted that the otherwise incomprehensible formation and repetition of specific chart patterns was fully explained by the assumed model, lending still further credence to the theory upon which the model is based.

In this Appendix, more powerful tools will be applied to the problem which demonstrate not only the remarkable breadth and consistency of the phenomena involved, but also bring to light new aspects, understanding of which can help extricate one from the occasional difficult situation.

## THE IMPLICATIONS OF FOURIER ANALYSIS OF STOCK PRICES

A hint of the unusual spectral order involved can be obtained from a high resolution harmonic analysis. Figure A I-1 is a plot of the results of such a project.

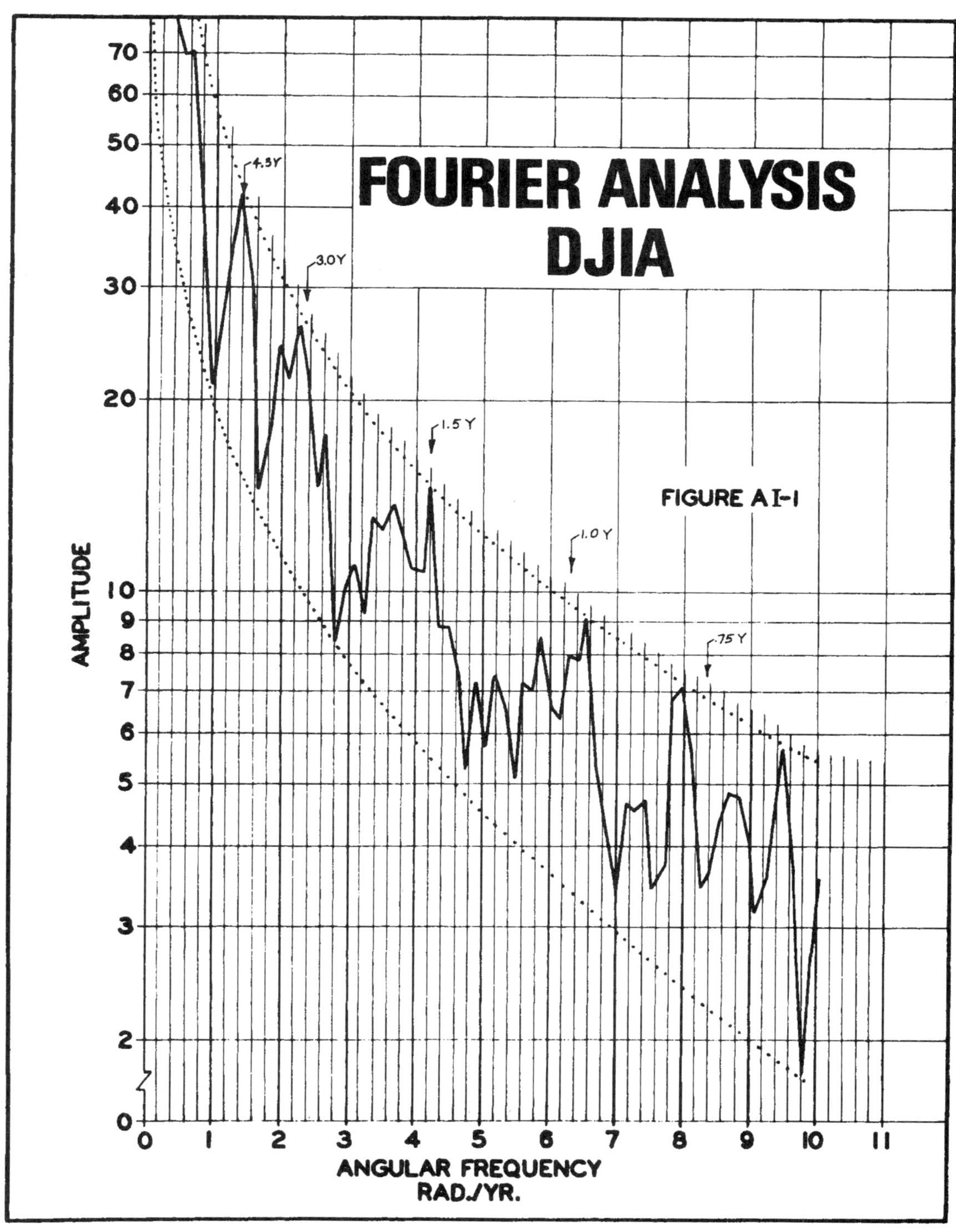


44 Years Of Market Cyclicality

This analysis was conducted on the weekly closing values of the Dow Jones Industrial Average over the time period 29 April 1921 through 25 June 1965. The resulting 2229 data points provided a frequency resolution of .568 radians per year.

Three major elements of spectral order are to be noted from the plot:

1. The resolution of spectral amplitudes into several broad segments with minimums approximately located at .95, 1.65, 2.8, 4.75, 7.0, and 9.8 radians per year.
2. The regularity of the fine frequency structure between the above major separation points.
3. The shape and smoothness of the upper envelope bound of the broad segments as drawn from peak to peak of each.

Let's discuss the significance of these unusual symptoms in order.

## COARSE FREQUENCY STRUCTURE

The coarse structure is seen to be divided into sections of increasing range of frequency as frequency increases. One is immediately forced to ask why this bit of order should exist in the spectra of a time series that is widely held to be randomly generated. Of even greater interest is the fact that the frequency peaks central to these large segments correspond to periodic price motion in the time domain that is readily observable (as demonstrated in several of the examples of Chapter Two). The sinusoidal periods associated with the central frequencies of these lobes is indicated (in years) in the figure, and each of these can be visually noted in the various samples of the DJIA presented in the chapters.

However, in the observational samples, fairly short periods of time are involved. In this case, we see evidence that the observationally isolated periodicities have persisted for at least 44 years. Any significant deviation from such a consistency would otherwise have averaged out both the broad peaks noted and the associated valleys.

## FINE FREQUENCY STRUCTURE

The regularity of the fine lobular structure between the coarse structure valleys is very apparent. In fact, these peaks average close to .8 radians per year in separation. It is significant that the broader lobes increase in width as frequency increases while the fine structure maintains equal spacing regardless of frequency. Although not shown in the figure, this statement applies all the way up to frequencies that can be resolved only by the use of trade-by-trade data.

The important observation that can be made is the fact that any degree of regularity is present at all. We arrive at the tentative conclusion that we may be dealing with a so-called "line" spectrum in the analysis of stock prices, and once again we are forced to ask why this element of spectral order should exist, let alone persist over long periods of time as we have seen demonstrated. Such order implies possible predictability in the time domain, and cannot be present if price fluctuations are randomly generated.

## AMPLITUDE-FREQUENCY RELATIONSHIPS

Fourier analysis results have one further surprise in store—the equation of the dotted upper boundary connecting coarse structure peaks in Figure A I-1 is:

$$a_i = \frac{k}{\omega_i}$$

Where "k" is a constant.

If we now assume the reality of a line spectrum, and ignore the possible existence of modulating lines for the sake of simplification, each component of the coarse structure is denoted as follows:

$$C_i = a_i \sin(\omega_i t + \phi_i)$$

Differentiating:

$$\dot{C}_i = a_i \omega_i \cos(\omega_i t + \phi_i)$$

And considering the previously noted relationship between $a_i$ and $\omega_i$:

$$\dot{C}_i = k \cos(\omega_i t + \phi_i)$$

This relationship implies that the maximum time rate of change of each spectral element in the coarse structure is identical to that of every other line in the spectrum—and that this delicate balance is maintained over many calendar years by a precise and particular relationship between amplitude and frequency!

Once more we are forced to question why such an orderly and interesting relationship should exist in the spectra of stock prices. And what about the implication regarding the nature of human decision processes which are responsible for price change and the resulting ordered spectral signature observed?

The above finding regarding equality of the maximum time rate of change of prices due to each spectral component is quite useful in applications, and is the basis of the simple technique of noting how many components are up or down at a given time in order to resolve chart patterns, etc. The very fact that this technique works constitutes a test of the general hypothesis. A detailed study of Figure IX-4 reveals just how effectively this test is passed.

## THE USE OF COMB FILTERS

The results of Fourier analysis are useful, but quite general in nature. In addition, numerical analysis based on equi-spaced digital data can sometimes lead to erroneous conclusions.

The results obtained can be validated and considerably extended through the use of overlapping combs of digital filters.

A typical such comb of filters is shown in Figure A I-2. In this particular case, the response bands of the individual filters were arranged with identically equal frequency spacings, and so constructed that each frequency was viewed by at least four separate filters. In this way, if spectral energy is not separated into discrete lines (as implied by the Fourier analysis), we should expect filter output more or less equally in all regions

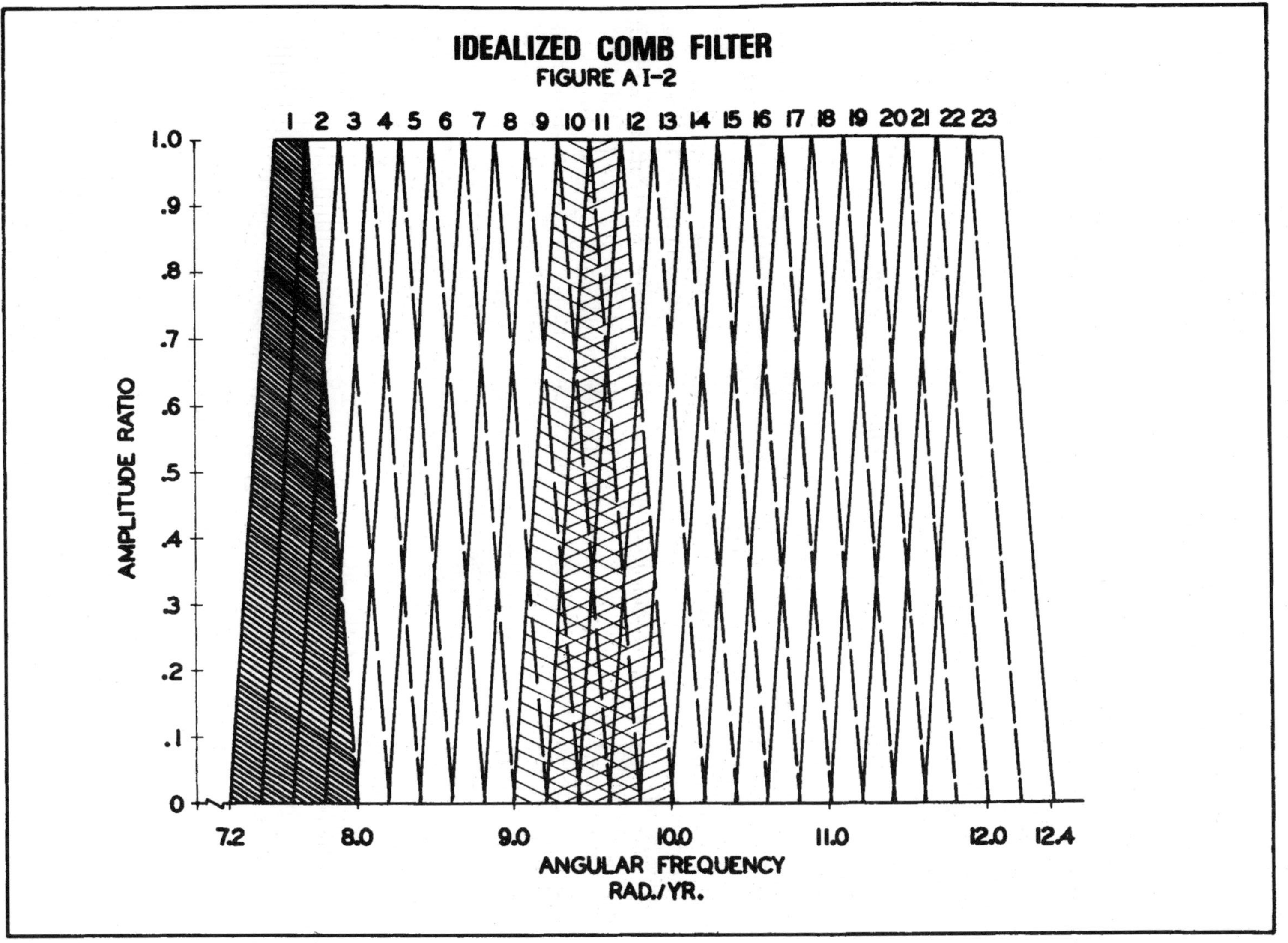


Setting Up Overlapping Band-Pass Filters

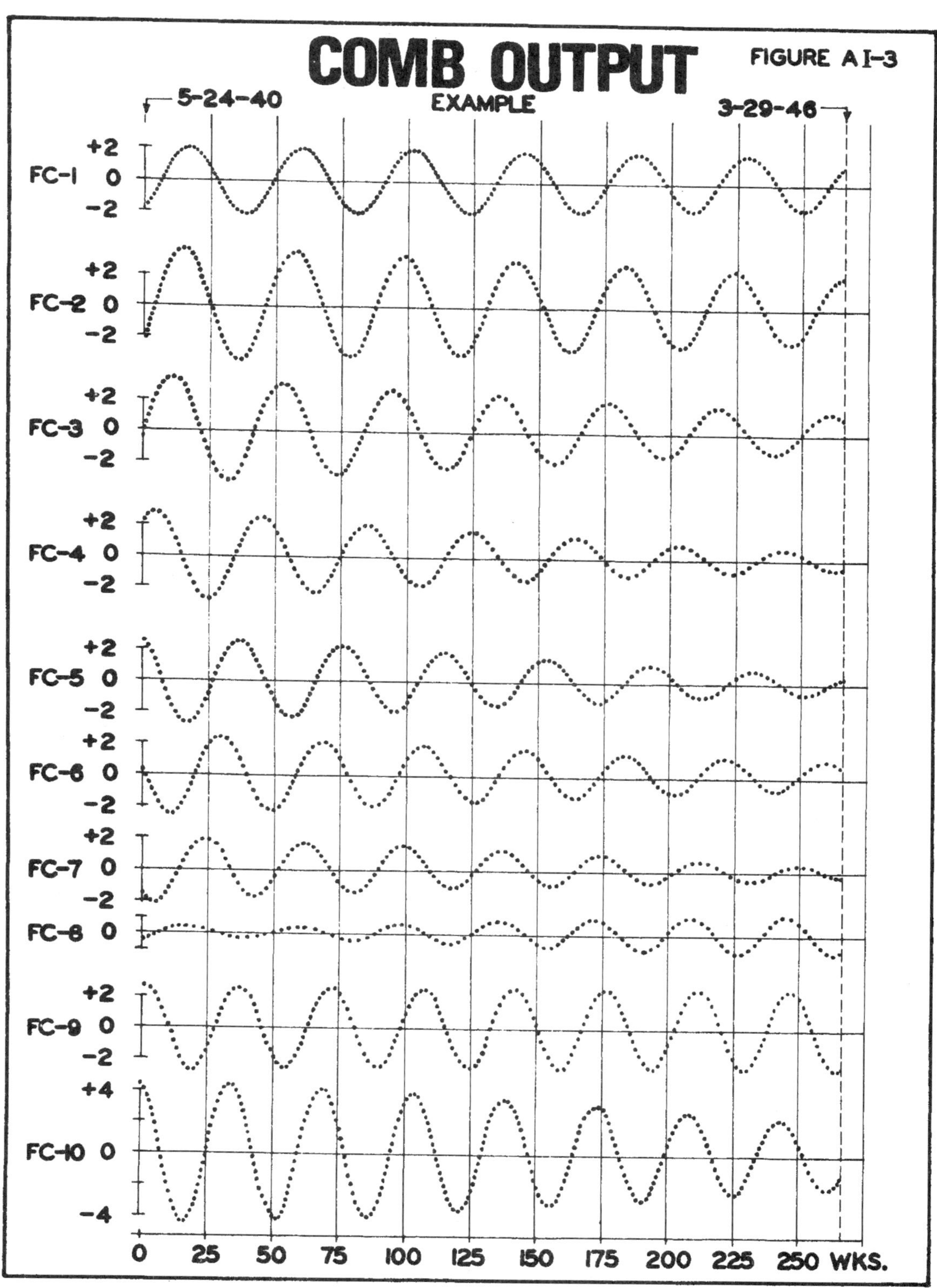


Typical "Comb" Filter Results

of the frequency domain. Likewise, we can hope to learn whether such lines (if they exist) tend to shift slowly with time or not. If sharp over short segments of time as indicated by filter output, the blurring of such lines indicated by the Fourier analysis would indicate slow drift with time.

Figure A I-3 is typical of the output generated from such combs. Each sine curve in time was frequency analyzed to permit study of frequency variations as a function of time.

Results for the 23 filters of this example are shown in Figure A I-4. Here, it is noted that the output of filters 1,2, and 3 are clustered in a narrow frequency band, then there is a "leap" in frequency to the output of filters 4, 5, 6, and 7. Outputs from several filters in the comb (such as 8, 12, and 16), whose response curves straddled the frequency gaps shown, fell completely outside the possible response pass-bands of the respective filter and were discarded as meaningless. All other filters provided outputs well within their response range.

It is seen that over the frequency range of 7.5 to 12 radians per year, filter outputs clustered in frequency bands. If the bands of these clusters are shaded in and

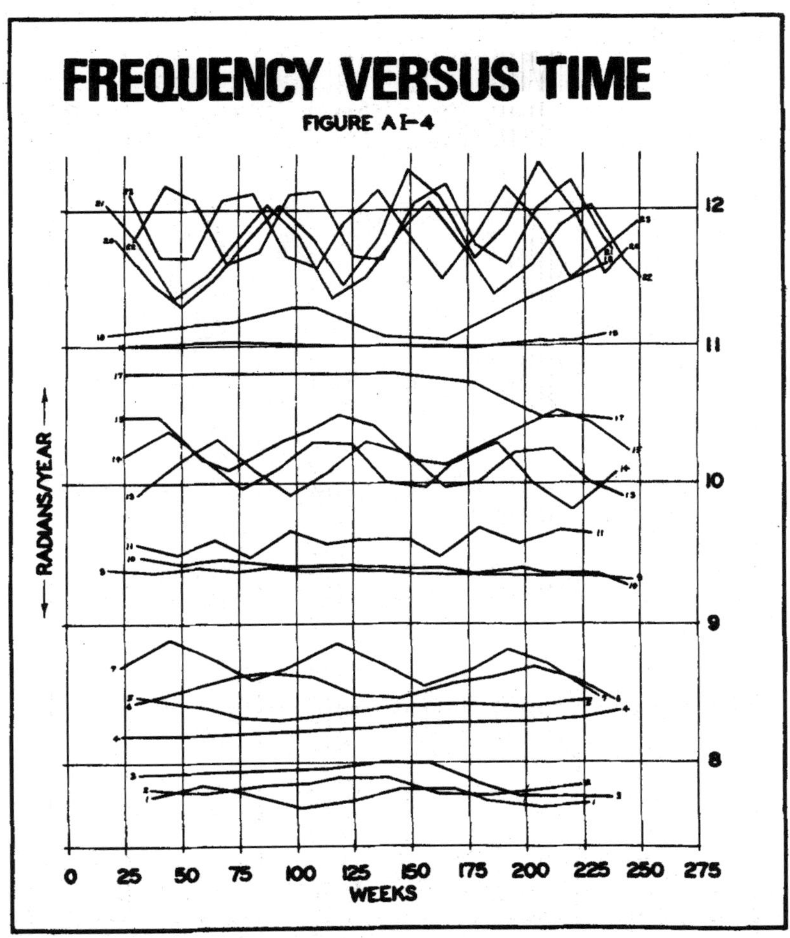


**The Incredible Frequency-Separation Effect!**

center lines are drawn an arbitrary .8 radians per year apart through them (the spacing of the fine structure noted in the Fourier analysis), the results appear as in Figure A I-5. Returning to Figure A I-1, it is seen how well these spectral "clumps" correspond to the fine frequency structure of the last coarse-frequency structure lobe of the Fourier analysis.

Furthermore, band definition is very sharp, lending credence to the suspicion that a slow drift of discrete spectral lines takes place with time. This effect can be tracked with special purpose filters and proven to exist.

Such comb filter analysis has been conducted over varying time periods for the DJIA, a number of individual issues, and over the entire frequency range from approximately .4 radians per year to the highest frequencies resolvable by daily data—with unvarying results.

The rate of time variance is a negligible factor in applications, as was to be suspected from the fact that the line character of the spectrum was not masked by a Fourier analysis over a 44-year interval. It nevertheless exists and in some situations can be profitably taken into account.

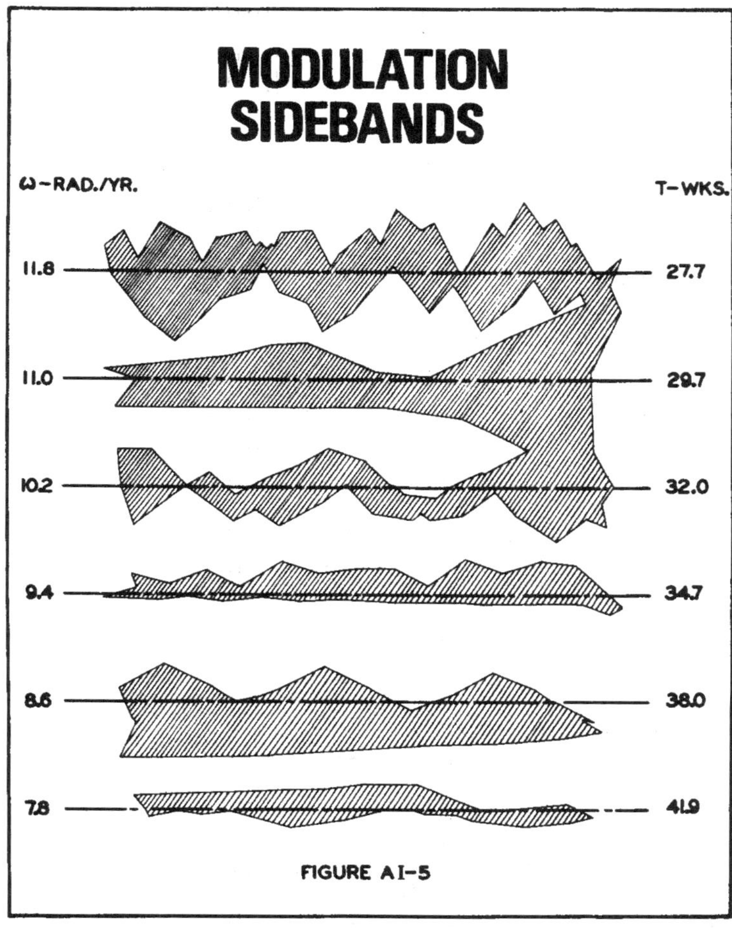


FIGURE A I-5

**The "Line" Frequency Phenomena**

## THE VARIABLES INVOLVED

The potential conclusion, of course, is that the spectrum of at least the DJIA consists of discrete frequency lines. (This conclusion is extended to a large segment of individual issues in Appendix Two.) This in turn leads to potential for predictability in the time domain, and to considerable amazement that the phenomena should exist at all!

However, before drawing such a conclusion, test of the invariance of the spectral signature is required over a large range of variables.

For example, in order to be sure that the noted effects are not a product of the analytical method or of the process of sampling a possible continuous function, results must be verified using random filter pass-bands in the combs, random variation of equal digital data spacing, variations in the degree of filter overlap, and non-equal digital data spacing. This was completed for the entire useful frequency range, and a sample of the results is shown in Figure A I-6.

Here, each filter output was frequency analyzed as a function of time. Additional smoothing of the results was obtained by passing a least-square-error straight line through the frequency versus time data. Each line on this figure represents such an output from one filter—and these outputs are taken from filters designed to sample the variables mentioned above.

The results show the same spectral grouping effects in the same frequency regions as for the Fourier analysis and for the equi-spaced filters working on equal digital data spacing. The conclusion reached is that the spectral signature effects noted are real and not due to vagaries of method of analysis.

## BEST ESTIMATE OF SPECTRAL LINE SPACING

If we now make the assertion that the hypothesis of a line spectrum is a valid one, we may obtain a highly smoothed best estimate of the minimum spacing between such lines by ranking the means of the least-square-error lines through frequency versus time data in order of increasing frequency.

This is done in Figure A I-7, where the resulting mean frequencies are plotted against the index number "N." The scatter along this curve is very small and the slope of the least-square-error straight line through the data points is the desired line spacing estimate. This does not mean, of course, that still more closely spaced lines do not exist, beyond the resolution of the filters used. The implication is certainly strong, however, not only that stock prices (or at least the fluctuations in the DJIA) exhibit a line frequency spectrum, but also that the lines are equally spaced.

The minimum line spacing is seen to be .3676 radians per year—just about one-half the spacing estimated from Fourier analysis. Going back to Figure A I-1, traces of such lines are seen to be visible between the peaks of the fine structure. Presence is, of course, largely inhibited by the limiting resolution of the analysis of approximately .5 radians per year.

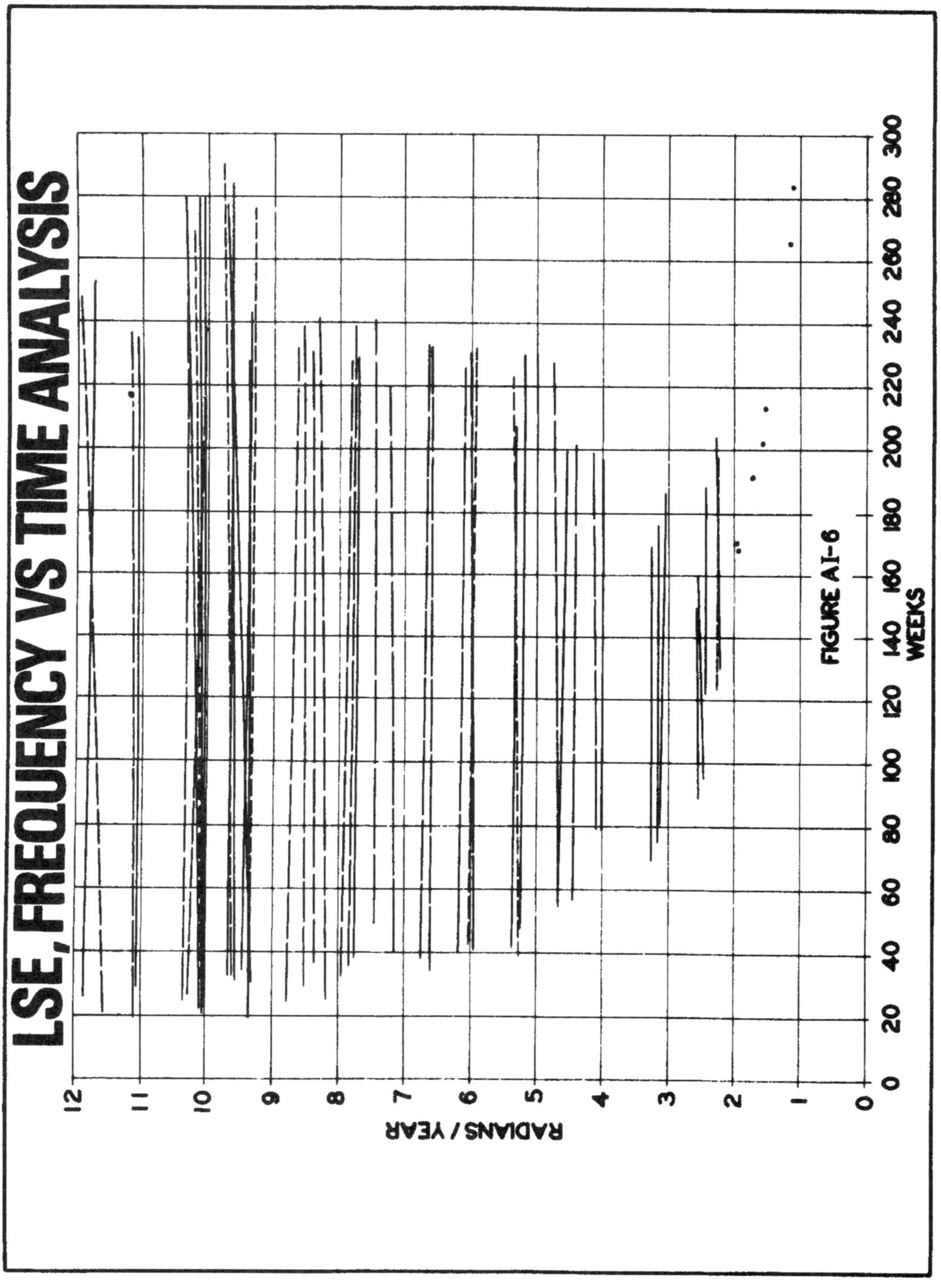


Smoothing Filtered Outputs

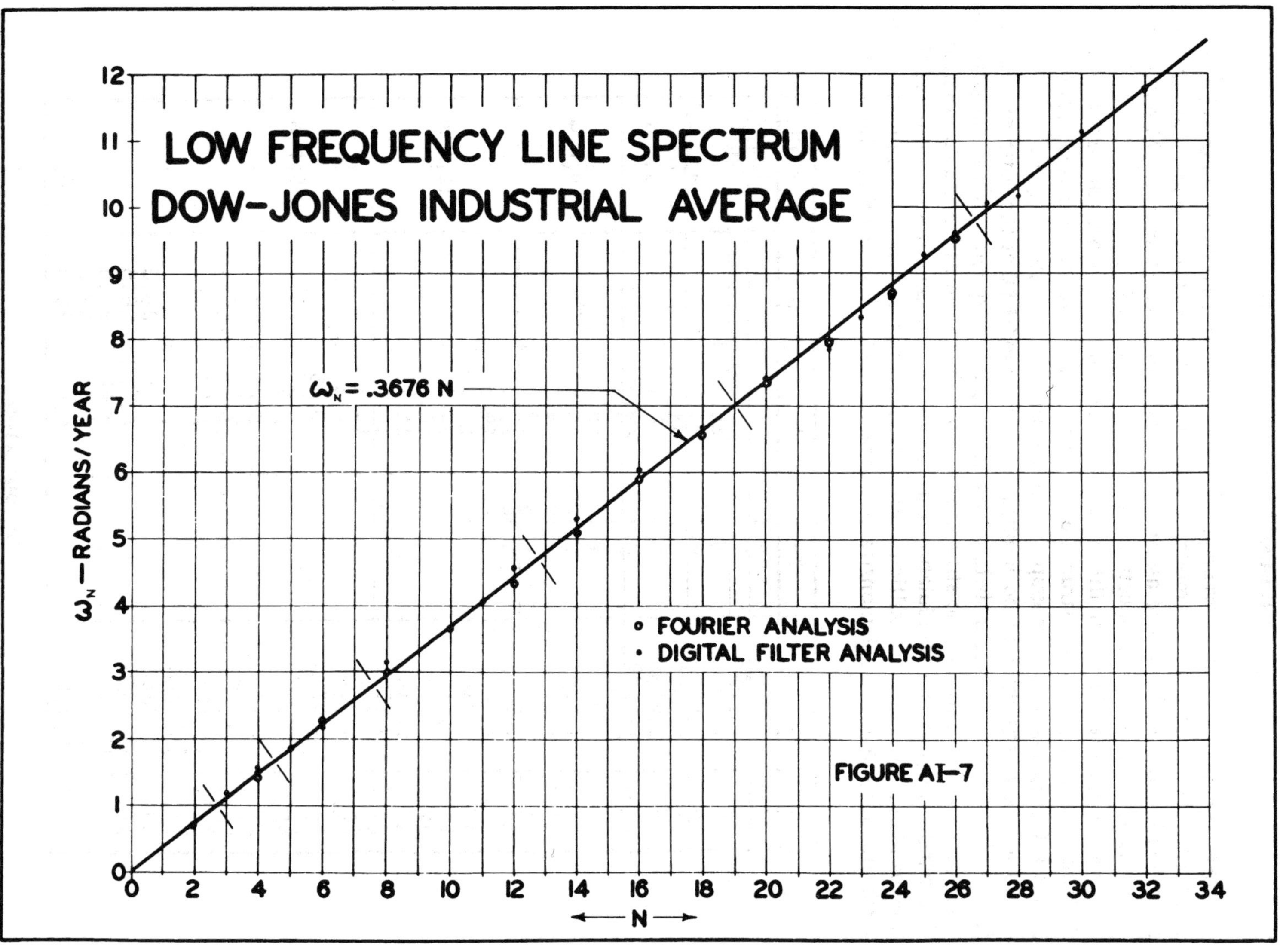


Best Estimate Of Line-Spacing

## THE LINE SPECTRAL MODEL

We can now use the presumed minimum regular spacing of spectral lines to establish a nominal spectral model of considerably more character than the one described in Chapter Two. The assumption of regularly spaced lines (.3676 radians per year separation) leads to the spectral groupings of Figure A I-8.

The horizontal lines on the chart are taken directly from the low amplitude dividing points of the coarse structure of the Fourier analysis. Results are completely in line with expectations from graphical, observational, and filter analysis.

The coarse structure to be implied from this model takes the form of a central group of spectral lines which behave like a "carrier" frequency in communications. Each of these has sets of fine structure lines which behave as amplitude modulation side bands. Some of the modulation side bands are also amplitude modulated (have side bands of their own), resulting in frequency modulation of the composite coarse structure wave form. As demonstrated repeatedly in the body of the book, this is

| N | $\omega_N$ | $T_Y$ | $T_M$ | $T_W$ | T, NOM. |
|---|---|---|---|---|---|
| 1. | .3676 | 17.1 | | | 18.0 Y |
| 2. | .7352 | 8.5 | | | 9.0 Y |
| 3. | 1.1028 | 5.7 | 68.5 | | |
| 4. | 1.4704 | 4.3 | 51.3 | | 4.3 Y |
| 5. | 1.8380 | 3.4 | 41.1 | | |
| 6. | 2.2056 | 2.9 | 34.2 | | 3.0 Y |
| 7. | 2.5732 | 2.4 | 29.4 | | |
| 8. | 2.9408 | 2.1 | 25.7 | | |
| 9. | 3.3084 | 1.9 | 22.8 | | |
| 10. | 3.6760 | 1.72 | 20.6 | | 18.0 M |
| 11. | 4.0436 | 1.60 | 18.7 | | |
| 12. | 4.4112 | 1.43 | 17.1 | | |
| 13. | 4.7788 | 1.32 | 15.8 | | |
| 14. | 5.1464 | 1.22 | 14.6 | | |
| 15. | 5.5140 | | 13.7 | | |
| 16. | 5.8816 | | 12.8 | | 12.0 M |
| 17. | 6.2492 | | 12.1 | | |
| 18. | 6.6168 | | 11.4 | | |
| 19. | 6.9844 | | 10.8 | | |
| 20. | 7.3520 | | 10.3 | | |
| 21. | 7.7196 | | 9.8 | | |
| 22. | 8.0872 | | 9.35 | | |
| 23. | 8.4548 | | 8.95 | | 9.0 M |
| 24. | 8.8224 | | 8.57 | | |
| 25. | 9.1900 | | 8.22 | | |
| 26. | 9.5576 | | 7.80 | | |
| 27. | 9.9252 | | 7.63 | | |
| 28. | 10.2928 | | 7.38 | | |
| 29. | 10.6604 | | 7.10 | | |
| 30. | 11.0280 | | 6.85 | 29.6 | |
| 31. | 11.3956 | | 6.65 | 28.8 | |
| 32. | 11.7632 | | 6.42 | 27.8 | |
| 33. | 12.1308 | | 6.22 | 27.0 | |
| 34. | 12.4984 | | 6.06 | 26.2 | 6.0 M |

**FIGURE A I-8**

**Low-Frequency Portion: Spectral Model**

exactly the observed nature of the periodic fluctuation of price with time. Special purpose filters can now be designed to isolate and study individual side bands. This has been done and the results confirm the detailed nature of the spectral model as described above. It is even possible to assemble a modulation model which links the elements of the spectral model in such a way as to explain the relationship $a_i = \frac{k}{\omega_i}$ noted in the Fourier analysis! Yet once again the question is posed: whence comes all this order in the spectral signature of a time series that is so widely believed to be random? It is clearly impossible for such relationships to exist in the frequency domain without counterpart order being present in the time domain.

The spectral model of Figure A I-8 indicates a lower limit to the cyclic portion of price motion in the vicinity of 18 years' duration. This is not necessarily the case. This limit is imposed simply because resolution of the analytical methods used to date show .3676 radians per year to be a possible minimum spacing. Other cyclic components may be crowded between .3676 radians per year and zero frequency, but their existence is academic to the applications. This is true not only because fluctuations of such long periods can be approximated over any reasonable transaction interval by a linear function, but also because of the constant maximum time rate of change relationship derived previously. This relationship essentially gives the vast number of high frequency components (whose periods grow ever more closely packed together as they decrease) dominance in the description of price fluctuations over the sparsely spaced, longer period components. In effect, each modulated component of the model has exactly the same maximum impact on price motion as that of any other, no matter what the disparity in amplitude may be.

Regarding the high-frequency end of the spectral model, no limit has been found to the order and precision of the spectral signature—right up to frequencies so high that they can be resolved only by using trade-by-trade data.

While the above results would seem to be strictly true only for the DJIA, extension of each finding to individual issues is possible. The results shown used samplings from many specific issues as well as the Averages, and are substantiated by some thousands of cases of graphical analysis and inferential testing. While it is impractical to repeat such extensive analysis on all of the listed issues, a good feeling for the commonality of the phenomenon is provided in Appendix Two.

# appendix two

# Extension of "Average" Results to Individual Issues

- **A Basis for the Principle of Commonality**
- **Spectral Signatures, Fundamentals, and Time Synchronization**

## A BASIS FOR THE PRINCIPLE OF COMMONALITY

The problem of demonstrating that the unusual and useful traits of the spectral signature of the Dow Jones Industrial Average apply to individual issues as well seems an overwhelming one. This would be most convincingly accomplished if a repetition of the studies summarized for the DJIA could be completed for every stock for which there is sufficient recorded data. This, of course, is a problem common to all generalizations. For example, Newton's famous law concerning the force of attraction between masses could scarcely be verified for every mass in existence. The procedure in such cases is to note effects from small samples, draw conclusions, extend the range of applicability to as large a sample as practicable, and then test the resulting hypothesis or "model" by forcing it to produce predictions which can be verified by real world action. In this situation, the DJIA constitutes the small sample, what follows is the extension to a large sample, and the predictive results of previous chapters are a sampling of real world tests of the hypothesis.

## SPECTRAL SIGNATURES, FUNDAMENTALS, AND TIME SYNCHRONIZATION

Figure A II-1 is a plot, on a logarithmic scale, of the weekly closing values of the DJIA and the S&P "500" average from 1949 into 1961.

The S&P "500" has each weekly value modified by a constant scale factor so that the total range of value over this time period matches that of the DJIA. This was done to provide direct comparison of the timing of value fluctuations without regard for relative volatility.

The implications are unmistakable. The long, sweeping undulations of each average are, of course, the nominal 4.5-year modulated cycle of the spectral model. This clearly exists in both.

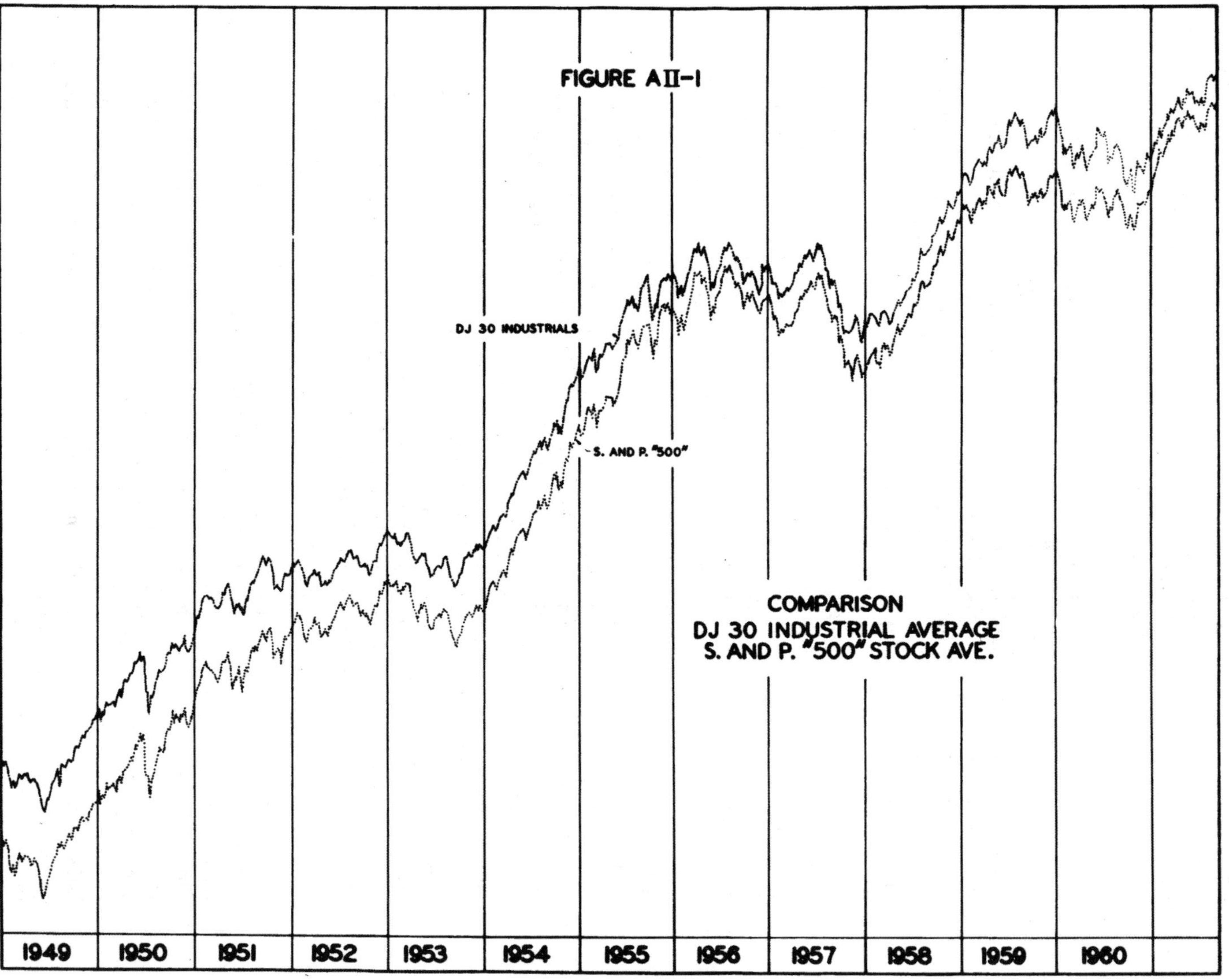


The Law Of Commonality; Generalized

As the eye follows each fluctuation of the DJIA, long or short, it is also found that the same identical fluctuation appears in the more comprehensive average. This is true down to the finest detail resolved by weekly data, and can be shown to be true also for oscillations resolvable only by daily data.

From this really incredible chart, the following conclusions are inescapably drawn:

- The time series of the two averages are so nearly identical that only minor spectral signature differences are possible between them.
- All results, conclusions, and implications derived from the spectral studies of the DJIA are now seen to apply (with but minor variations possible) to at least one-fourth of all the issues on both the New York and the American Stock Exchanges.
- At any given moment of time, the earnings and earnings potentials for the various issues of the S&P "500" are in all possible states. Some of the issues comprising this broad average have extremely good fundamental situations, some have extremely bad ones, and others exhibit all possible variations in between. If these considerations truly were the basis of price change, we would expect an average of some 500 resulting prices to show no coherency and order at all. In fact, we would expect the resulting price average to be quite smooth, with price variations due to all different fundamental situations averaged out. On the contrary, we now see that the average has a spectral signature with all the precise order shown for the DJIA!
- The above reasoning does not negate completely the potential of fundamentals to influence prices. Remember the scale factor difference that has been removed from the data in Figure A II-1 before conclusions were drawn. However, the evidence is clear that such factors do not have more than a negligible relationship to price fluctuations. The impact, if any, has to be in the area of volatility or the long-term, smooth price motion upon which the fluctuations of the spectral model ride. Given a lower frequency limit of the fluctuation model corresponding to periods of 18 years (or even of 9, or 4.5 years) it is seen that the remaining effect of fundamental factors must be quite smooth and slow changing indeed!
- Further, the same lines of reasoning apply to the DJIA. Again the earnings, earnings potential, and all other fundamental factors vary widely between the 30 issues involved at any given time, and certainly are not the same as for the constituents of the S&P "500." Again, not only do price changes supposedly due to these factors fail to average out, but the spectral signature displays coherency–*and goes beyond to show the same coherency exhibited in the larger average!* The conclusion is unavoidable that those fundamental considerations that are widely held to be so very effective in causing price change–and in fact are used as the basis for stock purchases and sales by individuals and institutions alike–simply are not the principal reason for the price motion that occurs!
- Finally, inspection of the timing of the turns of the fluctuations of the two averages demonstrates vividly the incredible degree of time synchronization of the spectral components involved in the fluctuations. Once again, if significant differences in spectral component phasing existed between individual issues, the fluctuations in the DJIA should at least be "smeared." This thinking would be even more valid for the average of 500 stocks, and the near-perfect identicality of fluctuations between the two averages would be simply impossible. This attribute of the principle of commonality was demonstrated with a single issue (Standard Packaging) in Chapter Two, and is dramatically extended by the implications of Figure A II-1.

# appendix three

# The Source and Nature of Transaction Interval Effects

- **Theoretical Yield-Rate Maximums vs. Transaction Interval**
- **The Impact of Compounding**
- **The Effect of Sinusoidal Rate Summation**

In Chapter One, it was demonstrated on a single issue that, given perfect transaction timing, yield rate is inversely proportional to transaction interval.

The effect demonstrated using a single stock can be quantified further. The same procedure was applied to 300 stocks, selected at random from both the New York and American Exchanges in equal numbers. Yield rate versus transaction interval was determined for each and the results averaged. The results appear on the left in Figure A III-1.

## THEORETICAL YIELD-RATE MAXIMUMS VS. TRANSACTION INTERVAL

The curve is inversely exponential with a significant "knee" between ten and 20 weeks. For transaction intervals of less than ten weeks the potential yield rate increases very steeply.

The significance of this, of course, is that it is worth almost any resource expenditure required to achieve significant shortening of average transaction intervals.

## THE IMPACT OF COMPOUNDING

In the same figure, on the right, are plotted two samples of the yield rate versus transaction interval directly from the compound interest law. It is obvious that the curve on the left derives its principal shape from the compounding effect. The lower of the two compound interest curves applies for average transaction profits of ten %each, while the upper one is derived for average transaction profits of 20% each. The

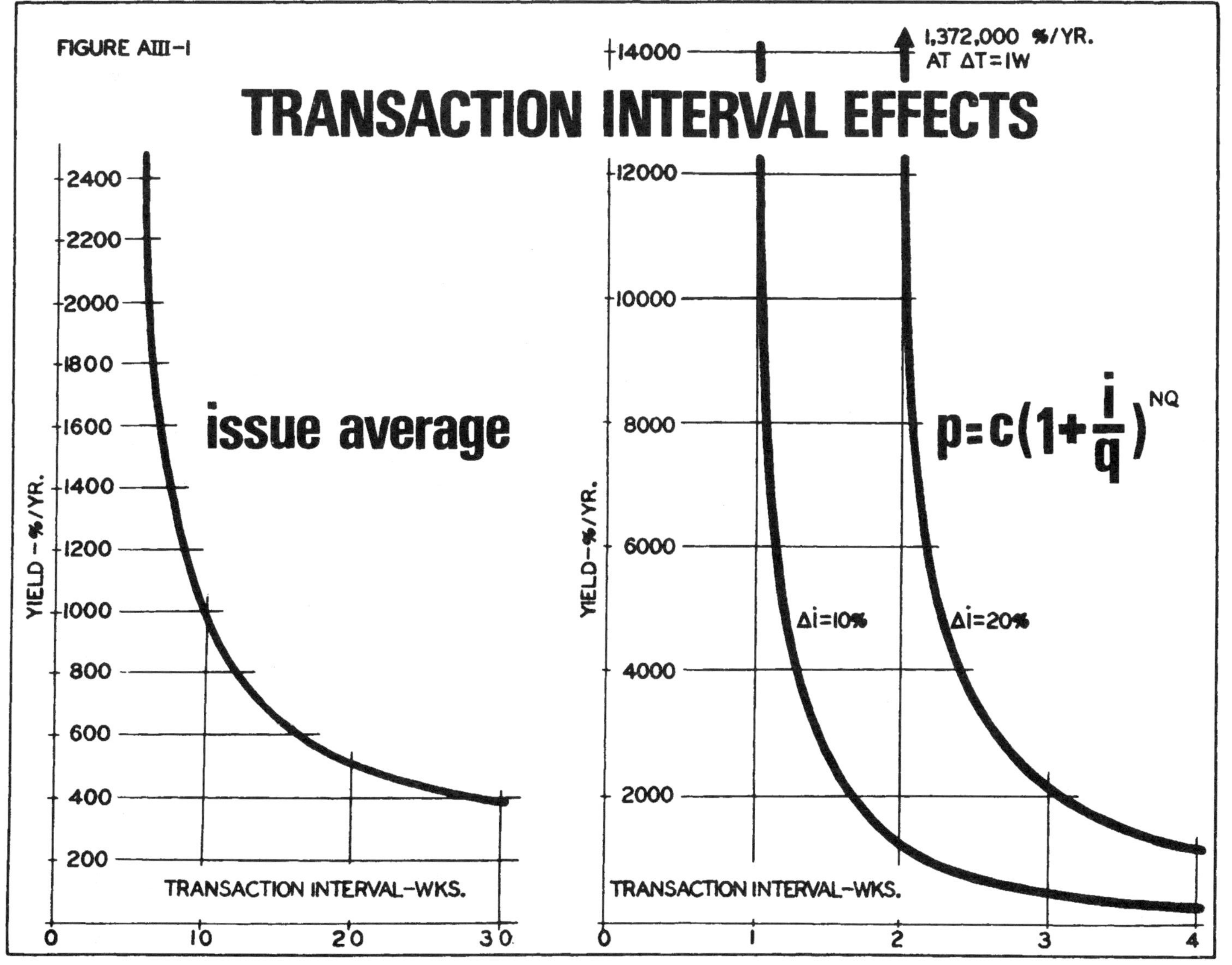


Why The Trading Interval Must Be Short

equivalent annual yield rates, for these very short transaction intervals, are seen to be astronomical. It is interesting to note that the restriction of transaction intervals to more than 26 weeks (the six-month favorable tax situation) neatly leaves one stranded on a very flat portion of the yield curve. It is obvious that favorable tax treatment is an insignificant parameter in the equation for making money in the market by comparison with the profit potential implications of shortened transaction intervals. The important thing is to find a way to so reduce risk of loss that one can operate on a less than ten-week basis. The existence of a unique stock price spectral signature makes this goal a practical possibility.

## THE EFFECT OF SINUSOIDAL RATE SUMMATION

The compound interest law does not account for all of the yield performance permitted by stock price fluctuation as transaction interval is shortened. The remaining performance is due to the manner of combination of spectral components. When sinusoids are added algebraically, the slope of the resultant is the sum of the slopes of the individual components. Obviously, longer-term transactions average out the time rate of change of short period components, eliminating the contribution of these to profit. That this is not insignificant is clear from the amplitude-frequency relationship derived in Appendix One. It is seen that both the unique spectral signature of stock price motion and the compound interest law force serious consideration of short-term trading, and the reduction of risk by improved transaction timing. The rewards are worth all effort required.

# appendix four

# Frequency Response Characteristics of a Centered Moving Average

- **Response Derivation**
- **Response Characteristics**
- **Application Implications**
- **Response of the Inverse Centered Moving Average**

In order to apply moving averages effectively, the design parameters and response characteristics to be expected must be known. These are simply derived as follows:

## RESPONSE DERIVATION

1. Defining $e_i$ as a cosinusoidal input to the averaging operation:

   $e_i = A \cos(\omega t)$

2. Determining $e_o$ = the output to be expected from the averaging operation (under the assumption of centering, and taking $t_o$ at the mid-span point):

$$e_o = \frac{1}{n}\Big\{A\cos(\omega t) + A\cos[\omega(t+t_n)] + A\cos[\omega(t-t_n)]$$
$$+ A\cos[\omega(t+2t_n)] + A\cos[\omega(t-2t_n)]$$
$$+ \cdots\cdots\cdots$$
$$+ A\cos\left[\omega\left(t+\left\{\frac{n-1}{2}\right\}t_n\right)\right] + A\cos\left[\omega\left(t-\left\{\frac{n-1}{2}\right\}t_n\right)\right]\Big\}$$

Where: $n$ = number of elements of the moving average,
$t_n$ = digital data spacing of the data against which the average is applied.

3. This expression can be rewritten as follows:

$$e_o = \frac{1}{n}\Big\{A\cos(\omega t) + 2A\cos(\omega t)\cos[(1)(\omega t_n)]$$
$$+ 2A\cos(\omega t)\cos[(2)(\omega t_n)]$$
$$+ \cdots\cdots\cdots$$
$$+ 2A\cos(\omega t)\cos\left[\left(\frac{n-1}{2}\right)(\omega t_n)\right]\Big\}$$

4. Factoring and combining terms:

$$e_o = \frac{1}{n}\left\{A \cos(\omega t)\left[1 + 2\cos(1)(\omega t_n) + 2\cos(2)(\omega t_n) + \cdots + 2\cos\left(\frac{n-1}{2}\right)(\omega t_n)\right]\right\}$$

5. Defining: $f = \cos(1)(\omega t_n) + \cos(2)(\omega t_n) + \cdots + \cos\left(\frac{n-1}{2}\right)(\omega t_n)$

$$e_o = \frac{1+2f}{n} \cdot e_i$$

6. And amplitude ratio is:

$$a_r = \frac{e_o}{e_i} = \frac{1+2f}{n}, \text{ where:}$$

$$f = \cos(1)(\omega t_n) + \cos(2)(\omega t_n) + \cdots + \cos\left(\frac{n-1}{2}\right)(\omega t_n)$$

## RESPONSE CHARACTERISTICS

From the derivation we note the following:

- Output is precisely in phase with input over the entire frequency range: $0 \leqslant \omega \leqslant \infty$ (except for reversals of phase in the high attenuation areas).
- $n \cdot t_n$ is the span of the filter (in units of time). The time lag is a constant: $L = \left(\frac{n-1}{2}\right)t_n$ (units of time), or one-half of the span.
- The cutoff frequency occurs when $f = -\frac{1}{2}$, or at a frequency:

  $$\omega_{co} = \frac{2\pi}{nt_n}$$

  This frequency corresponds to a cutoff period of:

  $$T_{co} = nt_n = \text{span of the average}$$

- The form of the amplitude response curve is a damped sinusoid, but the major pass-band lobe repeats itself at frequency intervals of $2\pi$. This implies a first high frequency window that can induce frequency-folding effects at:

  $$\omega = \frac{2\pi}{t_n}, \text{ or at a frequency whose period is: } t_n.$$

- The amplitude ratio of the first error lobe following cutoff frequency is a constant −.23, independent of design parameters. Subsequent error lobes alternate in sign as they diminish in size. Thus, high frequencies appear in the output damped, and either in phase with the input or 180 degrees out of phase with the input, dependent upon design parameters and frequency.
- The characteristics of a centered moving average are totally fixed by the span of the average, $nt_n$, which is the only design variable.

## APPLICATION IMPLICATIONS

The derived response curve for a centered moving average is plotted in Figure A IV-1.

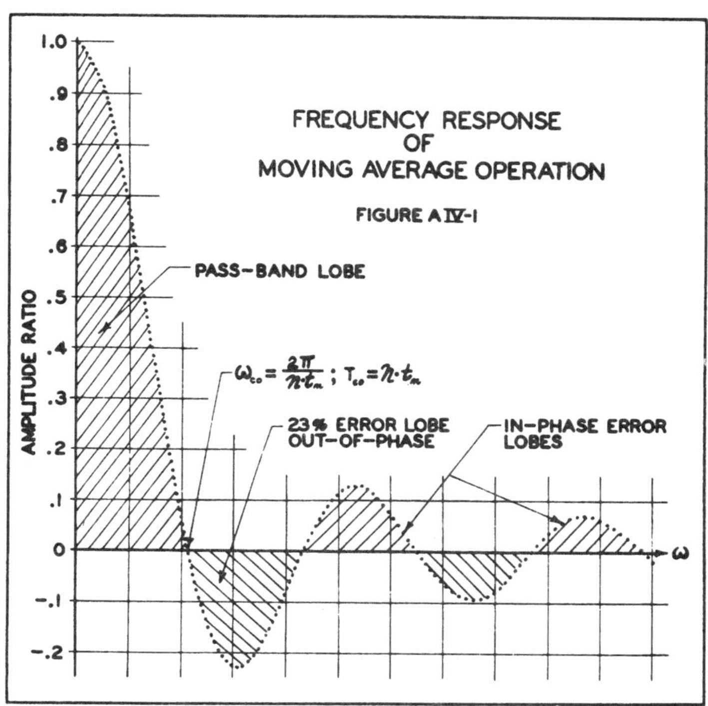


**How A Moving Average Works**

The simplicity of the function tells us that we need never plot it again for a specific design. Knowing that amplitude ratio is 1.0 at zero frequency, 0.0 at a frequency of $\frac{2\pi}{nt_n}$ (corresponding to a period of $nt_n$), and that the following error lobe is negative and reaches a peak of $a_r = -.23$ is sufficient to allow the curve to be visualized with sufficient accuracy for all practical purposes.

We note that selection of a span of $nt_n$ forces the output to contain no trace of spectral components whose period equals this span. We further know that slightly lower frequencies will come through attenuated, the attenuation diminishing as frequency decreases, reaching zero attenuation at zero frequency. Similarly, slightly higher frequencies (than that of cutoff) come through attenuated and 180 degrees out of phase. At a still higher frequency, output is again zero. At higher frequencies yet, output is obtained that is still more attenuated and in phase with input again.

It is clear that the centered moving average behaves as a low-pass filter with large-amplitude Gibbs-oscillation error lobes (due to the infinite discontinuities of the derivatives of the square-wave weighting function). Actually, the high-frequency suppression characteristics are sufficiently poor that such an average would not be very effective as a "smoother" of stock price data—except for the fact that the spectrum of stock prices consistently displays the $a_i = \frac{k}{\omega_i}$ relationship between amplitude and frequency derived in Appendix One. It is only the sharp attenuation of high-frequencies characteristic of stock price motion that permits the utilization of a filter with such relatively poor characteristics.

The combination of knowing the spectral behaviour of a given design of moving average and knowing in advance the general nature of the signal against which it is to be applied (per the price-motion model), generates a terrific advantage in the applications. Moving averages can now be designed to clarify and allow inference of spectral status of stock prices at any given time, thus providing insight into the future of the price time-series. This is the basis of the several applications of the chapters.

In using moving averages to help define the turning points of price-motion model components, one is now aware of the potential for high-frequency "creep-through"—either in phase or 180 degrees out of phase. Such knowledge permits identification of these unwanted residuals, so that they do not mislead conclusions.

## RESPONSE OF THE INVERSE CENTERED MOVING AVERAGE

The chapters have pointed up the utility of this version of centered moving averages. Knowledge of the frequency response associated with them can be used to sharpen your ability to interpret results obtained through their usage.

The phase response and lag characteristics of such an operation are similar to that of the conventional moving average. The principal difference lies in the fact that no phase inversion is experienced at frequencies output via error lobes. The output is, therefore, perfectly in phase with input across the entire frequency spectrum, and time lag remains precisely one-half the span of the filter.

Amplitude is simply derived by taking 1.0 minus that for the conventional moving average, with the result shown in Figure A IV-2.

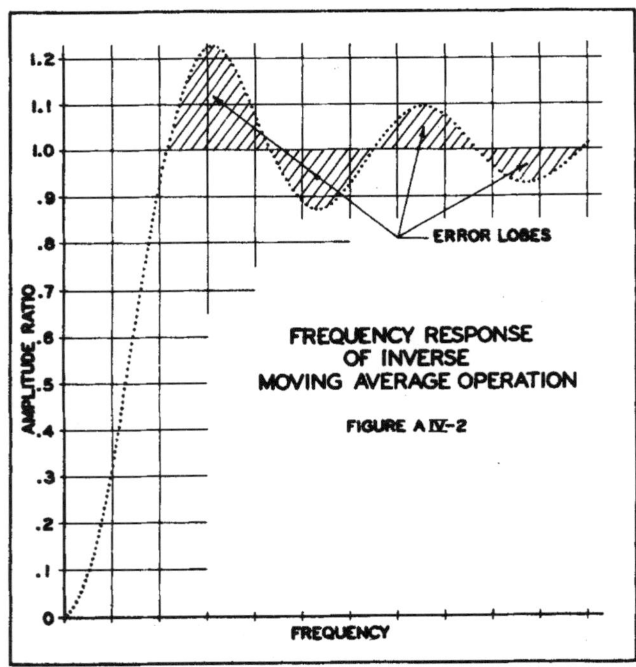


**How An Inverse Moving Average Works**

From this figure it is noted that the inverse moving average behaves like a high-pass filter–again with error lobes to 23%. The frequency for which amplitude ratio first become 1.0 is $\frac{2\pi}{nt_n}$, or the frequency corresponding to a period equal to the span of the average, $nt_n$. The actual maximum response point occurs at a frequency somewhat higher. You will sometimes want to correct output for the nearly one-fourth excess amplitude of the output at these frequencies in order to arrive at a true estimate of the magnitude of a spectral model component.

# appendix five

## Parabolic Interpolation

- **Three-Point Interpolation**
- **Equation Derivation**

As indicated in Chapter Eleven, digital data spacing of the time series of numbers on which a numerical filter operates is a design parameter of the filter. As such, it must be varied according to need, along with other factors, in order to achieve the desired filter characteristics.

This is sometimes inconvenient, as when the outputs of two filters must be combined or compared numerically, but the output of one is spaced at five-week intervals, while the other is spaced at three (for example).

In such cases, parabolic interpolation is useful. This process defines the equation of a least-square-error parabola fitted through any specified number of filter output data points. The equation is then solved for best-estimate intervening values that are a common interval apart. The results of the two or more incompatible filter outputs may then be compared directly, or operated upon together numerically.

The following material is intended for use with the output of band-pass filters where the high frequency content is small. Interpolation of high-pass (or otherwise non-smooth) data may require adaptation of the methods to use more data points, or even the use of other forms of curve fitting. If the need arises, a representative sample of the literature on such additional methods is to be found in the bibliography.

### THREE-POINT INTERPOLATION

The process operates as follows:

Consider any three consecutive data points in the output of a filter spaced "$t_n$" time units apart. Assign $t = 0$ at the central point, and symbolize this point as $S_0$. Call the one just preceding it in time $S_{-1}$, and the one following it $S_{+1}$. Form the least-square-error parabola fitted through $S_{-1}$, $S_0$, and $S_{+1}$. Solve the resulting equation from $t = 0$ to $t = t_n$ to find the interpolated values of "$s$" at any required time intervals.

Now move the whole process in time forward by one data point. Thus, $S_0$ in the preceding computation becomes $S_{-1}$ in the new one; $S_{+1}$ in the preceding computation becomes $S_0$ in the new one; and the next later data point becomes the new $S_{+1}$. Redefine $t = 0$ at the new $S_0$ and complete a new segment of interpolation. Proceed in this manner until the data to be interpolated are exhausted.

## EQUATION DERIVATION

The standard form of the equation of a parabola is:

$$S(t) = a_0 + a_1 t + a_2 t^2$$

where: $t$ = time

$S(t)$ = function to be interpolated

$a_0, a_1, \& \ a_2$ = constants to be determined for each set of three values of $S(t)$ between which interpolation is desired.

The least-square-error equations for the values of $a_0, a_1, \& \ a_2$ are:

$$\left.\begin{aligned} \Sigma s &= a_0 N + a_1 \Sigma t + a_2 \Sigma t^2 \\ \Sigma t \cdot s &= a_0 \Sigma t + a_1 \Sigma t^2 + a_2 \Sigma t^3 \\ \Sigma t^2 \cdot s &= a_0 \Sigma t^2 + a_1 \Sigma t^3 + a_2 \Sigma t^4 \end{aligned}\right\}$$

$N$ = Number of data points to be fitted and the summations to be carried out over the time interval corresponding to the fitted data.

For our case, where $N = 3$ and $t = 0$ is chosen to correspond with $S_0$:

$\Sigma t = 0$ and $\Sigma t^3 = 0$

So that the coefficient equations reduce to:

$$\begin{aligned} \Sigma s &= (3)a_0 + (0)a_1 + (\Sigma t^2)a_2 \\ \Sigma t \cdot s &= (0)a_0 + (\Sigma t^2)a_1 + (0)a_2 \\ \Sigma t^2 \cdot s &= (\Sigma t^2)a_0 + (0)a_1 + (\Sigma t^4)a_2 \end{aligned}$$

With a digital data spacing of "s" equal to $t_n$, the summations are evaluated and substituted as follows:

$$\begin{aligned} S_0 + (S_{+1} + S_{-1}) &= (3)a_0 + (0)a_1 + (2t_n^{\,2})a_2 \\ t_n(S_{+1} + S_{-1}) &= (0)a_0 + (2t_n^{\,2})a_1 + (0)a_2 \\ t_n^{\,2}(S_{+1} + S_{-1}) &= (2t_n^{\,2})a_0 + (0)a_1 + (2t_n^{\,4})a_2 \end{aligned}$$

Solving these three equations simultaneously for the values of $a_0$, $a_1$, and $a_2$ yields:

$$a_0 = S_0$$

$$a_1 = \frac{(S_{+1} - S_{-1})}{2t_n}$$

$$a_2 = \frac{(S_{+1} + S_{-1}) - 2S_0}{2t_n^2}$$

The desired equation of the least-square-error parabola fitted through any set of $S_{-1}$, $S_0$, and $S_{+1}$ is then:

$$S(t) = S_0 + \left[\frac{S_{+1} - S_{-1}}{2t_n}\right] t + \left[\frac{(S_{+1} + S_{-1}) - 2S_0}{2t_n^2}\right] t^2$$

Substitution of the values of $S_{-1}$, $S_0$, $S_{+1}$, $t_n$ and any desired values of time: $0 < t < t_n$ provides the needed interpolation values of the function $S(t)$ (output from a specific filter).

# appendix six

# Trigonometric Curve Fitting

- Generalized Least-Square-Error Methods
- Solving For Frequency
- Computing Amplitudes
- Determining Composite Amplitudes and Phases

The use of numerical filters on stock price data results in the generation of sampled functions which contain a reduced number of spectral components. In manipulating these functions it is often desirable to determine analytically the frequencies, amplitudes, and phases of the summed sinusoids present. This can be accomplished (and high frequency smoothing gained at no cost in additional time lag) by the trigonometric curve-fitting method described here.

## GENERALIZED LEAST-SQUARE-ERROR METHODS

The technique to be described requires a generalized form of the least-square-error curve fit method. This procedure will be demonstrated using the trigonometric functions of interest to us; however, the process is quite general and can be used to fit data with any kind of rational function.

Suppose we have utilized a band-pass filter to obtain a function of time containing "$m$" of the components of our spectral model. The approximation equation of the filter output is then:

(1) $S(t) \approx (A_1 \cos \omega_1 t + B_1 \sin \omega_1 t) + \cdots + (A_m \cos \omega_m t + B_m \sin \omega_m t)$

Let us say we have $N > 2m$ filter output data points. We write the set of $N$ equations which postulate that equation (1) is true at each of the times corresponding to the $N$ filter outputs:

$$\begin{aligned}
(2)\quad & (A_1 \cos \omega_1 t_1 + B_1 \sin \omega_1 t_1) + \cdots + (A_m \cos \omega_m t_1 + B_m \sin \omega_m t_1) = S(t_1) \\
& (A_1 \cos \omega_1 t_2 + B_1 \sin \omega_1 t_2) + \cdots + (A_m \cos \omega_m t_2 + B_m \sin \omega_m t_2) = S(t_2) \\
& \cdots\cdots\cdots\cdots\cdots\cdots\cdots\cdots\cdots\cdots\cdots\cdots \\
& (A_1 \cos \omega_1 t_N + B_1 \sin \omega_1 t_N) + \cdots + (A_m \cos \omega_m t_N + B_m \sin \omega_m t_N) = S(t_N)
\end{aligned}$$

To demonstrate the generalized process of least-square-error curve fitting, we will assume that we know the $\omega$'s. (The method of computing them also uses such curve fitting and is described in the next section.) We wish to solve equations (2) for the $A$'s and the $B$'s in such a way that the resulting equation will best fit the data points $S(t_1)$, $S(t_2)$, etc., in the least-square-error sense.

To do so, we must derive from the $N$ equations (2), $2m$ new equations in the $2m$ unknowns of interest (the $A$'s and $B$'s). We proceed as follows:

Form a matrix from the coefficients of the $A$'s and $B$'s in equations (2)—and the right-hand equation members—as follows:

$$\begin{aligned}
(3)\quad & \cos \omega_1 t_1 \quad \sin \omega_1 t_1 \cdots \cos \omega_m t_1 \quad \sin \omega_m t_1 \quad S(t_1) \\
& \cos \omega_1 t_2 \quad \sin \omega_1 t_2 \cdots \cos \omega_m t_2 \quad \sin \omega_m t_2 \quad S(t_2) \\
& \cdots\cdots\cdots\cdots\cdots\cdots\cdots\cdots\cdots \\
& \cos \omega_1 t_N \quad \sin \omega_1 t_N \cdots \cos \omega_m t_N \quad \sin \omega_m t_N \quad S(t_N)
\end{aligned}$$

From this matrix we now form a second matrix by the following rules:

- Multiply the elements of each row of the first matrix by the element of that row which lies in the first column. Sum the products by columns to get the elements of the first row of the second matrix.
- Multiply the elements of each row of the first matrix by the element of that row which lies in the second column. Sum the products by column to get the elements of the second row of the second matrix.
- Continue in this manner until you have converted the entire first matrix. The new matrix will consist of $2m + 1$ columns and $2m$ rows.

The second matrix is the set of coefficients and right-hand members of a new group of equations in the unknown $A$'s and $B$'s, located in the same positions in the members of these equations as in equations (2). Simultaneous solution of the new equation set yields the desired $A$ and $B$ coefficients. Substituting these in equation (1) completes the least-square-error data fitting process.

## SOLVING FOR FREQUENCY

From equation (1), it can be shown that the equation determining $\omega$ is of the form:

$$(4)\quad 2\cos[m\omega] - 2\alpha_1 \cos[(m-1)\omega] - \cdots - 2\alpha_{m-1} \cos[\omega] - \alpha_m = 0$$

Equation (4) must now be expressed in terms of Chebyshev polynomials and the parameter "$m$" as follows:

$$(5)\quad T_m(\cos\omega) - \alpha_1 T_{m-1}(\cos\omega) - \cdots - \alpha_{m-1} T_1(\cos\omega) - \tfrac{1}{2}\alpha_m = 0$$

The Chebyshev polynomials to be used in this expression ($T_m(\cos\omega)$, $T_{m-1}(\cos\omega)$, etc.) are as follows:

$$
(6) \quad \left.\begin{aligned}
T_0(x) &= 1.0 \\
T_1(x) &= x \\
T_2(x) &= 2x^2 - 1 \\
T_3(x) &= 4x^3 - 3x \\
T_4(x) &= 8x^4 - 8x^2 + 1 \\
T_5(x) &= 16x^5 - 20x^3 + 5x \\
&\cdots\cdots\cdots\cdots \\
T_{R+1}(x) &= 2xT_R(x) - T_{R-1}(x)
\end{aligned}\right\} \quad \text{where: } x = \cos(\omega), \text{ in this case.}
$$

Next, the $\alpha$'s in equation (5) are solved for by a technique known as Prony's method. Application of this method in this situation results in $(N - 2m)$ equations in the unknown $\alpha$'s, where the $S$'s are our filter output data points $S_0, S_1, \cdots S_{n-1}$. We now set up these equations as follows:

$$
(7) \quad (S_1 + S_{2m-1})\alpha_1 + (S_2 + S_{2m-2})\alpha_2 + \cdots + (S_{m-1} + S_{m+1})\alpha_{m-1} + S_m\alpha_m = S_0 + S_{2m}
$$

$$
(S_2 + S_{2m})\alpha_1 + (S_3 + S_{2m-1})\alpha_2 + \cdots + (S_m + S_{m+2})\alpha_{m-1} + S_{m+1}\alpha_m = S_1 + S_{2m+1}
$$

$$
\cdots\cdots\cdots\cdots\cdots\cdots\cdots\cdots\cdots\cdots\cdots\cdots
$$

$$
(S_{N-2m} + S_{N-2})\alpha_1 + (S_{N-2m+1} + S_{N-3})\alpha_2 + \cdots + (S_{N-m-2} + S_{N-m})\alpha_{m-1} + S_{N-m-1}\alpha_m = S_{N-2m-1} + S_{N-1}
$$

As the next step, the generalized least-square-error curve-fit procedures of the preceding section are used to obtain the $m$ values of $\alpha$ from equations (7). The step-by-step process is exactly the same as before, except that the coefficients of the $\alpha$'s of equations (7) are now used to set up the first matrix.

Substituting the derived values of the $\alpha$'s in equation (5) results in an equation of degree $m$ in ($\cos \omega$) as the unknown. From the $m$ roots of this equation, the desired values of $\omega$ are found.

## COMPUTING AMPLITUDES

The $\omega$'s may now be substituted in equations (2), and the generalized least-square-error method of the preceding section used to solve for the amplitude coefficients ($A$'s and $B$'s) as in the example of the first section.

## DETERMINING COMPOSITE AMPLITUDES AND PHASES

The frequency and amplitude of each of the $m$ sinusoid-cosinusoid pairs that best fit the filter output data are now known. Each pair can be further combined into a single sinusoid of the form:

$$
[A \cos(\omega t) + B \sin(\omega t)] = C \sin(\omega t + \phi)
$$

$$
\text{Where: } C = \sqrt{A^2 + B^2} \quad \text{and: } \phi = \tan^{-1}\left(\frac{A}{B}\right).
$$

With this step, the task is complete—and the frequency, amplitude, and phase of each of the $m$ sinusoidal components in the data has been identified. The final approximation equation is:

$$
S(t) \approx C_1 \sin(\omega_1 t + \phi_1) + C_2 \sin(\omega_2 t + \phi_2) + \cdots + C_m \sin(\omega_m t + \phi_m)
$$

# bibliography


## I. DIGITAL FILTERING AND SMOOTHING METHODS

*A New Technique for Increasing the Flexibility of Recursive Least-Squares Data Smoothing,* Bell Telephone Laboratories Technical Memorandum, No. MM-60-4435-1 September, 1960.

*Correlated Noise in Discrete Systems,* J. D. Musa, Bell Telephone Laboratories Technical Memorandum, No. MM-62-6421-2, May, 1962.

*Design Methods for Sampled Data Filters,* J. F. Kaiser, Bell Telephone Laboratories.

*Design of Numerical Filters with Applications to Missile Data Processing*, Joseph F. A. Ormsby, Space Technology Laboratories, Inc. Technical Memorandum, No. STL/TR-60-0000-09123, March, 1960.

*Digital Filters for Data Processing*, Marcel A. Martin, General Electric Technical Information Series, No. 62SD484, October, 1962.

*Filtering Sampled Functions*, E. D. Fullenwider and B. I. McNamee, U. S. Naval Ordnance Laboratory Technical Memorandum, No. 64-104, July, 1956.

*Frequency Domain Application in Data Processing*, Marcel A. Martin, General Electric Technical Information Series, No. 57SD340, May, 1957.

*Practical Aspects of Digital Spectral Analysis*, W. Lloyd, Great Britain Royal Aircraft Establishment Technical Note, SPACE 11-AD-284-243, May, 1962.

*Recursive Multivariate Differential-Correction Estimation Techniques,* V. O. Mowery, Bell Telephone Laboratories Technical Memorandum, No. MM-64-4212-4, February, 1964.

## II. NUMERICAL, STATISTICAL, AND SPECTRAL ANALYSIS (TEXTS)

Lanczos, Cornelius. *Applied Analysis*. Englewood Cliffs: Prentice-Hall, Inc., 1956.

Blackman, R. B. *Linear Data Smoothing and Prediction in Theory and Practice.* Reading, Mass.: Addison-Wesley Publishing Co., Inc., 1965.

Stuart, R. D. *Introduction to Fourier Analysis.* New York: Barnes & Noble, Inc., 1961.

Hildebrand, Francis B. *Introduction to Numerical Analysis.* New York: McGraw-Hill Book Company, 1956.

Ezekiel, Mordecai, and Karl A. Fox. *Methods of Correlation and Regression Analysis* (3rd ed.). New York: John Wiley & Sons, Inc., 1959.

Siegel, Sidney. *Nonparametric Statistics for the Behavioral Sciences.* New York: McGraw-Hill Book Company, 1956.

Milne, William E. *Numerical Calculus.* Princeton, N. J.: Princeton University Press, 1949.

Hamming, R. W. *Numerical Methods for Scientists and Engineers.* New York: McGraw-Hill Book Company, 1962.

## III. TECHNICAL ANALYSIS OF THE STOCK MARKET

Jiler, W. L. *How Charts Can Help You in the Stock Market.* New York: Trendline, Inc., 1962.

Markstein, D. *How to Chart Your Way to Stock Market Profits.* Englewood Cliffs: Prentice-Hall, Inc., 1967.

Edwards, R. D., and J. Magee. *Technical Analysis of Stock Trends.* 5th ed. Springfield: John Magee, Inc., n. d.

Cootner, Paul H., ed. *The Random Character of Stock Market Prices.* Cambridge: M.I.T. Press, n. d.

# Index

**TRADERS PRESS, INC.® IS THE PUBLISHER AND THE EXCLUSIVE DISTRIBUTOR OF THE FOLLOWING MATERIALS BY AND ABOUT J. M. HURST:**

## *J. M. Hurst Cycles Training Course*

Complete course written by J. M. Hurst which teaches how to apply the principles of his work to actual trading and investing, including trade selection, entry, management, and exit. See full description in the following 3 pages. Available exclusively through **Traders Press, Inc.®** **Item# 1400 $495**

---

## *Cyclic Analysis: The Dynamic New Approach to Technical Analysis in Stocks and Commodities*

By: J. M. Hurst

Legendary pioneer in cyclical price analysis explains the concepts derived from his extensive computer research into market price movements. Elaborates on concepts in his groundbreaking work, *The Magic of Stock Transaction Timing*, and gives an overview and description of the material in his comprehensive cycles training course which is described in the three following pages. Buyers of this book receive credit for price paid towards purchase of Hursts' full training course. **Item# 1500 $19.95**

---

## *Channels and Cycles: A Tribute to J. M. Hurst*

By: Brian Millard

Thorough examination and explanation of cyclic price movements and how they may be applied to trading and investing. Summarizes the work of Hurst as presented in The Magic of Stock Transaction Timing in nontechnical, more easily understood terms and explains each topic thoroughly. Teaches methods that make it possible to predict some turning points months before they occur. **Item# 1401 $45**

## HERE IS WHAT WELL-KNOWN INVESTMENT EXPERTS FAMILIAR WITH THE WORK OF J.M. HURST HAVE TO SAY ABOUT IT

"The work of J. M. Hurst is highly regarded by technical analysts interested in the cyclical approach. Those who want a thorough education on this topic should avail themselves of the opportunity to acquire his full length course, which has been unavailable for many years until recently. The principles it teaches are just as valid today as they were 25 years ago."

—Tim Slater, President, Dow Jones Telerate Seminars

---

"In the world of channels, bands, and envelopes, J. M. Hurst stands out as a primary source. (*THE PROFIT MAGIC OF STOCK TRANSACTION TIMING* constitutes the earlier stock-market citation for envelopes I have found.) So it is with great pleasure, and not a little excitement, that I greet 'lost' material from this venerable source. Long out of print and known to but a few, Hurst's course should prove to be an invaluable asset to the research-oriented technical analyst."

—John Bollinger, CFA, CMT

---

"My copy of *The Profit Magic of Stock Transaction Timing* by J. M. Hurst was only $5.95 when purchased in March of 1979; it remains one of few treasured and frequently referenced volumes. Being an engineer, it is gratifying to find a book that is not full of hocus-pocus and magical methods. Hurst's tone clarifies cycles and channels, and brings a host of believable and useful methods for price analysis. Ed Dobson should be 'publisher of the decade' for uncovering and producing a course written by such a major contributor to market analytics. If you have not read his book, you need this course. If you have read his book, you have probably already ordered the course."

—Gregory L. Morris, CEO MURPHYMORRIS, Inc.,
author of *CandlePower and Candlestick Charting Explained*

---

"Jim Hurst's original cycle work laid the foundation for most of the cycle analysis being done in today's futures and stock markets. The cycle concepts and forecasting techniques are as valid today as they were then. His book and course should be read and studied by all serious students of the markets."

—Walter Bressert, Co-founder of Computrac

---

"Ever since I read about Hurst's method of 'phasing,' I have looked forward to learning more about his work. His apparently pragmatic approach to technical analysis is very appealing and should adapt well to the more advanced tools now in our hands."

—Perry Kaufman, author of *Commodity Trading Systems and Methods* and numerous other financial titles

"I am delighted that Ed Dobson is preserving the *Hurst Cycles Course* for posterity. It is superb material and should be in the library of every serious technician. I have relied heavily on this material in my own cyclical analysis and in my writings on the subject."

—John J. Murphy, noted technical analyst, author of *Technical Analysis of the Futures Market* and *Intermarket Technical Analysis*

"Anyone interested in stock or commodity cycles should be enlightened by the work of James Hurst. His pioneering into the cyclical nature of stocks and commodities is the background of modern cyclic theory. Hurst's entry and exit methods are by themselves worth the price of the course."

—Larry Pesavento, professional trader and author of numerous financial titles

"After studying technical analysis for several years my perspective was changed forever by reading Hurst's book on cycles and studying his course in the early 1970's. This was the first true explanation of the rhythm in chart formations and has been a valuable tool to this day. It adds tremendously to an understanding of the markets."

—Jim Tillman, publisher of *Cycle Trend Market Letter*

"When Ed Dobson told me he had located the workbooks and audio tapes of J. M.Hurst's course on market cycles, I felt as if a past market master had been resurrected from the dead. Hurst was such a brilliant original thinker that I can't imagine anyone who is serious about technical and cycle analysis would be without this material if given the opportunity to acquire it. Hurst's original book written in the late 1960's was the genesis of my career in cycles and contributed to a significant degree to any success I have enjoyed in this business."

—Peter Eliades, StockMarket Cycles

"...carefully researched work on cycles and envelopes, backed up by solid and verifiable facts... Brilliant application of mathematical analysis to the stock market... He developed a simple technique, which we now call channel analysis, which could easily be applied by the pencil and paper investor. ...a man whose work must be considered a landmark in the field of investment."

—Brian J. Millard, author of *Channels and Cycles: A Tribute to J. M. Hurst*